Old Time Radio's Comedy Couples

Dan McGuire

Old Time Radio's Comedy Couples
© 2018. Dan McGuire. All rights reserved.

All illustrations are copyright of their respective owners, and are also reproduced here in the spirit of publicity. Whilst we have made every effort to acknowledge specific credits whenever possible, we apologize for any omissions, and will undertake every effort to make any appropriate changes in future editions of this book if necessary.

No part of this book may be reproduced in any form or by any means, electronic, mechanical, digital, photocopying or recording, except for the inclusion in a review, without permission in writing from the publisher.

Published in the USA by:
BearManor Media
P O Box 71426
Albany, Georgia 31708
www.bearmanormedia.com

Printed in the United States of America

ISBN   978-1-62933-257-4 (paperback)

Book & cover design and layout by Darlene & Dan Swanson • www.van-garde.com

For Joy, with nostalgic appreciation
for the patient love
that has made our years together
so memorable.

Contents

Foreword   vii

Introduction   xi

Goodman and Jane Ace   1

Phil Harris and Alice Faye   39

Ozzie Nelson and Harriet Hilliard   105

George Burns and Gracie Allen   173

Jim and Marian Jordan   247

Acknowledgements   361

References   365

About the Author   367

Foreword

Over the years, I've had occasion to speak with a handful of people who were part of the early years of radio—that era we refer to as "the Golden Age." The memories span different decades and different locations, but one thing that comes up repeatedly is an appreciation for how simple radio was. As Bob Newhart once explained, if you wanted to set a television show at Grand Central Station, you'd need to build sets, hire extras and possibly even rent a train engine to put in the background—and that's not counting the makeup and costuming you'd need for everyone who appeared on camera. By comparison, to set a scene at Grand Central Station on radio, you needed only some train sounds, maybe some crowd sounds, and someone telling you they were at Grand Central Station. The listeners' imagination would do the rest.

In addition to its reputation as a "theater of the mind," radio had other professional benefits for a performer. Many of radio's early stars were vaudeville comedians or orchestra leaders who were used to the often-grueling schedules that accompanied tours of theaters or nightclubs. New York actor Jackson Beck (later the narrator on *The Adventures of Superman*) recalled being stranded in Philadelphia while performing *The Drunkard* because the management had skipped town with the box office receipts. Radio allowed a performer to stay in one place and broadcast across the nation. That stability, in turn, allowed a performer to think about the long-term plans people sometimes like to make: getting married, starting a family, buying a house, and so forth.

That stability was perhaps especially important for couples who came to radio as husband and wife. When you performed on radio with your spouse, you not only got twice the family income, you also got to share your bond without the marital strains that were frequently encountered in the high-pressure worlds of vaudeville and television. Many of radio's best-known couples came to radio from vaudeville, where having your spouse with you offered economic advantages (that is, two salaries instead of one); but it also meant that you had the luxury of working together to establish a bond as performers. That bond was at the center of some of radio's most beloved comedies.

Those comedies, and the couples who starred in them, are at the heart of this book by Dan McGuire. I've enjoyed Dan's writing for years, whether the subject was his own wryly humorous boyhood (chronicled so perfectly in his first book, *Now, When I Was a Kid*) or the performers and shows that he grew up enjoying and remembering. His affection for this era and the sounds it produced is obvious, and his enthusiasm for it contagious. You may finish this book and find yourself eager to hear an episode of *Fibber McGee and Molly* or *The Burns and Allen Show*. I think that would be an appropriate way to honor Dan's efforts. Knowing Dan, I think he'd tell you it would be an appropriate way to honor the couples whose work has meant so much to him. Either way, enjoy this visit to those thrilling—and hilarious—days of yesteryear.

Steve Darnall

Foreword

Steve Darnall is the publisher and editor of Nostalgia Digest, *where he has had the pleasure of publishing Dan McGuire on numerous occasions. Since 2009, he has also served as the host and producer of* Those Were the Days, *the weekly old time radio showcase founded by Radio Hall of Famer Chuck Schaden, which is heard Saturday afternoons on Public Radio station WDCB, Glen Ellyn, IL (wdcb.org). Information about* Those Were the Days *and* Nostalgia Digest *is available at nostalgiadigest.com.*

Introduction

Having grown up in the years before the arrival of the "boob tube" changed our lives and lifestyles, I spent many hours being entertained by that wonderful medium called radio. For a kid in the 1940s, the afternoon hours between 4:30 and 6:00 p.m., Monday through Friday, afforded a selection of 15-minute serial adventure series on three Chicago stations. *Superman, Orphan Annie, Terry and the Pirates, Captain Midnight, Straight Arrow, Tom Mix* and the rest made for difficult choices and sometimes some switching back and forth from one station to another to catch a little of the action from two different favorites. For good measure, *The Lone Ranger* and *The Green Hornet* alternated with complete half-hour programs at six o'clock.

All three stations devoted a good portion of Saturday morning to programs aimed at us kids. Smilin' Ed McConnell performed before a live studio audience, along with his pals Squeeky the Mouse, Midnite the Cat and Froggy the Gremlin. The mix of comedy and adventure shows included *Archie Andrews, Meet Corliss Archer* and *The Adventures of Frank Merriweather*. *Let's Pretend* dramatized familiar fairy tales before a live studio audience. To this day, faithful listeners still can sing the Cream-of-Wheat song that was part of the commercials:

Cream-of-Wheat is so good to eat that we have it every day.

We sing this song, it will make us strong, and it makes us shout: "Hurray!"

It's good for growing babies, and grown-ups, too, to eat.

For all the family's breakfast, you can't beat Cream-of-Wheat!

Depending upon my parents' preferences, I was entertained by an assortment of mystery, drama, variety, and comedy programs in the evening. I could work on my homework sprawled on the floor in front of the radio. If an all-music program was on, I might leave the room to go work at the dining room table. Most of the others were worth a listen, even if they didn't get my rapt attention. *Suspense* and *Lights Out* occasionally resulted in my pulling the covers over my head when I went to bed.

Comedy shows ranked as my favorite genre, even if some of Fred Allen's and Henry Morgan's humor went over my head. Sunday night was special, because I would have no homework to do as we listened to cast members deflate Jack Benny's ego with one gag after another. Afterward, Jack's band leader, Phil Harris, joined his wife, singer/actress Alice Faye, for a half hour of nonsensical situations that Phil got himself into with the help of his pal Frankie Remley. My folks viewed these as somewhat silly, but humorous. From my less critical juvenile perspective, they were hilarious.

Programs that featured husbands and wives were a common commodity on radio. Dozens of serialized daytime programs, dubbed "soap operas," followed the trials and triumphs of various families, usually headed up by a husband and wife. On nighttime dramas we had two married detective teams, *Mr. and Mrs. North* and Nick and Nora Charles on *The Thin Man*. Parents were key characters on *Date With Judy, Meet Corliss Archer* and *Henry Aldrich*. Mickey Rooney, in a brief stint on radio as Andy Hardy, was blessed to have two very patient and understanding parents.

Introduction

There were numerous couples in the comedy category. William Bendix and Paula Winslowe portrayed Chester A. Riley and his wife, Peg, on *The Life of Riley*. Richard Denning teamed with Lucille Ball as the subject of *My Favorite Husband*. As Blondie and Dagwood, Penny Singleton and Arthur Lake brought the popular comic strip characters to life on radio, as they did on the screen. Don Ameche and Francis Langford had hilarious squabbles on *The Bickersons*. Art Van Harvey and Bernadine Flynn, billed as "radio's home folks," were *Vic and Sade*, the couple who lived in "the small house halfway up the next block."

Phil and Alice, though, shared a unique trait with four other of radio's most popular comedy couples. Like Goodman and Jane Ace, Ozzie and Harriet Nelson, George Burns and Gracie Allen, and Jim and Marian Jordan, they were married both on the air and in real life. Except for the Jordans (alias Fibber and Molly McGee), they even portrayed themselves, or comedic variations thereof.

From all accounts, it was a joyful experience for these couples to be able to perform side by side. Their husband/wife status lent a special appeal to many of their listeners, and their programs were among the most popular on radio. The sections that follow are a fond remembrance of the lives and careers of these comedy couples who entertained and endeared themselves to so many millions of listeners in "the Golden Age of Radio."

Dan McGuire

Goodman and Jane Ace pose for a studio photo. Smile, Goody, smile!
CREDIT: Nostalgia Digest collection

Goodman and Jane Ace

(*Easy Aces*)

As Jane Ace was wont to say, "Let's begin at the beguine."
In the game of Bridge, two sets of partners sit across from each other at the table. When each hand is dealt, they bid for the right to earn points by taking a certain number of tricks. The high bidder gets to select a "trump" suit, meaning if Diamonds are trump, a two of Diamonds beats (or trumps) any card of any other suit, regardless of face value.

Sometimes, because of the assortment of cards held, the high bidder will call for a hand to be played as "No Trump." In a "No Trump" hand, no matter what suit is led, the highest card in that suit takes the trick. Should it happen that the high-bidding partners hold all four aces in their hands, they are viewed as four sure tricks. Thus the term "easy aces."

In an era before television, having friends over for an evening of Bridge was a popular way to combine socializing with a little fun. (The radio could provide some background entertainment without distracting players' attention from the game.) On week nights, it might be just one couple playing their hosts, or switching partners for each game. On a weekend, six or more couples might gather and move from table to table, playing with different partners and opponents in successive games. Typically, the hosts would provide prizes for couples who won the most games, had the highest score or scored the most points in all games combined.

Jane and Goodman Ace were ardent Bridge enthusiasts, meeting often with friends to play the game. Thus, when presented with the opportunity to perform together on radio, coming up with a name for the program was not a challenge. *Easy Aces*!

So, now we've cleared up the question that has long puzzled many fans of the Aces who are not Bridge players. But who *are* Jane and Goodman Ace? Well, not who your might think if you were listening to them at the peak of their popularity.

Not much is recorded about their early years other than the fact that both were born in Kansas City, Missouri. Jane was born Jane Epstein on October 12, 1897. Goodman Aiskowitz, as he was originally named, was born on January 15, 1899, the son of Latvian immigrants.

They both apparently were comfortably middleclass. Jane's father, Jacob Epstein, was the owner of a clothing store. Goodman's father ran a haberdashery. The young Aiskowitz may have earned a few dollars as a delivery boy, mowing lawns or assorted odd jobs typically available to boys. Once out of high school, his first real job, not surprisingly, was as a hat salesman.

Although the two lived in the same town, fate did not bring them together until they attended the same high school. Goodman was smitten from the moment that they met. Unfortunately, it was not to be a boy-meets-girl, love-at-first-sight, storybook romance.

In addition to her pleasing personality, Jane was a quite attractive young lady. She had numerous boys vying for dates with her, and she paid little attention to Goodman's advances. The fact that he was two years younger probably was an added disadvantage in his amorous efforts. A male junior might date a female freshman. When the roles are reversed, the maturing young woman is likely to view her pursuer as "just a boy."

However much he may have been disheartened in the romantic arena, Goodman appears to have done well in school. Already having felt an urge to write, he joined the staff of the school paper. Somewhere along the way he was promoted to the role of editor.

No examples of his contributions to the paper appear to have been saved, but one can assume that his pieces often drew chuckles from schoolmates, provided they could tune in to his droll sense of humor. Given his talent for delivering sharp barbs, albeit with a humorous twist, he also may have occasionally drawn frowns or been censored by the adult monitors of the paper's content.

His parents managed to send him to college, but like many students he took on some part-time jobs to help defer the cost. While studying journalism at Kansas City Polytechnic Institute, he spent some time dashing about town as a roller-skating messenger for Montgomery Ward. He also found time to write a weekly column that he called "The Dyspeptic" for the school newspaper.

Not long after Goodman graduated, his father died. To help support his mother and sisters, he worked at a local Post Office in addition to selling hats.

It was his experience writing and editing the school paper, however, that helped align his career path. His cousin, Hy White, was a press agent. In 1919, with help from Cousin Hy, Goodman acquired a job at the Kansas City *Journal-Post* as a reporter.

Perhaps because of his writing aspirations, he at this time took on the *nom de plume* Asa Goodman. Given the prevailing prejudices of the time, the name does not seem meant to disguise his ethnic background. Writers often use pen names, especially if their own is prone to mispronunciation. The name Asa Goodman has a nicer ring than Goodman Aiskowitzis, and it flows more smoothly off the tongue. Since he was working in his home town, he may also have wanted to have his work judged on its own merits by those who would remember him from high school or the neighborhood.

It's not clear whether he ever was successful in dating the elusive Jane Epstein in the interval between high school and his new profession, but he evidently did maintain contact. His golden opportunity came when the popular entertainer Al Jolson was scheduled to perform at a Kansas City theater. Jane was an enthusiastic Jolson fan and desperately wanted to see the show. The performance was sold out, and none of her current boyfriends was able to wrangle tickets.

Asa Goodman, however, had a press pass that got him into a lot of otherwise inaccessible events. Voila! Whether he passed her off as an assistant or was able to bring her along as a guest, he escorted a jubilant Jane to see and hear the nation's favorite minstrel singer wow the audience with his "You ain't heard nothing yet, folks!" performance.

Thereafter Asa's stock increased as he was able to gain entry for himself and Jane at other shows for which tickets might have been costly or unavailable. More important, though, the two found that they were quite compatible, and Jane gradually came to feel the same affection for Asa that he had long felt for her. They were married in their home town on November 16, 1922.

Jane's father had hoped that his daughter would provide him with a son-in-law who could join him as an assistant in the clothing store.

Disappointed when he learned that Goodman was in the newspaper business, he reportedly asked, "Where's your newsstand?"

The newlyweds' days of marital bliss appear to have been somewhat foreshortened. Not long after they were married, Asa lost his job at the newspaper. Several sources agree on this misfortune, but none seems to know the reason.

In any event, it made for some trying times in their early days together. Jane was in charge of their finances, and was adept at making the dollars stretch. She also was an excellent seamstress. She made almost all of her own clothes while they endured what must have been a trying period, and no doubt felt more keenly because of the comfortable lifestyle they had enjoyed until then. They distracted themselves to some extent by playing Bridge more frequently than ever.

Whatever the reason for Asa's departure from the *Journal-Post*, we know that it was not because of any disagreement with management or his failure to satisfy his editor. For a few years later, we find him working again at the same newspaper.

It appears this also was the time when he elected to again rename himself. This time he once more flip-flopped his first and last name and changed Asa to Ace. Goodman Ace became his permanent name. Thereafter, most of his friends and close associates affectionately called him Goody.

It's not clear whether Ace returned to the *Journal-Post* to pick up where he left off as a reporter. Somewhere along the line, however, he became the paper's movie and drama critic. Whether his judgment of a film or play was complimentary or a thumbs down, the reviews were always witty and enjoyed by readers. He noted that a certain vaudeville comic could not be heard beyond the third row and advised anyone attending the show to sit at least four rows back. He once reviewed a road show musical whose advertisements had boasted of its many magnificent stage scenes. Ace wrote: "The sets were beautiful...both of them."

The reviewer's role indirectly led to his initial entry into the world of that popular new medium, radio. Intrigued by radio's potential, Ace visited the manager of station KMBC (the local CBS affiliate) and outlined an imaginative suggestion. The manager liked the idea and took him on at ten dollars a week to read the Sunday newspaper comics.

With his creative flair and droll sense of humor, Ace gave an entertaining presentation of various comic strips for the kiddies who tuned in. This offbeat endeavor was almost two decades before the newspaper strike that prompted Mayor Fiorello H. La Guardia to take to the airwaves in New York City and win the hearts of future voters by reading "the funnies."

The funny paper gig led to another opportunity. In 1928, on the same station, Ace began a weekly program on Friday nights that was dubbed *Ace Goes to the Movies* (or, according to some accounts, *The Movie Man*). It was partly gossip, but mostly involved Ace reading his own reviews. It required no rehearsal, since he'd written the material himself, and Ace's delivery rendered the reviews enjoyable even for those who had already read them in the paper. For this he pocketed another ten bucks.

It was on the latter program that Goodman and Jane received their big break.

One night in 1930, Ace wrapped up his program and was gathering up his script when he observed that he was getting frantic hand signals from the engineer and producer in the control booth.

The cast of a 15-minute program that was to follow his had for some reason failed to show up. In the brief interval while station announcements were being made, the producer dashed in to explain the problem and urge Ace to stay on and fill the 15-minute segment. Ace was willing, but had no excess material with him to extend his own program format.

Jane often accompanied her husband to the studio and listened from a lobby area outside the on-air booth. As luck would have it, she was there that night. Ace called her in, quickly briefed her on the emergency and suggested that they chat.

They did. As though carrying on a casual conversation in the living room at home, they chatted idly, as married couples often do, about a few inconsequential things. Then they touched on a topic that had been much in the news recently. A woman had murdered her husband, reportedly over a dispute that occurred while they were partners during a Bridge game.

As a serious Bridge player, Ace observed that under certain circumstances it could be deemed justifiable homicide. That led to a discussion of a recent visit with friends in which they had enjoyed an exhilarating evening of Bridge. As their ad lib chatter interwove the two subjects, Jane at one point chirped, "Would you like to shoot a game of Bridge, dear?"

That drew guffaws from the guys in the control booth, and probably from listeners at home, certainly those who were Bridge players. Goodman Ace, whose keen wit always enlivened his reviews, probably got off a few more good one-liners camouflaged as part of the conversation.

No question that the folks at home enjoyed the spontaneous tête-à-tête. Many may not have known who or what they were listening to, but the response was so heavy and so favorable that the station management invited the Aces to create a program involving a domestic comedy along the lines of their impromptu performance.

Jane had never even been in a school play. Although attractive enough to be taken as a starlet when she was a young woman, she never had any aspirations to perform on the stage, on radio or anywhere else. Still, she was game.

For his part, Ace saw the potential of the new medium and recognized the possibilities it offered. Already comfortable at the microphone and a seasoned writer of material that incorporated much humor, he had no doubt that he could produce the required scripts. He may have perceived it not so much as a long-term assignment, but rather as an open-ended project that would be fun to do and bring in a few extra dollars for its duration.

Easy Aces, in its early format, was like a continuation of that first impromptu conversation with the addition of a plot line, albeit a rather minimal one. The station promoted it as "radio's laugh novelty." Someone else described it as an urban and urbane flipside to *Vic and Sade,* familiar to many listeners as the folks in "the small house halfway up the next block." The Aces played themselves, with personalities modified somewhat by Goodman Ace's imagination.

An announcer would introduce each episode, sometimes setting the scene with a hint of what was being discussed. His comments always would refer to "the Aces," or to "Mr. Ace and Jane." Later in the evolution of the show, when it became necessary to give Jane a little more background, we learned that her maiden name had been Sherwood.

Goodman cast himself as a realtor, with various problems that were sometimes woven into the script. Jane was cast as a well-meaning but somewhat addle-headed gal, who described herself as "his awfully-wedded wife." She would listen sympathetically to his laments and offer suggestions or encouragement that only worsened Ace's headache. For the most part, though, the show centered on Jane's misadventures and Mr. Ace's efforts to distract or rescue her.

The show was enthusiastically received from the very outset. Listeners were no doubt sympathetic toward Jane, even as they laughed at her foolishness. Males in the audience may also have empathized with her put-upon husband. The response overall was so favorable that the Aces found themselves still doing the show more than a year later.

A Kansas City advertising executive who was an early listener to the program was certain that the couple would prove popular. After talking it up with several of his clients, he convinced a local drug store chain to sponsor the program for thirteen weeks. That, too, probably helped to secure their place at KMBC.

At some point, the success of the program attracted the attention of people at the network level. A potential sponsor, the makers of the mouthwash Lavoris, offered to bring the Aces to Chicago and air their show as a network program on a trial basis. If the show earned good ratings, the sponsor would negotiate a salary for the duo.

Goodman saw it as a great opportunity and was all for taking up the offer. In the early days of radio, many performers worked for a token fee, or even for free, in hopes of being "discovered." KMBC may have doubled the amount they were paying him when Jane came on board, but local stations using local talent usually had limited resources with which to reward them.

Jane, on the other hand, said absolutely not. If they were good enough to go on network radio, she reasoned, they deserved to be paid. After all, wouldn't the sponsor be airing commercials on the program to sell his product? Moreover, she had a specific dollar amount in mind: $500 per week. She would consider no less.

Given the social norms of the day, Goodman had to do the negotiating. In doing so, he was bolstered by the recollection that practical Jane's skill in handling their finances had helped them weather some lean times. It may well be that the Lavoris people were prepared to pay more than $500, but simply opened with a trial balloon offer to see if this Kansas City couple was naive enough to accept it. They weren't. The Aces got what they asked for. *Easy Aces* became the first KMBC program ever to achieve network status.

In October, 1931, *Easy Aces* began its 13-week trial run as a network program. It was broadcast from the CBS station in Chicago, WBBM. As was often done, some sort of promotional gimmick was used to test the show's appeal by getting listeners to write in. The response was overwhelming—more than 100,000 letters came pouring in. That convinced their sponsor. Near the end of the trial period, the Aces were able to cut a deal for the years 1932 and 1933.

From the start, *Easy Aces* became a favorite of many in the radio audience. The program continued as a network feature for fifteen years, with a number of moves, various sponsors and announcers and, over time, an expanded cast.

In 1933, Franklyn MacCormack, an announcer and program director at WIL, a small independent station in St. Louis, joined CBS and auditioned for the role of announcer on *Easy Aces*. He won out over twenty-eight other hopeful competitors.

MacCormack later was announcer for the long-running kid's adventure series *Jack Armstrong, the All-American Boy* and for the *Orphan Annie* series. To Chicago radio listeners, he is perhaps best remembered for *The All Night Showcase*, sometimes referred to as *The Meister Brau Showcase,* because its primary sponsor, back when that was allowed, was a beer company. The program aired six nights a week from 11:05 p.m. until 5:30 a.m.

MacCormack, who had a deep but soothing voice, introduced himself as "host and companion" and filled the hours with classical, big band and Broadway music. He also unabashedly read romantic and sentimental poetry. Even irregular listeners came to relate him to one poem that he recited hundreds of times, "Why Do I Love You?" MacCormack hosted the program to a faithful audience from 1959 until 1971, when he died during a broadcast.

By the summer of 1933, the Aces had decided that if they were to continue in radio they should be represented by an agent. Their search led them to the Blackett, Sample and Hummert agency in New York City. It was a fortuitous connection.

Frank Hummert headed the agency. Frank and his wife, Anne, were best known for bringing numerous serialized melodramas ("soap operas") to radio. They were, nonetheless, a prolific team that produced mystery, music, juvenile adventure, sports, news, comedy, dramatic theatre and quiz programs. In his book *Frank and Anne Hummert's Radio Factory*, radio historian Jim Cox notes that the Hummerts brought more than 125 different programs to the airwaves. For a time during the 1940s, they filled four and a half hours of the three networks' weekly scheduling.

Hummert liked the Aces. He enjoyed their unique style and was aware of their proven audience appeal. As a producer and agent, he also realized that potential sponsors would appreciate the show's low overhead: only two performers, and one of them writing all the scripts. He soon had them doing their shtick four times a week in an afternoon time slot on CBS.

In 1934, the Aces signed a contract to do a series of two-reel comedies for Educational Pictures. Yes, Educational Pictures. The company originally was formed to produce instructional and informational films for schools. It later branched out into more profitable one- and two-reel comedies and other short features. Its comedies featured such stars as Bob Hope, The Ritz Brothers and, in an era when "darkie" comedy was still acceptable, The Two Black Crows. Their musical shorts introduced Bing Crosby to movie audiences, singing "I Surrender, Dear," and included a young starlet named Shirley Temple.

Although doing a film meant performing in front of a camera, Jane, the non-actress, had no qualms, since she and Goody would still be playing themselves. Their first film, *Dumb Luck*, was not a box-office smash, but radio fans probably enjoyed seeing the Aces on screen, even though the plot departed from the brisk back-and-forth that personified their on-air encounters. Others in the audience, unfamiliar with the Aces' style, may not have had time to tune in to the low key humor of Jane's wackiness and Goody's frustration.

Unfortunately, Educational Pictures already was experiencing financial trouble when Goodman and Jane signed with them. *Dumb Luck*, released in January, 1935, proved to be their one and only film before the company went bankrupt.

They did, however, manage to continue briefly as film stars... sort of. RKO Radio Pictures hired them to work with The Van Beuren Corporation, another small producer of live action features and shorts, including Frank Buck's *Bring 'Em Back Alive* series. During 1936-37, the Aces were heard, but not seen, as narrators for the "Van Beuren Vagabond" travelogues, a series of novelty shorts produced by Van Beuren Studios and filmed by RKO Radio Pictures.

In 1935, with some help from Frank Hummert, the Aces acquired Anacin as a sponsor. They moved to New York, and the show moved to the Blue Network of NBC. The show was switched to an evening slot at seven o'clock three times a week.

Unfortunately, the Monday night airing put the Aces up against *Amos and Andy*, one of the most popular shows on radio. Ratings-wise, there was no way they could compete. Nonetheless, they succeeded in building a loyal audience. Those listeners followed them and were joined by others when they moved back to CBS in 1942, in a 7:30 p.m. slot on Wednesdays and Fridays.

Though the program moved around a bit, the formula that earned *Easy Aces* its following never changed. Its appeal derived mainly from two facets that played upon each other and were continually woven into the scripts. Jane portrayed a homebody much like her real self. But in Ace's scripts she was a bit scatterbrained, prone to be meddlesome, and given to misinterpreting situations or concocting schemes that led to comical mayhem. As her loving but long-suffering helpmate, Ace would do his best to redirect her or repair the damage of what he called her "undoings." Faithful listeners grew accustomed to hearing him moan, in a throwing-up-of-hands voice, "Isn't that awful?"

In addition to her misadventures, Jane because famous (notorious?) for uttering comments of fractured logic and mangled verbiage, all skillfully scripted for her by her writer/husband. A typical example was Jane explaining what a rough day she's had: "I've been working my head to the bone." On a hot summer afternoon she might suggest to Ace, "Dear, why don't we go down to the ice cream shop and have a chocolate soldier." Or she might diagnose her malingering brother Paul's ailment as "intentional flu."

Expounding at length on some disconcerting incident, she once commented, "You could have knocked me over with a fender."

Ace: (groaning) Now *there's* an idea.

Jane: What, dear?

Ace: Nothing.

Despite her comical talent for inserting the wrong word or phrase, it was always clear what Jane meant. Certainly she knew what she meant, and her husband's exasperation would perplex her. Yet it seldom slowed her down.

One contributing factor to the success of Jane's persona was her voice. It was slightly high pitched with a tendency to sound a bit whiny, even when she was being sympathetic or just carrying on a friendly discussion. It made her come across as all the more comical when trying to explain her way out of a self-made dilemma and spouting what a *New York Times* critic referred to as "Jane-isms."

The program began with the announcer saying simply: "Ladies and gentlemen, *Easy Aces*." The "Easy" was uttered with a drawn-out "e" that gave it a sort of lazy, laid-back sound. This was followed by a brief portion of "Manhattan Serenade" played on an accordion. With a few words from the announcer to set the scene, Ace and Jane would take over.

Amazingly, Ace was able to concoct countless shows that required just the two of them to chronicle his wife's misadventures. Occasionally an off-stage character would be brought in via the telephone. Most often it was Jane on the phone and only her end of the conversation would be heard. In the background, Ace would mutter comments that expressed his exasperation.

Sometimes he would suggest things for Jane to ask or say to the caller. This required her to stop and say, "What, dear?" Then, after relaying the comment or question to the caller, she had to relay his or her response to her husband. While helping to carry the story along, this added to the comic effect of Ace's irritation and Jane's confusion. It also succeeded in sometimes filling much of an episode with the three-way conversation.

Gradually, a few supporting characters began to appear from time to time. Soon after going on the network, Ace introduced Jane's lazy, ne'er-do-well brother, Paul, one of those characters you love to hate.

He hasn't worked in years and, although married to a wealthy tycoon's daughter, he visits Ace's tailor for a new wardrobe and charges it to Ace's account.

Ace observes that Paul is a sensitive fellow who objects to the use of four-letter words, especially the word "work." Jane steadfastly defends him, explaining that Paul is waiting for the dollar to stabilize before seeking employment.

In an interview some years later, Ace was asked why Jane's brother was perennially unemployed. Goodman noted that Paul had been in a car accident ten years ago and sustained an injury for which he's been receiving an annuity of ten dollars a month. If he gets a job, the insurance company stops paying him. So he can't work. He was lucky enough to have escaped alive, and now he wants to get paid for it. A case of robbing St. Peter to pay Paul.

The wit of Goodman Ace was such that few humorists would reach as far as he for a pun.

In addition to playing a sort of caricature of himself, Goodman wrote all of the scripts. Many involved incidents that were resolved or not in one episode. Others would carry over for two or three episodes or even for a couple of weeks. Sponsors liked these "to be continued" series because the listening audience was "hooked" and had to tune in again next time to find out what happens.

In a typical example of these "more to come" series, one episode has Jane wanting to redecorate the living room. So she sells all of the furniture to a second-hand dealer for $400. Much to her husband's distress. In the next installment, she goes to attend the auction where the furniture will be sold. Irritated by the low bidding from the audience, she begins bidding herself, and manages to buy back everything for a total of $250.

The next episode opens with Jane sitting at a desk in the refurnished living room, scribbling on a piece of paper.

Ace: What are you doing there, Jane?

Jane: Hmm? Oh, I'm doing some figuring. I sold our furniture for $400 and bought it back for $250. So I figure I made a profit of approximately $150.

Ace: Approximately.

Jane: So I figure if I can do that nine more times, I can make a total profit of approximately $1,500.

Most of the episode is then taken up with Ace trying to convince her that it ain't going to work. Before that is completely resolved, the episode ends with Jane's niece arriving to announce that she has had a fight with her husband, will never speak to him again, and she's come to live with them. Ace tells her to go home, kiss and make up. Jane, however, says of course she can stay with them.

To be continued....

The most enduring supporting character on *Easy Aces* was Jane's old school chum, Marge Hale. Jane referred to her as "my insufferable friend." The part was played by Mary Hunter, who had been a receptionist at the radio station. When Goodman wrote the character into a script for the first time, there was no actress standing in the wings hoping for a part. He showed the script to Mary and asked if she's like to be Marge. Like Jane, Mary had no previous acting experience and no aspirations in that field. Whether she saw it as a career opportunity or just a lark, she allowed as how she'd enjoy giving it a try. She proved perfect for the role.

The Aces sit at their specially designed table with partially hidden microphone.
CREDIT: CBS/Photofest

Like Jane, Mary was a bit self-conscious and nervous speaking into the microphones. Ace drew up a plan for a special table, which the station constructed. It was essentially a card table with a partially-hidden microphone. When the cast of three sat around it reading their scripts, it felt as though they were simply carrying on a normal conversation. Mic fright for the ladies ceased to be an issue.

During her tenure, the Marge character lived with the Aces, although it's never explained why. Ace never interposed Marge in the real "action" of the various episodes. Her role, as one reviewer explained it, was to serve as a sort of Greek chorus. When Ace was necessarily off stage, Jane could explain to Marge her latest wacky scheme or self-induced dilemma. Marge responded with chuckles, questions and half-hearted attempts to get Jane to see what difficulties she was creating for herself. That enabled Jane to brush her off with one of her comically twisted clichés ("If I'm wrong, I'm not far from it") and continue to expound on where the story was going.

Marge never interfered, but also stubbornly refused to be part of Jane's schemes. Later, though, she often sympathetically attempted to help explain to Ace how Jane's good intentions had again gone awry. In an age long before canned laughter, Mary Hunter's spontaneous laughter at Jane's nonsense and Ace's exasperated retorts served as a sort of laugh track for the no-audience presentations.

Another more short-lived character was a Southern maid named Laura (played by Helene Dumas) who apparently managed to roam about the Ace's bungalow without ever really cleaning anything. She can best be imagined by recalling a scene from the Don Ameche/Francis Langford show *The Bickersons*.

Blanche: We need a maid, John.

John: We had a maid.

Blanche: Yes, but how long was she with us?

John: She was never with us. She was against us from the start!

Other characters, who appeared as needed to fill a plot line, included Ethel Blume as the Aces' niece, Betty; Alfred Ryder (best remembered as Sammy on *The Goldbergs*) as her husband, Carl Neff; and none other than Martin Gabel as Marge's love interest, newspaper reporter Neil Williams.

Ann Thomas played Mr. Ace's secretary, Sally Anderson. Her typing, messaging and organizational skills were minimal to nonexistent. She was unable to grasp the concept of an office intercom, forever asking, "Is that you, Mr. Ace?" or announcing, "It's me, Miss Anderson." Still, she was irreplaceable, because she was Jane's cousin.

From the beginning, Mr. Ace never had a first name, or rather it was never uttered. Like most married couples, he and Jane could carry on long conversations without addressing each other by name. From time to time, if trying to stress a point or calling him from another room, Jane simply called him "Dear." He frequently used the same term of endearment when speaking to her. More often, though, especially when she was beginning to rattle his nerves, he called her Jane.

Even as the cast grew, Goodman adhered to the unique aspect of his having no first name, or at least never being addressed that way. In Jane's conversations with Marge, when he was mentioned, Jane resorted to "he/him/his." Marge invariably referred to him as "Mr. Ace;" i.e., "I don't think Mr. Ace will approve of that." When other incidental characters spoke with or about Ace, they managed to do so without addressing him by name. Or, like Marge, they called him "Mr. Ace."

The avoidance of using his first name surely must have been a challenge in his writing. Nevertheless, Goody coped, and no doubt took pleasure in the coping. Listeners may at times have wondered about it, but their attention to the stories made it inconsequential. No one ever wrote in asking "What the heck is that guy's name?"

Goodman Ace had a keen sense of what made the program format work. To keep things fresh and spontaneous, he insisted that the cast would have only one rehearsal of each episode. It was a quick read-through shortly before the program went on the air.

From time to time, listener polls were conducted to determine radio program ratings. *Easy Aces* typically received respectable, if modest, ratings. Never shy about self-promotion, Goody took out ads in the trade papers pointing out that the polls were taken by phoning people while the programs were on the air. *Easy Aces* fans, he said, were not going to answer the phone while they were listening to the show.

In 1943, probably at the behest of the sponsor, the program was converted to a half hour offering. Ace had perfected the 15-minute format and was quite comfortable with it, but he was game.

Fiercely independent and confident in his work, Ace steadfastly avoided meetings with sponsors. He broached no interference from them, insisting that keeping writer and cast apart from sponsors was essential to the integrity of the program. Even so, if the expanded format was the sponsor's idea, Goody did not balk. He may have seen it as an opportunity for the Aces to attract more listeners and renegotiate their contract.

With no apparent stress, he began cranking our half-hour scripts. Like any seasoned writer with assorted tricks in his bag, he also drew upon old programs, fluffing them up, stretching them out, adding a few twists and inserting new bits of garbled clichés for Jane to utter.

On November 24, 1943, the *Easy Aces* program premiered in its new half-hour format. It continued as such, airing just one night a week, until January 10, 1945. The show's popularity had not suffered. Its end came as the result of an unpleasant incident that should not have occurred.

The show's sponsor, Anacin, had mostly honored Goody's hands-off requirement during their long association. Then an ill-advised executive sent a note to Ace complaining about, of all things, his choice of a musical bridge used in the program. Goody was offended and responded with a note saying that the packaging of his show was his business. In a tone uncharacteristically harsh, he suggested that Anacin should pay more attention to the packaging of their own product. Their use of cardboard boxes in lieu of tin was, he declared, a gyp. Anacin executives were furious and the show was abruptly cancelled. Recalling the incident, Goodman said, "They sent me a two-word answer: 'You're fired.'"

Suddenly unemployed, Jane and Goody took it in stride and were not deterred. They began a pleasant collaboration on a new project. As both writer and co-star, Goodman Ace had the foresight to retain all rights to their program. Most of the shows had been "transcribed," the term then used for recording. From a wealth of transcriptions in their possession, he and Jane picked and chose favorites, put together a package of over 300 episodes for syndication, and released it through the Frederick W. Ziv Company. Their contract brought in $75,000 a year, a tidy sum in those days.

Their abrupt dismissal by Anacin was not the end of *Easy Aces*. Although the show never regained its former status, it managed to make several comebacks in the next few years. In 1948, CBS put the Aces back on the air. Initially, the show's unlikely sponsor was the U.S. Army Recruiting Service; however, it was soon picked up by Jell-O.

For purposes of promoting the show, it was renamed *mr. ace and JANE*. The lower-and-upper-case combination was Goodman's doing, intended to emphasize Jane's persona as the main comedy feature. In its promotions of the show, CBS billed the Aces as "radio's original comedy couple."

During the years that the program aired, several highly regarded announcers followed in Franklyn MacCormack's footsteps, including Ford Bond, Truman Bradley and Ken Roberts. Roberts returned for the renewal of the program, and Goodman worked him into the cast as well, playing a next-door neighbor who just happened to be—of all things—a radio announcer. This enabled Ace to do some spoofing of radio in general, radio executives and especially radio commercials. One example had Roberts proudly declaring: "Fifty years ago, Blycose began selling the public its high quality-products. And today, just as it was fifty years ago, it is March 20."

This time around the network insisted that the show be done with an orchestra and a live studio audience. Goody went along, but was not pleased. He felt both additions detracted from the quiet style that was part of the show's appeal. His sense of what worked is borne out by comparing the first episode, recorded as an audition show with no music or audience, to subsequent shows. Ace wrote new material and revamped old shows. The style and low-key humor were still there, but the show lasted only one season.

Goody wasn't initially impressed with that newcomer medium, television. He referred to it as "terrible vaudeville." Still, when invited to adapt *Easy Aces* for the little screen, he agreed to give it a whack. The fact that the program would be filmed may have appealed to him. He and Jane could do the show at a convenient time and join their fans in watching it at home later.

Again he created some new scripts and remodeled old ones from radio. The program, which would be aired by the DuMont Television Network and syndicated in some areas, would again be fifteen minutes, a format in which both Ace and Jane felt more comfortable.

Keeping it simple, Ace concocted scripts that mostly involved just himself and Jane and an old friend for Jane, who (for reasons unknown) was named Dorothy rather than Marge. The latter was played by Betty Garde. (From all indications, Mary Hunter did not pursue an acting career after the Anacin incident that knocked the original program off the air.) The show debuted on December 14, 1949, airing on Wednesdays from 7:45 p.m. to 8:00 p.m. Response was tepid and the last episode aired on June 14, 1950.

With a few interruptions and changes of format, *Easy Aces* enjoyed a lifespan of almost nineteen years. During that time, Goodman and Jane Ace played their respective roles in some 2,400 episodes. It's an impressive number, made even more so when one considers that Goodman Ace wrote every script.

For the most part, the Aces moved out from behind the microphone after that. Jane was a homebody at heart, and was quite happy to return to that venue. As she explained, "Be it ever so hovel, there's no place like home."

Jane never had considered herself an actress. Although reading from scripts created by her husband, she never thought of it as acting.

Early on, after *Easy Aces* took hold, she was offered several other radio roles. A producer asked her to play the lead in a radio version of *Dulcy*. Originally a play by George S. Kaufman and Marc Connelly, *Dulcy* had opened in 1921 and ran for 241 performances. It was then made into a film starring Constance Talmadge in 1923. The producer thought Jane was perfect for the role, but Jane didn't feel she could play anyone but herself. She declined.

Apart from her one big screen appearance in *Dumb Luck*, Jane had never harbored any ambition to venture beyond her role as the pleasantly ditzy wife on *Easy Aces*.

As for Goody, he had proven himself as a writer both in the print media and on radio. In 1946, prior to the several attempted revivals of *Easy Aces*, CBS hired him to be "supervisor of comedy and variety." Describing his role as head of a writing team, Ace said, "I tell them how to do things and they say yes and don't do them." To illustrate his point, an early assignment had him working on the ill-fated *Little Show* starring Robert Q. Lewis.

In a departure from his steady outpouring of comedy scripts at CBS, Ace demonstrated his imaginative and serious side with a program that began on radio and evolved into one of CBS-TV's most memorable programs.

The idea came to him almost fully formed. Various historical events would be recreated on radio and reported by a modern day on-the-scene newsman who had somehow been transported back in time. Ace was certain that William Paley, the brilliant head of CBS, would take to the idea. His problem was that no mere writer was going to get in to see Paley.

Robert Metz, in his book *CBS: Reflections in a Bloodshot Eye*, recounts how Ace got bumped from one executive to another, none of whom warmed to the idea. At one point he got as high up the ladder as Paley's No. 2 man, Vice President Davidson Taylor. Taylor essentially told Ace to forget it.

Ace, however, was certain he had something worth airing, and he was determined. One afternoon he was scheduled to join Taylor in a meeting with Paley to outline a proposed summer replacement program that Ace would be writing. When Ace finished his presentation, Paley nodded and gave his approval. Ace then politely said that he had another idea that he thought Paley might like. Before Taylor could interrupt and usher him out the door, he began elaborating.

Taylor gave him an icy stare that said "Stop!" Ace ignored him and forged ahead. For his part, Paley listened attentively and appeared impressed. As Ace wrapped up his pitch, Paley turned to Taylor and asked, "Why aren't we doing that?"

Taylor may have been lacking in vision, but he wasn't stupid. He quickly responded, "Oh, we're going to...."

On radio, the program was called *CBS Was There*. It drew an attentive audience and earned critical approval. When the program made the transition to television, it was narrated by none other than Walter Cronkite. He stepped in after an announcer's introduction: "CBS asks you to imagine that our microphone is present at this unforgettable moment. All things are as they were then, except... *You... Are... There!*"

In the comedy arena, Goody seemed to still be on a roll when, for reasons unknown, CBS fired him. Stopping him in the hall later, a sympathetic network executive said to Ace, "I'll tell you a secret. We haven't got a man who understands comedy." Ace replied, "I'll tell *you* a secret. That's no secret."

Goody's wit and productive writing ability were well established. He had no trouble finding work, providing gags for such varied styles as those of Milton Berle, Robert Q. Lewis, Abbott and Costello, Ed Wynn and Bob Newhart. As head writer for Perry Como's television show, he put funny lines into the mouth of the laid-back singer. The show achieved top ratings in its first season, and Ace was twice nominated for Emmy awards in 1956 and 1959.

At one point, the producers of *The Danny Kaye Show* hired him at the rate of $3,500 a week. One day during rehearsals, Danny became upset that too many of the funny lines were going to other cast members. He sarcastically expressed his displeasure to Ace: "I must be the highest paid straight man in radio." As if scripted, Goodman responded, "Jack Benny makes three times what you do."

Benny was noted for giving a major portion of the gags to his cast members. Often the gags were at his expense: jokes about his stinginess, his imagined sex appeal, his ancient Maxwell automobile, lying about his age, etc.

Goody enjoyed a long-running connection to Jack Benny. While Ace was still working as a reporter/columnist and Benny had not yet risen to star billing, Ace had an opportunity to interview him. Benny had read and enjoyed some of Ace's witty columns and invited him to write some jokes for his stage act. Goody agreed, and later sent him a packet of ten jokes.

Benny liked them all and even used one for his opening line. He was playing a theater as the number two act, coming on after a Chinese magician. His opener was: "My, how vaudeville has changed. It used to take Japs or better to open."

Jack used all of Goodman's jokes and was so pleased with the audience response that he sent Ace a check for $50. He included a note that said, "Your jokes got lots of laugh. If you have any more, send them along." Ace returned the check and enclosed a note of his own: "Your check got lots of laughs. If you have any more, send them along."

Thus began a lifelong long-distance friendship. Throughout the years, Ace continued sending gags to Jack, always free of charge.

Meanwhile, he became a regular columnist for *The Saturday Review of Literature* in the early 1950s. Two weeks after his debut column, the magazine shortened its name to *The Saturday Review*. Goody liked to claim that there was a direct cause and effect. Nevertheless, his column became a favorite feature of the publication for many readers.

His "Top of My Head" column initially dealt mostly with the world of television. Some pieces were gentle and approving. More often they were tart but funny critiques of performers and programs, with the sharpest barbs reserved for behind-the-scenes TV executives. Still, the pieces never contained any genuine malice. One publisher described it as "nibbling the hand that feeds him." In 1955, Goody collected some of his favorite pieces and they were published as *The Book of Little Knowledge: More Than You Want to Know About Television*.

Ace gradually broadened his field of vision to cover many contemporary concerns. Neither frivolous nor overbearing, his essays became as popular as the radio show had been. Indeed, he frequently found ways to include his beloved Jane into the discourse. His output was received warmly enough to prompt the publication of another collection, this one called *The Better of Goodman Ace*.

In his introduction, Goody explains to readers: "The title I chose raised some eyebrows and doubts at the publishers' office. They suggested a stronger title, but I wasn't going to leave myself open to the sneer of some browser in a bookshop, opening a page at random, reading one of the chapters, and saying, 'Is that his best?' Nobody ever says, 'Is that his better?'"

Meanwhile, radio audiences were being lured away in droves by the novelty of television. In spite of the imperfections and limitations that Ace often teasingly mocked, families were crowding around the small screen rather than around their radios. In 1950, NBC Radio launched a last-ditch effort at survival by premiering *The Big Show*, a 90-minute variety program.

The program boasted an impressive weekly line-up of top performers, dramatic, comic, and musical, who appeared on a rotating basis. The premiere broadcast boasted such stars as Jimmy Durante, Ethel Merman, Danny Thomas, Frankie Laine, Paul Lucas and Jose Ferrer. Meredith Willson and his orchestra provided the music. Subsequent broadcasts included the likes of Fred Allen, Bob Hope, Louis Armstrong, Lauritz Melchior, Groucho Marx, Joan Davis, Ezio Pinza, Edith Piaf, Ginger Rogers, Ethel Barrymore, Phil Silvers and Benny Goodman.

Tallulah Bankhead, the deep-voiced actress, known for calling everyone "dah-ling" and for her seductively superior attitude, was the show's hostess. Some reviewers' recollections credit her bigger-than-life personality for the show's initial success. Goodman Ace, a prominent member of the writing staff, provided Bankhead with many of the lines that made her come across as charmingly comical in spite of her gruff exterior.

The Big Show burst upon the radio waves November 5, 1950, a Sunday, airing from 6:00 p.m. to 7:30 p.m. Eastern time. In its second season it shifted to 6:30 p.m. to 8:00 p.m., still on Sundays. The program got mostly good reviews and earned respectable ratings, but it could not stop the ebb tide of radio listeners drifting over to the new visual medium. The cost per show was sometimes as much as $100,000. After two seasons, the network decided the results were not worth the cost.

In another move to save the medium, NBC Radio introduced *Weekend Monitor* in 1955. The premier broadcast on Sunday, June 12, aired from 4:00 p.m. to midnight Eastern time. Subsequent weekend broadcasts ran continuously for forty hours, from 8:00 a.m. Saturday morning until midnight Sunday. Featuring news, sports, comedy, interviews, music, and remote pick-ups from around the world, the show was touted as "a true magazine of the air."

As various features were aired, they were presented by a team of hosts referred to as "communicators." It included a veritable *Who's Who?* of NBC Radio personalities (some of whom were already, or would later be, performing on television). Goody became one of them, and Jane came out of retirement to join him as a "co-communicator."

Unlike *The Big Show*, the *Monitor* innovation was a tremendous success. Even though the midnight-to-dawn segment was later eliminated, it afforded listeners the opportunity to tune in at random for a wide range of entertainment and information throughout the weekend. There was no way it could defeat the attraction of TV, but it achieved a large and loyal audience. Even as NBC ramped up its involvement in the new visual medium, *Monitor* enabled the network to retain much of its radio audience until its last broadcast on January 26, 1975.

The Aces' participation in *Monitor* led to them becoming part of the NBC Radio *Weekday* program, which made its debut not long after *Monitor*. Aimed mostly at a female audience, it was a daytime program that aired Monday through Friday. Finding himself and Jane back in the radio mainstream again, Ace began writing commercials, which the two of them performed together.

After awhile, however, Jane tired of it all and she again retreated to the coziness of her favorite role: homemaker. It was, after all, the role she had signed up for before that fateful day at station KMBC.

She returned to radio only one more time. In 1952 she briefly accepted an uncharacteristic solo role as hostess of a recorded music program. It required no acting, so Jane could be comfortable just being herself as she introduced and commented upon musical selections. Goody had a bit of fun at her expense. He described her venture in his column as "a former comedienne now making her come-down as a disc jockey."

As for Goody, he continued in his dual careers as a radio writer and columnist for *The Saturday Review*. To those who can remember the early years of television and the fading signal of radio, Goodman Ace may not be a name they readily remember among writers. But his low-key style and literate way with words made him one of the most sought-after writers in both media. Like Fred Allen and Henry Morgan, he was admired for his intelligent wit, as opposed to those in both media who aimed for snappy gags and belly laughs. At one time he was earning $10,000 per week, the highest salary of any comedy writer at the time.

As television slowly squeezed the life out of radio, he found a new outlet for his skill at creating comedy. In the mid-1960s, CBS recruited him when it sought to develop a sort of school for young comedy writers for television. As Ace told it in one of his later columns, he was "placed in charge of half a dozen young writers who wanted to make all that easy money." A *Time* reporter noted that when a CBS comedy or variety show was floundering, it often was Ace who was called in to the rescue.

Radio was in his blood, though. When the opportunity arose, he took on a small but regular slot at New York station WPAT in which he offered his trademark witty commentaries. This was picked up by National Public Radio and went out over the full network during the 1970s.

When not kept busy enough by his regular duties, Goody sorted through old *Easy Aces* scripts, selecting eight favorites. He added some wry comments and a few short essays and assembled it all into a book. In 1970 it was published as *Ladies and Gentlemen: Easy Aces*. The book sold enough copies to confirm that many one-time listeners still fondly remembered the program.

In today's politically correct society, when one listens to a typical *Easy Aces* episode, Mr. Ace comes across as a bit huffy and put-downish toward Jane, although not as harsh as Archie Bunker chastising Edith. Today's feminists might be inclined to take offense. Yet in an era when husbands were deemed to be the head of the household, no complaints were raised. Listeners who found Jane to be a charming diversion from life's doldrums may actually have sympathized a bit with Goody, who had to live with her.

In real life, there is no question that Goodman Ace adored his Jane. She died while in New York's Doctors Hospital on November 11, 1974, after a prolonged illness that left her mostly unaware of what was going on around her. The Aces were just five days away from their fiftieth wedding anniversary.

They had no children. Jane's two brothers still lived in Kansas City. Goodman Ace arranged for services to be held there for family members only.

In the February 8, 1975, issue of *Saturday Review*, Goody devoted his "Top of My Head" column to a heart-breaking tribute to his beloved Jane.

He spoke of being alone at the funeral home, answering the usual barrage of questions about arrangements. Debating burial versus cremation, he pondered "a tisket, a casket?" and "we are all cremated equal." He recalled the lonely train trip to Kansas City, transporting Jane in her casket. At the burial, there was a light snowfall, the first of the season. Ace closed by saying, "He had the grace to celebrate her arrival with a handful of His confetti...."

The response was overwhelming. Hundreds of *Easy Aces* listeners, both men and women, wrote letters saying how much joy Jane Ace had brought into their lives. "Your loss is our loss," they said. "She will be remembered in our prayers."

Goody plodded on. Doing what had become second nature to him, he continued producing humor wherever he could. Both a gagsmith and a wordsmith, he poked fun at anyone and anything; but his was a gentle humor, never malicious. As one observer noted, "He was funny, but he never made fun of people."

Goodman Ace was still working when he died at the Ace home in New York City on March 25, 1982. He was interred next to his life's companion in the cemetery near their hometown, Kansas City.

Norman Cousins, who was then editor of *The Saturday Review*, wrote a tribute to him which appeared three months later. In it, he shared a story that had long circulated among the magazine's staff.

Supposedly, Ace received a call one day from a lady representing the Westminster Dog Show at Madison Square Garden. She invited him to be a speaker at one of their events. Ace at first demurred, explaining that he had never owned a dog in his life. No matter, said the caller. He could speak on any topic he chose, and it need not involve dogs. When she mentioned that there was a $2,500 honorarium, Goody said that he would be delighted to speak.

On the day of the show, he started out the door, telling Jane that he would be gone for a few hours. She asked where he was going, and he said, "The dog show."

"That's all right, Goody," she replied. "You don't have to tell me if you don't want to."

In 1971, the CTV Television Network of Canada adapted some of the *Easy Aces* scripts and attempted to bring them back to life in a series dubbed *The Trouble with Tracy*. It didn't work. Changing attitudes about feminism may have been a factor. The primary problem, however, was the players' inability to recreate Jane's natural dizziness or Ace's droll wit and long-suffering exasperation.

Saturday Review once ran a poll asking well-known Americans to nominate persons they thought worthy of being made members of a contemporary Hall of Fame. Ace playfully responded, saying, "I respectfully suggest the name of Goodman Ace...if he's still around. If he isn't," he added, "I wouldn't dig him up for this."

With all due respect, the Radio Hall of Fame chose to disregard him on this. In 1990, the *Easy Aces* programs and the Aces themselves were together inducted therein.

Books by Goodman Ace

The Book of Little Knowledge: More Than You Want to Know About Television, Simon & Schuster (1955)

The Fine Art of Hypochondria; or, How Are You? Doubleday (1966)

Ladies and Gentlemen: Easy Aces (8 scripts with added essays and comments), Doubleday (1970)

The Better of Goodman Ace, Doubleday (1971)

POSTSCRIPT: Jane-Isms

For those familiar with *Easy Aces*, the term "Jane-ism" has come to be familiar and understood to refer to those comically twisted utterances of Jane Ace. Every reference book that chronicles the Aces' careers mentions them and gives some examples. One such has worked its way into the vernacular as a classic cliché. Almost everyone has heard it or even uttered it themselves. Yet very few are aware that it was Jane Ace who first said: "Time wounds all heels."

In the presentation of the *Easy Aces* episodes, listeners chuckled over Jane's slightly skewed observations and mangled bits of wisdom, but then quickly lost track of them in the ongoing development of her latest predicament. For the enjoyment of those who loved hearing them, and others who missed out, here is a sampling, far from complete, from the hundreds of jumbled and juxtaposed clichés that were uttered with a straight face by Mr. Ace's beloved Jane.

Begin at the beguine.
Congress is back in season.
If I'm wrong, I'm not far from it.

You could have knocked me down with a fender.
Up at the crank of dawn.
Now, there's no use crying over spoiled milk.
The way things are these days, a girl's gotta play hard to take.
I'm completely uninhabited.
Seems like only a year ago they were married nine years!
I am his awfully-wedded wife.
He blew up higher than a hall.
He flew off the coop.
He shot out of here like a bat out of a belfry.
I'm sitting on pins and cushions.
The coffee will be ready in a jitney.
This hangnail expression…
I don't drink. I'm a totalitarian.
We'll be together like Simonized twins.
There's a time to and a time not to, and this is it.
As honest as the day is born.
I look like the wrath of grapes!
I wasn't under the impersonation you meant me!
No sooner said the better.
I can't find hide nor seek of it.
Making a mountain out of Mohammed.
Let me tell you, my tar-feathered friend.
I gave him my peace of mind.
Don't take any wooden Indians.
A fly in the oatmeal.
Stop batting around the bush.
Keep a stiff upper cut.

Goodman and Jane Ace

Come down off your high hat.
In a sort of roustabout way.
I went on a wild goose egg.
The fable of the dog and the manager.
Don't have that hangman look.
Keep your nose to the tombstone.
Sitting on Pretty Street.
It's high noon something is done.
He (Lincoln) was tall and emancipated.
Speaks with a Southern drool.
We were insufferable friends.
Burning your camel at both ends.
I have them by the galore.
In all my bored days.
I'd give my right name to (marry him).
We'll just nosey around.
No matter how you slice it, it's still blarney.
A baffle of wits.
To be contrary.
Too humorous to mention.
A woman's tuition.
I got an interior complex.
You know the way the gospel travels.
You're becoming historical.
To tidy him over until...
I hate people who are impromptu.
I await your answer with dated breath.
Simple as the day you were born.

Don't cross bridges in midstream.
I'm always in there punchy.
Can't they at least be Masonic friends?
Shaking like a thief.
That cock-and-wool story.
He'll pay back every tin dime.
Bawling and cooing.
Taking little catnips.
Just wrecking my brain.
I had him in the hollow of my head.
A mediocre castle in Spain.
Running around like a chicken with its hat off.
A girl is only young once in a while.
Make it short and sappy.
I've always wanted to see my name up in tights.
I'm a member of the weeper sex.
Home wasn't built in a day.
What you don't know about wouldn't take much.
A person can stand so much and not a step further.
I wasn't born yesterday for nothing.
I don't know if I'm going or on horseback.
You have to take the bitter with the batter.

Phil and Alice get cozy for a studio photo. CREDIT: Nostalgia Digest collection

Phil Harris and Alice Faye

Alice Faye got her start in show business as a child star... sort of. Born May 5, 1915, Alice Jeanne Leppert was the daughter of one of New York's finest. Charley Leppert, her father, was of German descent. His wife, Alice, was Irish-American. The family lived in a rough part of town known as Hell's Kitchen.

Though not poor, they lived on a modest income, with Mrs. Leppert often using a bit of creative cookery to keep her family fed. Charley Leppert chose to be an honest cop in an era when policemen were paid a barely living wage, and being on the take was considered a normal supplement to a cop's income. Once Alice and her two brothers were in school, their mother took on an unskilled labor factory job.

When she was twelve years old, young Alice found a job working in the dressing room of a dancing school. Unable to afford her own lessons, she watched the classes closely and later practiced the dances at home. She seemed to have a natural talent for dancing, which would contribute to her later career success.

Alice attended Public School No. 84, where she was a good student. She graduated with a perfect attendance record. Like most of her classmates, she was due to enroll for the coming semester at Washington Irving High School. But Alice had other ideas.

She and her mother had begun a weekly practice of meeting once a week for a visit to a nearby vaudeville theatre. The glamour of show business had instilled in young Alice a yearning to be part of that.

Not yet quite fourteen, she nonetheless was endowed with a figure more like that of a maturing young woman. With no mention to her parents, she auditioned for the Earl Carroll Vanities and was hired as a chorus girl at the handsome salary of $35 per week.

Strict child labor laws weren't yet in place back then. For a job that required performing in skimpy costumes and being out late at night, the arbitrary minimum age probably was eighteen. That surely didn't prevent a lot of ambitious young ladies who were sixteen or seventeen from getting hired. If the kid had a good figure, could dance and/or sing a little, and could reasonably pass for eighteen, the people doing the hiring weren't likely to ask to see a birth certificate.

Alice certainly wasn't the first kid with Broadway ambitions to fudge her age, but she may have been the youngest. Unfortunately, although her ruse got her hired, she let slip her real age to another chorus girl and was overheard by one of the bosses. When the Earl Carroll people learned her true age, they gently but firmly showed her the backstage door.

Notwithstanding the shortness of her time behind the stage lights, Alice's brief taste of show biz only whetted her appetite. Disappointed but undeterred, she tried again two years later when she was just fifteen. This time, claiming to have been born in 1912, she succeeded in landing a spot with the Chester Hale Vaudeville Unit. That led to her appearing in the 1931 edition of *George White's Scandals*.

Years later, Faye laughed about the fact that reviewers and others always made her out to be older than she was because of the phony birth year she gave to avoid being pulled off the stage. New York City public school records confirm that her birth year was 1915, not 1912, as often stated.

The star of that year's *Scandals* was Rudy Vallee. The megaphone-wielding singer and his dance band already had a number of hit recordings on their resume. With his mellow, if wavering, tenor voice, and his college boy good looks, Vallee was especially popular with the ladies. He made his radio debut in 1928 on a variety revue program called *The Fleischmann Hour*. In the relatively new medium, he drew 200 million listeners. In recognition of the star's popularity, the program later was renamed *The Rudy Vallee Hour*.

Vallee let it be known that he would like to have a female vocalist as part of his ensemble, and a number of hopefuls auditioned. Alice beat out the competition with a recording on which she did an imitation of Maurice Chevalier singing "Mimi." Rudy Vallee was impressed, finding her not only attractive but talented. He later said of Alice, "She was a cute blond, with a smile warm enough to melt the heart of an Eskimo."

Rudy was a perfectionist. He fined his musicians who played a flat note and singers who muffed a lyric. On the other hand, his popularity earned him one of the highest incomes of his peers, and his people were paid well. On the basis that Alice would be a featured singer on his Fleischmann show, he twisted the sponsor's arm to pay her $120 per week.

It was a hefty income for a Depression-era girl still in her teens. Alice already was attempting to help her family by sending money home to her mother. This enabled her to send a bit more.

By the time Vallee brought her onto *The Fleischmann Hour* in 1932, she had adopted the name Alice Faye. She later professed that she had played with a number of names, and chose this one because she liked the way it sounded. It rolled off the tongue nicely and it would fit easily on a theater marquee.

Alice began touring with Rudy and his "Connecticut Yankees" band. Audiences responded warmly to her rich, husky singing voice.

Her popularity grew during 1932-1934 as she became a regular vocalist on the radio program. Although no sparks ignited on contact, it's believed that she met future husband Phil Harris for the first time in 1933, when he made a guest appearance on the show. Harris was married at the time.

Faye was appearing on stage in the 1933-1934 edition of *George White's Scandals* when the Fox Film Corporation decided to produce a film version. Rudy Vallee was signed to play the male lead. At his insistence, Alice was given a small part that would enable her to do one song. Late in 1934, the two headed for Hollywood.

The film's female lead was to be played by Lilian Harvey. An English/German actress, Harvey already enjoyed a star status in Germany. The Fox people had persuaded her to come to America, and were attempting to establish her as a star here. She had by then appeared in four films for the studio.

Well into the movie's production, however, Harvey decided that she was being miscast, and that this film was unworthy of her talents. She summarily dissolved her contract and walked out. Years later, Faye sympathized with Harvey, saying in an interview that "the truth was that she simply was not right for the role as it had been written."

For Alice, it proved to be one of those rare moments when one is in exactly the right place at the right time. Fox had the film half made and suddenly found itself with no female star. No other known female lead was readily available. While scratching their heads over the dilemma, they noticed that there was an attractive young supporting actress standing in the wings.

Faye's one number, "Nasty Man," had already been filmed. Viewing it and then reviewing it, the execs agreed that she had done a superb job. She had a fine voice and came across well on the screen. Moving her up to the star role would be a gamble, but they were convinced that this girl had *something*.

They offered Faye $500 per week to take over Harvey's role and complete the picture. She, of course, accepted. Aware that she was already known as a popular singer, the studio played upon that and mounted a publicity campaign promoting her as the talented new discovery appearing in their forthcoming *Scandals* film.

Everything clicked. The film was a hit. As was Alice.

Notwithstanding Rudy Vallee's star status and his long connection with the stage version of *Scandals*, it clearly was Alice Faye who made a hit with the movie audiences. Louella Parsons singled her out as someone with great style and personality, high praise from Hollywood's noted gossip columnist.

Although she participated in a couple of production numbers, "Nasty Man" was her only solo. Nevertheless, more than one reviewer singled out that solo as a show-stopper. Calling her a flashy blond with great style, *The New York Times* gave a thumbs up to the picture and to Vallee, but saved their highest praise for Alice and her rendition of "Nasty Man." One reviewer described it as a "hot tune which comes closest to the cinematic patterns (created) by Busby Berkeley."

Sitting on her New York fire escape as a young school girl, Alice had dreamed of being a movie star. When she came to Hollywood with Rudy Vallee, she still thought of it as a dream. She saw herself as a singer coming to take on a small movie role that would be a brief but pleasant diversion. Suddenly she was offered and signed a contract with Fox.

A real life scandal threatened to sidetrack Alice's Hollywood career before it got rolling. Rudy Vallee was going through an unpleasant divorce. His bitter wife accused him of having affairs with at least three women, one of them being Faye.

Whatever the case with the other women, nothing was ever proven regarding Alice. She and Rudy steadfastly denied it. Nor did any third party ever come forward to support the accusation. Given that the band and singers traveled and roomed together, it is unlikely that any intimate relationship between Alice and Rudy could have gone undetected.

Nonetheless, a sudden storm of negative publicity had Fox execs on edge. Fortunately, the furor died before *George White's Scandals* premiered, and the public's memory is short. Rudy Vallee's career had about peaked along about here. Alice Faye's star had only begun to twinkle.

With Alice Faye in their fold, the Fox studios thought that they had their answer to Jean Harlow, albeit a singing version. Like Alice, Jean Harlow got an early start in show business. Born in 1911, she found her way to Hollywood while still in her teens. During the late 1920s, she appeared in numerous films, sometimes credited, sometimes not.

Her break-through came when Howard Hughes cast her in his 1930 epic about World War I, *Hell's Angels*. When the picture proved to be a smash hit, Harlow came to the attention of both audiences and studio reps on the lookout for potential stars. Hughes was approached by Metro-Goldwyn-Mayer and sold them Harlow's contract for $60,000.

Harlow was soon earning $1,250 per week. MGM cast her opposite numerous male stars, including several films with one of Hollywood's most popular leading men, Clark Gable. Between 1932 and 1937, she was one of MGM's biggest box office draws. Sadly, she died of a kidney ailment at the age of 26.

In her early grooming for potential stardom at Fox, Alice was given a new hair styling and, like Harlow, she became a platinum blonde. Her eyebrows were plucked, to be replaced by thin black pencil-line brows. The wardrobe people selected outfits for her to wear that accented her voluptuous figure. Faye once told an interviewer that she never thought of herself as beautiful when she was young, but her makeover and otherworldly costumes made her feel like another, more glamorous person.

Over the next year she appeared in three more films. Despite the grooming that gave her a somewhat sexy appearance, her parts mostly called for her to play a good-hearted gal whose main function was to win the hearts of audiences with her sultry voice and smooth delivery.

That she did well. Over the years, many new tunes became hits after being sung by Alice in one of her films. In a poll some years later, top songwriters of Tin Pan Alley were asked to name America's Number One female song-plugger. Irving Berlin, Cole Porter, and George Gershwin were among the celebrated composers who picked Alice Faye hands down. "There's something," they agreed, "about the way Alice projects a song that spells immediate success for it."

The first *Scandals* film had done well, so the Fox studios decided to ride upon its success. In *George White's 1935 Scandals,* George White appears as himself, along with the Scandals Beauties. Alice Faye, sans Rudy Vallee as leading man, received top billing for the first time. The film is best remembered, though, for the first screen appearance of a young dancer, already a Broadway star, named Eleanor Powell.

Trivia fans may know that actress Jane Wyman appeared in the film in an uncredited role as a chorine. Also, it's believed that Bill "Bojangles" Robinson filmed a dance routine, but it was cut before the film was released.

In 1935's *Every Night at Eight,* Alice co-starred with George Raft. She, Frances Langford and Patsy Kelly play a trio of singers looking to break into show business. Alice got in her star's share of vocals, but Frances Langford sang the film's big hit, "I'm in the Mood for Love."

For his book *Speaking of Radio*, old time radio historian Chuck Schaden interviewed both Alice Faye and Phil Harris. Speaking of those early years, Alice recalled a studio atmosphere that must have been a great comfort to a young woman 2,000 miles away from home and family.

"It was a wonderful job," she enthused. "I loved it. You live with those people. You get up at six in the morning and go right to the studio. You're made up and have breakfast on the set and shoot at 8:30. (Every day) the same wardrobe woman, the same make-up man and cameraman. You knew everybody. It was my home, and those people were my family."

Then, in 1935, the financially troubled Fox Film Corporation merged with 20th Century Pictures. Darryl F. Zanuck, the tough, demanding head of 20th Century Pictures became the kingpin of the new 20th Century-Fox Pictures.

The newly combined company would be cranking out low-budget films, called "B" pictures, from both its old and new lots to insure a steady flow at company-owned theaters around the country. Zanuck had a keen eye for spotting young performers who showed potential to star in these films. He quickly took an interest in Faye and decided to groom her.

To soften her image, he instructed that she be allowed to let her eyebrows grow back in and her hair to return to its natural color. Her wardrobe was modified, and Zanuck began casting her in roles where she could be more of a big sister or girl-next-door type. She even played a young, motherly type in some Shirley Temple films. Alice later noted that she was happier and felt much more comfortable when she was allowed to appear on screen looking more like her natural self.

Despite Alice's memories of a happy childhood home life, it seems her parents had some marital difficulties. At some point, after her move to California, they separated. Alice was by then the family's chief breadwinner and had been sending money home regularly. She continued doing so, but now made two separate contributions to her mother and father.

In 1935, she convinced her mother and her two brothers to join her. She found and rented a comfortable house that would accommodate all of them, and Alice Leppert became the unofficial housekeeper. When Alice Faye was obliged to attend some Hollywood event, her brothers took turns serving as her escort. Their mother, looking out for the best interests of her daughter, charged them with seeing that she got home at a reasonable hour so as to be rested for her next day at the studio.

For Alice, a plus side of her brotherly escorts was that it enabled her to be part of the Hollywood social scene without being linked to any male star in the town's gossip columns. If she was to achieve stardom, she was determined to do so on the merits of her own talent and efforts.

Alice's brother Charles, nicknamed Sonny, suffered from chronic arthritis. As a result, he was periodically unemployed. The California climate afforded him some relief from the illness. Alice helped him get hired as an assistant director at Fox. Older brother Bill had been a banker. Soon after his arrival, he became Alice's personal business manager. He schooled her in how to prepare a budget and live on it and put the bulk of her income in the bank.

Meanwhile, back in New York City, Charley Leppert had quit the police force. He had taken a job as a shipping clerk in a small company, but he was not a well man. In November, 1935, he collapsed and was admitted to Bellevue Hospital. When word reached Alice and the others, they hurriedly departed for New York. It was not a four-hour trip by jet plane in those days. They arrived too late to be at his side when he died on Thanksgiving Day.

After her father was buried in Woodlawn Cemetery, Alice lingered in New York to go to court and have her name legally changed from Leppert to Faye. Having worn that name for so long, she felt it had become her "real" name. Perhaps to maintain family unity, her mother and brothers had their names changed also.

Darryl Zanuck knew his business. In her modified persona, the studio's new star became a favorite of movie-goers. Her voice and singing style continued to win praise, both on the screen and off. Although not a trained actress, Alice demonstrated a degree of natural talent that sufficed to carry off her roles. She was able to hold her own with such co-stars as Rudy Vallee, Al Jolson and Edward Everett Horton, as well as leading men Don Ameche, Tyrone Power and John Payne. Though her early films were not box office blockbusters, they enjoyed respectable attendance.

Radio was a great boon to Americans during the Great Depression. It provided entertainment to suit almost every taste, and it was free. For those who could afford it, movies probably were the second most popular means of escaping from the harsh realities of a troubled time. The Hollywood studios cooperated by cranking them out with production line efficiency. During 1936, Alice Faye starred in four of them.

The story line in *King of Burlesque* is paper thin, but in addition to Alice's singing we get to see and hear the great jazz pianist Fats Waller perform. The film received no raves, but some critics much enjoyed Jack Oakie's comic efforts to avoid Arline Judge's matrimonial intentions; and Jane Wyman, apparently still waiting for someone to notice her, again appears as an uncredited dancer.

In *Poor Little Rich Girl*, Shirley Temple plays a rich kid pretending to be an orphan. Alice Faye and Jack Haley play a vaudeville couple who take her in. Tony Martin, in a bit of type casting, appears as a radio vocalist.

The 8-year-old Temple was already America's darling, riding on the rave waves of her success in *Little Miss Marker* and *Bright Eyes*. In the latter, the first film in which her name appeared above the title, she introduced her signature song "On the Good Ship Lollipop." The sheet music sold 500,000 copies.

Alice got to sing three songs in *Poor Little Rich Girl*, as well as demonstrating her motherly side. But *New York Times* reviewer Frank Nugent noted that the film was essentially "a display window for the Temple talents." In sympathy for Faye and Haley, he observed, "Short of becoming a defeated candidate for Vice President, I can think of no better way of guaranteeing one's anonymity than appearing in the moppet's films."

That didn't deter Alice from appearing with Temple again after first doing *Sing, Baby, Sing* with Adolphe Menjou and Tony Martin. Patsy Kelly was on board again to provide some comic relief.

In *Stowaway*, Alice collected her paycheck for singing just two songs. As the title suggests, the main character is a waif who's found aboard the yacht of rich guy Robert Young. He and Alice wed and adopt the kid. Arthur Treacher comes along for the ride as Young's valet.

Alice does get to display her motherly persona again. Meanwhile, Shirley Temple sings three songs and does impersonations of Eddie Cantor, Al Jolson singing "Mammy," and Ginger Rogers, dancing with a life-sized male doll attached to her toes.

Shirley Temple was not only enormously talented but precocious as well. At the premiere of *Poor Little Rich Girl* her mother was being interviewed by a reporter when the criminally cute cherub strolled over and said, "Why don't you talk to me? I'm the star."

Alice was by now making $1,500 per week. It was a hefty income for the era, but she earned every dollar. Her popularity was being utilized in a series of films, with one barely wrapped up before the next one got under way. Despite weariness that sometimes resulted in a down-time illness, she kept up the pace during 1937 and 1938, starring in seven—count 'em!— seven films.

On the Avenue
Wake Up and Live
You Can't Have Everything
You're a Sweetheart
In Old Chicago
Sally, Irene, and Mary
Alexander's Ragtime Band

Alice Jeanne Leppert, a.k.a. Alice Faye, the 13-year-old showgirl, was by nature a shy type, but she found the courage to stand up for herself when she felt the occasion demanded it. She was not reluctant to speak up when her instincts told her that something needed changing in a script. She was especially insistent when she felt that something in her role wasn't right.

For his part, Darryl Zanuck was not accustomed to having people question his judgment or his way of doing things. The product of a broken marriage, abandoned by both parents, he was a self-confident and strong-willed individual.

When he was fifteen, he lied about his age to join the U.S. Army, and fought in Belgium in World War I. During World War II, he took leave from 20th Century-Fox and was made a colonel in the Army Signal Corps. Frustrated when given stateside duty, he went to Washington, D.C. and demanded to see Chief of Staff General George

C. Marshall. That got him assigned as a liaison officer to the British Army, where he worked on training films as England endured frequent Nazi bombings. On one occasion, he talked his way into going along to film a naval night attack on a German radar site across the Channel on the shore of occupied France.

Whatever his autocratic failings, Zanuck had a strong social conscience. After the war, back at 20th Century-Fox, he began producing films with social messages that other studios had as yet avoided. Anti-Semitism was the subject of *Gentleman's Agreement*, starring Gregory Peck. Zanuck's films also addressed the issues of racism (*Pinky*), environmental destructiveness and abusive union tactics (*How Green Was My Valley*), poverty and unfair treatment of migrant workers (*The Grapes of Wrath*), and mistreatment of the mentally ill (*The Snake Pit*). After the latter was released in 1949, thirteen states passed new regulations regarding mental institutions.

Given his firm stance as the man in charge, Faye's outspokenness resulted in numerous clashes with her boss during her tenure with 20th Century-Fox. Zanuck clearly was the more immoveable of the two objects. Yet, though he may at times have been tempted to throw her off the payroll, he was loath to do so with a popular singer/actress whose name in the credits continually resulted in good box office for the films in which she starred. So the great man wisely curbed his wrath while Faye continued to help fill the studio's coffers.

Despite all the glitter of Hollywood, the studios seemed to have a fascination with Broadway, or perhaps found that audiences did. In the 1937-1938 series of films, three had plots involving Broadway shows. *Sally, Irene, and Mary* may have been a bit of déjà vu for Alice, being the story of three chorus girl friends, all determined to make it on Broadway.

Wake Up and Live was a satire on radio, with Jack Haley playing a singer who suffers from mic fright. Radio journalist Walter Winchell, playing himself, engages in a feud with bandleader Ben Bernie.

In *You Can't Have Everything,* Alice again makes it to Broadway, but this time as a playwright. Perhaps the most memorable aspect of this film was the first screen appearance of Rose Louise Hovick, better known as Gypsy Rose Lee. Robert Lowery, whose name probably won't ring a bell with most readers, has a small supporting role. Your reporter remembers him well as the star of a 1940s 13-week serialized adventure thriller titled *The Monster and the Ape.*

In Old Chicago was another turning point in Alice Faye's career. The film was a heavily fictionalized account of the great Chicago fire of 1871 and the lives of the O'Leary family, whose cow was blamed for the disaster. The beloved Jean Harlow was to have played the lead, but her untimely death occurred just as production got under way. Her role was given to Alice.

The film, which at the time was one of the most costly ever produced, was nominated for an Academy Award as best picture. Alice Brady, who played Mrs. O'Leary, actually won an Oscar for best supporting actress.

Alice Faye received no nomination, but her popularity soared as a result of the film's success. That later resulted in her being reunited with Tyrone Power and Don Ameche in *Alexander's Ragtime Band,* another film that received high praise and was a smash at the box office.

Alexander's Ragtime Band was an unabashed paean to the Jazz Age, from the ragtime saloon music of the early 1900s to the coming of the swing era, even recreating the Benny Goodman orchestra's performance at Carnegie Hall in 1938. Irving Berlin created some new arrangements for old favorites and combined them with new songs.

Among the film's hit numbers were "Blue Skies," "Easter Parade," "A Pretty Girl is Like a Melody," "Heat Wave" and, of course, the title song.

In addition to Don Ameche and Tyrone Power, Alice shared the credits with a parcel of co-stars that included Dick Powell, George Murphy, William Gargan, Brian Donlevy, Ethel Merman and Jean Hersholt. Comic relief was provided by the likes of Joan Davis, Patsy Kelly, Andy Devine, Fred Allen and Al, Harry and Jimmy Ritz (a.k.a. the Ritz Brothers).

Ethel Merman and Alice both had ample opportunity to display their vocal talents. Alice reprised or sang along with others in five songs. Her rendition of "When the Midnight Choo-Choo Leaves for Alabam'" was bouncy and sprightly. She followed that with two tender ballads, "Remember" and "All Alone." Her many fans had gotten their money's worth by the time the film reached its rousing finale. Alice fronted the chorus on the vocal as the band again played the title song.

Alexander's Ragtime Band was decidedly one of the best pictures in which Alice was featured or starred. It garnered six Academy Award nominations. Although it took no Oscars, both the press and the public heaped accolades on the film itself and in particular Alice's performance and singing. Her fan mail increased to second highest on the Fox lot.

Notwithstanding that she was already under contract, Darryl Zanuck recognized a valuable asset when he saw it. In September, he raised her salary to $2,500 a week.

In the midst of what would seem to be a continuous process of movie-making, Alice somehow found time to fall in love and get married. She and Tony Martin had worked together on a couple of films. As often happened in her pictures, something clicked, and they began dating, first casually and then more intimately. On September 4, 1937, after a short flight from Los Angeles, they were married in Yuma, Arizona. In spite of a prolonged on-and-off romance, it was an ill-fated and probably ill-advised union.

To their fans and the general public, the marriage of two popular singers probably seemed fairy-tale romantic. Reporters and gossip columnists made the most of the opportunity to quip about the couple making beautiful music together. In real life, the early harmony later gave way to some discord and sour notes.

From the beginning, their respective career paths caused a strain. Tony was very conscious that Alice's star shown more brightly than his own. That did not go unnoted by the press in their early dating, and continued after the wedding. Tony was determined to bolster his star status, and he concluded that singing, not acting, was his forte.

He had long been a popular nightclub favorite on the East Coast. He had his agent arrange a series of bookings for him there and in New York. It was a good career move. Before long, he was drawing in $2,000 per week.

Alice, of course, continued making movies in Hollywood. Tony returned for brief visits between engagements. They had purchased a comfortable little house, but the happy home life Alice had envisioned seldom occurred. Most often, after a long day on the studio lot, she returned to an empty house. Lonely and weary, she collapsed into bed, alone.

In December, 1939, she took time off to visit with Tony in New York. He gave her a large star sapphire for Christmas, and they spent as much time together as his engagement allowed. It appeared to be a pleasant holiday reunion.

Nevertheless, after returning to Hollywood, Alice announced in February that she was filing for divorce. Tony later said that the news came out of "darkest left field." On March 22, 1940, a judge granted Alice's petition.

Like many marriages made in Hollywood, this one apparently was not also made in heaven. Fortunately, their union had produced no children, so no one suffered save the principals.

Tony Martin later married the beautiful and talented dancer Cyd Charisse, and the two enjoyed one of Hollywood's most long-lasting marriages. Charisse died in June, 2008, not long after the couple celebrated their sixtieth wedding anniversary.

Regardless of any strains in her personal life, Alice kept busy during the next couple of years and continued to help enrich the studio. The 1939 film *Tail Spin* was a change of pace, a drama about the daring exploits of female pilots.

Rose of Washington Square was presented as a fictional story involving the *Ziegfeld Follies*. It carried a full-screen disclaimer stating that it was "entirely fictional and any similarity to persons either living or dead is purely coincidental." Nevertheless, the plot and principal characters could only have been inspired by Fanny Brice and her troubled marriage to gambler Nicky Arnstein. Not only was the film's title closely associated with Brice, but the producers had the audacity to include her signature song "My Man," sung by Alice. Brice sued 20th Century-Fox and an undisclosed settlement was reached out of court.

Notwithstanding, the picture was a success. Once again, Alice got to star with Tyrone Power, and the film offered such popular songs as "I'm Just Wild About Harry," "California, Here I Come," and "Toot, Toot, Tootsie, Goodbye," sung by Al Jolson.

Hollywood Cavalcade was another of Hollywood's many attempts to tout itself, with a story of the silent movie era, leading up to the challenges of adapting to sound. Alice helps sell the picture even though she does no singing. The flimsy plot is supported somewhat by the cameo appearances of such silent film favorites as Buster Keaton,

Ben Turpin and the Keystone Kops.

The studio rightly judged *Barricade* to be a mediocre picture. It was held on the shelf for awhile. Then the studio released it, hoping Alice's name in the credits might carry it over at the box office. Even Alice wasn't that popular.

Little Old New York, a romanticized story of Robert Fulton and his invention of the steamboat, starred Fred MacMurray, Ward Bond, Andy Devine and an attractive blonde actress named Brenda Joyce. She later became the Jane who took up with Johnny Weissmuller's Tarzan. The film was a non-musical, which caused many of Alice Faye's fans to express their disappointment. Alice, however, was pleased at the rare opportunity to perform as an actress rather than a singer.

Her fans were compensated when Alice starred as *Lillian Russell* in a bio-pic that offered such old time favorites as "After the Ball," "The Band Played On," and "Rosie, You Are My Posie." Co-stars included Henry Fonda, Don Ameche and Edward Arnold. The comedy team of Weber and Fields appeared as themselves.

Then came another biggie: *Tin Pan Alley.* There's singing and dancing aplenty, as John Payne and Jack Oakie play songwriters in the early 1900s. Alice does most of the singing, with Betty Grable taking the spotlight for the dance numbers.

Betty Grable was the gal with the million dollar legs—literally. A passable young actress and a great dancer, she was widely believed to have the most beautiful legs in Hollywood. As her popularity grew, the studio insured her legs for $1 million with Lloyds of London. Betty Grable came to be one of Hollywood's favorite pin-up girls. Thousands of male fans had pictures of her in poses that accented her famous legs. During World War II, she was portrayed on the fuselages of many an Air Force bomber.

Having bided his time, Darryl Zanuck sought to bring the rambunctious Alice Faye down a notch by giving her some competition. The lovely young dancer with the great legs seemed like just the right choice. Even before the film went into production, there was talk of a feud between the two, although in fact they had not met. Zanuck may well have floated the rumor himself.

In any case, he was doomed to be disappointed. On their first day together on the set, Faye and Grable hit it off nicely from the start. They not only worked well together during the film's production, but became lifelong friends, even though Grable later took Faye's place as the studio's box office darling.

In between the latter three 1940 films, Alice found time and energy to make her debut on *Lux Radio Theatre*. The June 3 program was a radio adaptation of *Alexander's Ragtime Band*. Ray Milland and Robert Preston took over the roles of Tyrone Power and Don Ameche respectively. With Ethel Merman absent from the cast, Alice got to sing seven numbers, including "Blue Skies," "Say It With Music" and the title song.

Faye kicked off 1941 by starring in the musical comedy *That Night in Rio* opposite Don Ameche. The Brazilian bombshell, Carmen Miranda, appeared in her outrageous costumes and hairdos and livened things up singing three numbers: "I, Yi, Yi, Yi, Yi, I Like You Very Much," "Chica, Chica, Boom Chic," and "Cai Cai."

Before the year was over, Alice also appeared in *The Great American Broadcast* and *Weekend in Havana*, two lighthearted and pleasant films. The first was a musical built around the early days of radio. The latter involved a pleasure cruise gone awry, and was graced by only one song from Faye.

For Alice, the real high point of 1941, a turning point in both her life and her career, was her second marriage to that fellow she'd met briefly on Rudy Vallee's radio program: Phil Harris.

Probably the most intriguing trivia tidbit about Phil Harris is his real name: Wonga Philip Harris. Yes, Wonga.

One might wonder if someone made a mistake when filling out his birth certificate, as happened to Oprah Winfrey. But then, what other name might his parents have meant to give him?

Phil was born June 24, 1904, in Linton, Indiana, the only child of Harry and Dollie Harris. As a young man, Harry had been a mine worker. Prior to their marriage, Dollie Harris was a buyer for a clothing company.

Harry was spared from a life down under by his multiple musical talents. He did some performing in vaudeville, and worked for several circuses, including Ringling Brothers. After their marriage, he and Dollie also did some performing in summer stock tent theater. Presumably, they were supporting players or the shows were not memorable. There appears to be no record of what roles they played or in what productions.

At one point in his career, Harry played the clarinet as leader of the circus band. He taught young Wonga to play several instruments, including the drums, which the boy favored. As bandleader, he was able to hire his young son for his first job, playing drums with the circus band. Dollie was not musically inclined, but she may have performed as one of the pretty costumed young women who marched around in the parade under the big top.

These days, some parents have no qualms about burdening their offspring with outrageous names that will hang around their necks like a millstone as they grow up. But in 1904, parents tended to give their children familiar, popular names, such as Joe or Mary. So what were little Wonga's parents thinking?

Harry chose the name to honor a performing Indian chief who became a good friend during his circus years. Phil used the name well into his teen years and apparently suffered no youthful repression as a result.

Wonga's grandmother also lived in Linton, at 190 E Street, NE. The boy spent a lot of time residing with her while his parents were on the road.

His parents' background in vaudeville no doubt influenced Wonga. It may have given him the initiative to acquire a job at Linton's Nicklo Theatre at the age of nine. Playing drums along side of a woman who played piano and another who played a fiddle and a horn, Wonga also provided sound effects for the silent films. Keeping an eye on the screen, he would blow a whistle, toot a car horn, crank a wind machine or give a drum roll. He got to see movies for free and was paid five dollars per week!

The family moved to Nashville when Wonga was eleven. Mr. Harris may have felt there was more opportunity for a musician there. Nashville already was a town noted for its country music. Whether the change of venue proved fruitful for Harry and Dollie, it was providential for their son.

Wonga attended Hume Fogg High School in Nashville. There he honed his musical talent as a trap drummer in the school band. Soon after graduation he was able to put his talent to use playing drums in the Francis Craig Orchestra.

With the instinct of a show biz pro, he recognized the distraction that his unusual name might present. He discarded the name Wonga, shortened Philip to Phil, and from then on became just Phil Harris.

Before long he decided to branch out. Parlaying his multi-musical talents and on-the-job experience unusual for one his age, he rounded up a group of fellow musicians and formed a five-piece Dixieland band called the Dixie Syncopators. Phil doubled as leader and singer of some comedy vocals.

The band signed with an agent, and soon they were playing one night stands and some longer engagements throughout the South. They even managed to wrangle a trip to Honolulu, where they helped open the new Princess Theatre. Phil recalled that experience in his interview with Chuck Schaden, saying "…they were hanging somebody on the screen and we're playing 'St. Louis Blues' and the Hawaiians are going crazy, 'cause they never heard music like that."

The Syncopators had steady work and enjoyed themselves for a couple of years before some grew restless and the group disbanded. Phil took a job with a band called the Palais de Dance just in time to join them for a tour of Australia.

Phil and several other musicians were recruited to augment the group. One of the newcomers was a left-handed ukulele player named Frank Remley, with whom Phil struck up what would become a long working relationship and friendship.

In Sydney, during the band's tour of Australia, Phil met Marcia Ralston, a popular screen star. A romance bloomed, and the two were married on September 2, 1927. When Phil returned to America, Marcia emigrated with him.

Their marriage seems to have gone along smoothly in its early years, generating no newsworthy stories, good or bad. At some point it was determined that Marcia was unable to have a child. She and Phil then adopted a son, Phil Harris, Jr., who was born in 1935.

In Hollywood, Marcia sought to pick up where she had left off. Arriving as an unknown, she did not achieve stardom here, although she appeared in almost two dozen films between 1933 and 1947. In a variety of bit parts and supporting roles, she shared the screen with such notables as Olivia de Havilland, Helen Hayes, Bonita Granville, John and Lionel Barrymore, Clark Gable, Jimmy Durante and Roland Young. She was a stewardess in W. C. Fields' last film, *Never Give a Sucker an Even Break*, and a USO girl in the Abbott and Costello film *Keep 'Em Flying*, with Martha Raye along for the ride.

In 1928, after returning stateside, Phil was working on the West Coast. Musical groups of all sizes were finding an appreciative audience there. Phil had no trouble initially finding work by returning to his drummer role. For a time he played with the Henry Halstead Big Band Orchestra.

Sometime during 1928, he met pianist Carol Lofner, and the two teamed up as co-leaders of the Lofner-Harris Orchestra. They were the first to perform at the new Rendezvous Ballroom in Balboa, California. Lofner directed the orchestra. Phil, on drums, was out front and center, rather than at the back of the group, and occasionally took a turn singing. The group's success at the Rendezvous led to an engagement at the St. Francis Hotel in San Francisco.

In those days, said music man Meredith Willson, San Francisco was a key place for musical groups to perform. A new medium called radio was attracting more and more listeners, and San Francisco was the major radio town on the West Coast. In his memoir *And There I Stood with my Piccolo*, Willson recalls that "Over at the St. Francis Hotel a curly-haired drummer by the name of Phil Harris was causing talk...." The Lofner-Harris Orchestra was such a hit at the St. Francis that they were held over for three years.

The orchestra's shows were being broadcast over one of the local radio stations. Many listeners were still tuning in on crystal sets, and in an as-yet unregulated medium, stations from various areas often interfered with one another. Phil recalled that his ensemble was fortunate in that the station carrying their music was one of the two most powerful on the air at that time.

In 1931, Victor Records approached Lofner and Harris about doing some recording. With the orchestra augmented by Muzzy Marcellino on violin, the group recorded six sides for Victor. Phil provided a vocal on one number called "I Got the Ritz from the One I Love (I Got the Big Go-By)." It may have been a precursor to the talk/sing novelty tunes for which he later become known.

Harris and Lofner separated in 1932. Harris formed a new band under his own name and based in Los Angeles. Phil led and sang as the group enjoyed a prolonged engagement at the Ambassador Hotel's glamorous Cocoanut Grove, with the shows being aired on radio.

In 1933, Phil appeared in a short novelty film for RKO Radio Pictures called *So This Is Harris!* Its plot centered on Phil's extraordinary appeal as a lady's man. It was a surprise hit and won the year's Academy Award for best live action short subject in the comedy category.

That led to his first part in a full-length film, RKO's *Melody Cruise*. Phil did only a little singing, instead co-starring this time as the wisecracking sidekick of womanizing millionaire Charles Ruggles.

He followed up with two more short films, *Romancing Along* in 1936 and *Harris in the Spring* in 1937. Both films proved popular, and they no doubt boosted Phil's recognition factor with moviegoers who had never seen him in person and had only limited exposure to his radio appearances.

In addition to the making of his first short film, 1933 proved to be an eventful year for Phil in a way he could not have anticipated at the time. That year he and his band performed on *The Fleischmann Hour*. The band had by then grown to twenty-five pieces and was renamed the Phil Harris Orchestra. The name change and the popularity of *The Fleischmann Hour* surely helped to increase Phil's name recognition. It also was during this guest appearance that he made the acquaintance of an attractive young singer named Alice Faye.

In 1934, the orchestra played in Chicago for the first time at the College Inn. They were replacing Ben Bernie and his orchestra. Bernie, the "yowsa, yowsa" man, was immensely popular and had enjoyed a long run. Phil worried that it was going to be a tough act to follow. Fortunately, the World's Fair was drawing people from near and far, and many of those people found their way to the Hotel Sherman to hear the Harris orchestra.

Despite the hard times of the Great Depression, or perhaps because of them, people craved entertainment. Phil and his orchestra managed to keep busy providing it. They did some recording for Decca Records in 1933, then again in 1935. During 1936 and 1937, they recorded sixteen sides for Vocalion, mostly hot swing tunes that sold well.

Along the way, Phil had made the acquaintance of many entertainment personages, including George Burns and Jack Benny. In 1936, he came this/close to providing the music for the *Burns and Allen* radio program.

When Chuck Schaden interviewed him, Phil recalled that Burns had suggested him for the spot. Music Corporation of America, Phil's agent at the time, inquired if he'd like the job. Phil agreed and the orchestra cut short its current engagement to prepare to move to New York. Unfortunately, George Burns apparently did not have the final say. Two days before they were scheduled to leave, Phil was told to unpack. The slot was going to be filled by Wayne King.

Barely a week later, Jack Benny invited Phil to dinner at Hollywood's famed Trocadero Restaurant. Jack was seeking a replacement for the departing band on his radio program. Unaware of the Burns near miss, Jack asked Phil where he was working now. Phil confessed that at present it appeared he was sort of between jobs. Scarcely missing a beat, Jack said, "You're with me!" Just like that, Phil and his orchestra became a regular part of *The Jell-O Show,* making their debut performance on October 4, 1936.

Phil undoubtedly could have maintained his popularity as band leader and singer long enough to retire comfortably when rock music began to drown out the big bands. But the Benny program definitely was a major turning point in his life.

Benny made it a practice to incorporate announcers, singers and band leaders into the cast with speaking roles. It did not take long for Jack's great team of writers to work Phil into the script.

Phil was possessed of a voice that projected well, and he was a handsome fellow with his naturally curly hair. The real Phil tended to be modest and soft spoken. Notwithstanding, he was built up as a rather brash, hip-talking wise guy whose comments invariably proved him not as smart as he thought.

No mention was ever made of his marital status. Instead, his persona on the Benny program became that of a would-be ladies man who believed that his curly hair and cute dimples made him irresistible to the gals.

Frank Remley had by that time joined Phil's orchestra. Having switched for a time from a ukulele to a banjo, he was now playing guitar. The fact that he was left-handed was deemed somehow humorous, and it was often mentioned in the script that he was a left-handed guitar player. Noting that Remley and Harris were pals, and playing on the conception that musicians often partied after a late-night gig, the writers began to feed Phil lines about raucous band parties. They portrayed Harris and Remley as heavy drinkers, which enabled a lot of hangover gags.

Jack even attempted to augment Remley's income by having the writers give him a couple of comic lines to read. Unfortunately, it quickly became evident that Remley was not comfortable at the mic and was not going to be able to pull it off. He did, however, provide what Phil referred to as a trigger laugh. When anyone in the cast read a gag line that tickled Remley, he instantly burst out laughing, even though he'd heard it during rehearsals. That triggered people in the audience to join in the laughter almost before they'd had time to grasp the punch line.

Phil had a bit of a Southern accent, acquired during his years in Nashville. He played upon that in some of his songs and in comic exchanges with Benny. When his recording of "That's What I Like About the South" proved to be a big hit, it prompted a running gag in which Benny couldn't believe that the song was so popular. In one program, a large portion of the show was devoted to Phil singing the song and explaining it chorus by chorus to Jack, who expressed uncomprehending disbelief.

A key element of Jack Benny's humor and the program's success was the fact that he mostly allowed himself to be the butt of jokes by his cast. Mary Livingston (Jack's real-life wife, Sadie), announcer Don Wilson, and Jack's supposed valet, Rochester, all took potshots at him. Singer Dennis Day's job was to drive Jack nuts with his wacky logic.

As Phil's character was developed, he made self-deprecating gags about his Southern upbringing. He took to giving people nicknames. Ignoring the fact that Benny was his boss, he dubbed him "Jackson." Talking to other cast members, he called Benny "ol' Jackson." Greeting

Jack himself, he said "Hi ya, Jackson." He usually spoke of and addressed Mary Livingston as "Livvy." He had a number of insulting but funny nicknames for notoriously overweight Don Wilson, including some that worked in the name of Jell-O, the show's sponsor.

For his part, Jack made Phil the goat of jokes about his ego, his inability to talk like normal folk, even his band's music. The subject of his supposed excessive boozing was a frequent source of Jack's jibes. Phil spouted gags that reinforced the illusion: "I can't die until the government finds a safe place to bury my liver." Asked if he had a favorite brand, Phil replied, "I never endorse any brand. Wouldn't want to slight the others. They're all great!"

Once Jack allowed that he might have been a bit too harsh on Phil and he apologized. Phil let on that he was not appeased.

Jack: Phil, I said I was sorry. Now let me go and tell some jokes, will you?

Phil: Well, don't expect my orchestra to laugh.

For the most part, though, Phil appeared impervious to joshing by Jack and any of the other cast members. In keeping with his self-admiring persona, he frequently hinted that the audience was really there to see him. A typical Harris entry line was: "The program's been dull, but now Harris is here. So come on, all your folks, prepare to cheer!"

A Benny/Harris exchange would involve Phil insulting the boss and doing some boasting about his own charms. Jack would respond with jabs that went over Phil's head. As his exasperation grew, Jack would mutter, "Alright, alright!" and ask Dennis what he was planning to sing. After enduring a bit of silliness from "the kid," Jack would cue the number by saying, "Sing, Dennis" or "Play, Phil."

In his autobiography, Jack Benny described Phil's on-air personality as "the brassiest, most worldly character...loud-talking, illiterate, rude, alcoholic, arrogant, boastful. He was completely immoral (yet) radiated vitality and a sheer gusto in animal pleasures that made him unique among all the characters on radio." Phil thus stood out and endeared himself to listeners, coming across as a novel and welcome change from the usual bandleader or announcer who doubled as a straight man for the star.

Becoming a regular on the Benny program made Phil's name a household word. It provided a steady income without one-night stands. It also meant that when Jack made his 1940 film, *Buck Benny Rides Again*, Phil would ride along with the other cast members who had featured roles: Eddie "Rochester" Anderson, Andy Devine and Dennis Day.

When *The Jell-O Show* took its summer break, Phil was free to book his orchestra out of town if he chose. Otherwise, he could stay put in one place, except when the show was broadcast from some other town.

Jack did like to broadcast from various locations. One of his favorite spots was the California desert town of Palm Springs. Doing a show there was like a mini-vacation for the cast and any supporting crew that went along.

An ardent golfer, Phil fell in love with the area in the early 1930s, and he purchased property at the Thunderbird Country Club in Rancho Mirage. It was part of a prototype development, the first community designed to be constructed surrounding a golf course. Phil became a dedicated promoter of golf charity events in the Palm Springs area, often chairing the event or doing commentary during a tournament. He also played in many of them, along side various Hollywood stars.

Phil was a regular member of the Benny cast almost from the time he came on board as orchestra leader. His participation in the goings-on became such an integral part of that show that his arranger, Mahlon Merrick, took over the actual conducting of the orchestra. Continuing the illusion for the folks at home, though, Jack still cued the musical interlude with his "Play, Phil."

Career-wise, things were going along swimmingly for Phil. Apparently that was not the case on the home front. His marriage to Marcia Ralston lasted nearly ten years, but there were tensions early on that increased over time.

As Phil capitalized on his growing popularity, Marcia was at first frustrated and then angry at the path her career was taking. The star status she had enjoyed in her homeland was not replicated in Hollywood. Neither did American movie-goers come to adore her as Australian audiences had.

Moreover, the romance that had blossomed there began to be strained here. Her own career and Phil's kept them apart so much that she was unable to enjoy the at-home togetherness she craved. One morning in 1940, Phil awoke to find Marcia and Phil Jr. gone. Marcia had left a note on his bedside table. With no elaboration, it informed him that she was filing for divorce.

It is possible that Marcia suspected Phil of having strayed from the nest. His good looks and boyish charm made him attractive to the ladies, and prior to their marriage he had had some brief romances. However, while married to Marcia, it does not appear that he ever was unfaithful. What seems more likely is that Marcia was unable to accept her diminished status in Hollywood after having been idolized by fans in her native country. This and their frequent separations may have combined to make her feel compelled to move on.

If there was any effort by Phil and/or Marcia to reconcile, it was unsuccessful. Phil apparently acceded to Phil Jr. going with his mother. He later helped Marcia get their adopted son enrolled at St. John's Military Academy in Los Angeles. In spite of some troubled teen years, Phil Jr. eventually straightened up and became a mature adult. He had no interest in show business, but found his calling as an air traffic controller. He worked at several major airports, eventually becoming a manager at Fort Worth. He died of a sudden heart attack a few days short of his sixty-sixth birthday on March 13, 2001.

Marcia Ralston continued, however reluctantly, to accept various supporting roles and bit parts into the late 1940s. As offers became fewer and less appealing, she forsook films and became an Arthur Murray Dance Studio instructor in the 1950s. While there, she met and married a man named Bud Henderson. His sister, Betty, was married to actor Robert Young. This connection later led to Marcia appearing as Nurse Donnelly on the 1970s television series *Marcus Welby, M.D.* In 1988, she died of a subarachnoid brain hemorrhage. She was eighty-two years old.

Phil may have sensed that his marriage was in trouble, but he was stunned by the abruptness of Marcia's departure with no prior discussion. The Benny cast and other friends observed a Phil they had never seen before, downcast and distracted. As the shock wore off, however, he gradually began to perk up and be more his usual upbeat self.

Then a lucky happenstance completed his recovery. He chanced to meet again that lovely girl singer he had met some years ago on *The Fleischmann Hour*. She looked even more attractive than he remembered.

This time he was free to ask for a date. She accepted. Another date followed, and they soon became an item. Alice found Phil as attractive as he found her, and they soon agreed that their romance was the real thing. Phil, however, was still married to Marcia until the divorce was finalized.

On April 30, 1941, gossip columnist Louella Parsons wrote: "The only thing that stands in the way is Phil's decree, which will not be final for several months. Phil is telling anybody interested that he'll marry her the minute he can."

A U.S. marriage was not yet possible, but on May 12, Phil and Alice traveled to Mexico and had a "quickie" wedding in Ensenada. On September 20, the court formally dissolved Phil and Marcia's marriage. The next day, at Alice's insistence, they flew to Galveston, Texas, and had the marriage "redone." Alice later quipped that she "wanted to be sure it would stick and be Americanized."

The newlyweds continued with their respective careers through 1941. However, Alice was pregnant during the filming of *Weekend in Havana*. She elected to take a break from film work and be a stay-at-home mom for a year. The Harrises welcomed their first daughter, Alice Faye Harris Jr., on May 19, 1942.

By then, of course, the Japanese had bombed Pearl Harbor, and the United States was a nation at war. Like most American males, Phil would have liked to pick up a rifle and join the fight for freedom. The "boys" in the band no doubt shared that yearning, but like Phil they all were past what the armed services considered the idle age group.

As the war progressed, the need for men would no doubt result in most of them being drafted one by one. Instead, they chose an alternative course. They enlisted en masse in the Merchant Marines. On December 6, Phil made his farewell appearance on the Benny program.

As might be expected, none of the group ever was assigned to sea duty. Instead, they were charged with establishing an entertainment center for the troops stationed on and passing through Santa Catalina Island. Once they had things organized and running smoothly, Phil demonstrated his own brand of G.I. ingenuity by designating one of the band members as a substitute leader on weekends. He then was able to arrange for weekend passes that allowed him to rejoin the Benny show.

In March of 1943, Jack Benny suffered a prolonged case of pneumonia and was off his show for five weeks. George Burns and Gracie Allen filled in for him on March 7. Unlikely as it seems, Orson Welles was then invited to take over. With his macabre sense of humor, he accepted. A listing for the March 14 program reads:

"Orson Welles fills in. Although Jack is still ill, the good news is that Phil Harris is back!" Thereafter, Phil was able to resume his place as a regular cast member for most broadcasts that were not done on the road . Back on his feet at last, Jack Benny returned on April 11.

Meanwhile, Alice decided that she was ready to go back to work. Despite her differences with Darryl Zanuck, 20th Century-Fox knew that Alice's fans were impatient for her return. When she agreed that she was ready, they starred her with John Payne in 1943's *Hello, Frisco, Hello*. Done in Technicolor, it is a tale of San Francisco vaudeville performers in the early 1900s.

Alice got to sing ten songs, including a heartwarming rendition of "You'll Never Know." For GIs scattered around the world, seeing the lovely Alice Faye on the screen, and hearing her wistful rendering of this song, evoked memories of the wives and sweethearts they had left behind. The song won an Academy Award. Even though Alice didn't record the number, it came to be associated with her and was considered her signature song. Over the years, she sang it again many times on her own program and as a guest on others. In 1962, she included it on a Reprise Records album along with many of her movie hits.

The picture proved to be one of Faye's highest-grossing films. With fans delighted at her return, the studio hastened to find a starring role for Faye in another Technicolor musical that year. The cast of *The Gang's All Here* included Benny Goodman and his orchestra and

Phil Baker, host of the quiz program *Take It Or Leave It,* as himself. The saucy Carmen Miranda sang "The Lady in the Tutti Frutti Hat," a number that was quite risqué for its time, with dozens of scantily clad women handling very large bananas. Whether or not these were meant to be phallic symbols, the film got a thumbs-down from the censors in Miranda's native Portugal and was banned from being shown there.

During filming, Alice learned that she was again pregnant. She waited until filming was done before making that known. In doing so, she also gave Louella Parsons an "exclusive," announcing that she planned to retire and begin living a "normal" home life. That was a blow to 20th Century-Fox and Darryl Zanuck. They had other big name stars and continued to groom new ones, but Faye was still their biggest, most sure-fire box office draw.

The announcement was not an easy decision for Alice. Performing was in her blood. She enjoyed her star status and immersed herself in her performances even when the script or her part were below par. Moreover, her social life was centered almost entirely on the stars with whom she worked and the many friends she had made on the set.

Still, the rigors of doing musicals was exhausting and often left her ill. Most other pictures were usually wrapped up in four to six weeks. Musicals could take months, with endless and tiring rehearsals of the singing and dancing segments.

Rather than ending her career, however, her announcement enabled her to do some renegotiating with the studio. Her fans pleaded for her to return. She was at the peak of her popularity and a top money-maker for 20th Century-Fox. When Darryl Zanuck personally asked her to reconsider, she came away from their meeting with a new contract that required her to do just one film per year. She could do two or more at her discretion, but would have the option to choose. She made it clear that her intent was for any additional pictures to involve dramatic rather than song and dance roles.

On April 22, 1944, Alice presented Phil with their second child, another girl, whom they named Phyllis Wanda.

Later that year, empowered to be selective about her films, she accepted a role as one of four guest stars in *Four Jills in a Jeep*. Carole Landis, Martha Raye, Mitzi Mayfair and Kay Francis starred as four USO gals in a more-or-less true story about entertaining American troops overseas. Dick Haymes made his screen debut and Alice again sang "You'll Never Know," which became even more popular during the war years.

With Alice back in the fold at 20th Century-Fox, the studio began sending her scripts that would afford her the opportunity to do some serious acting. After rejecting more than two dozen of them, she accepted a role in the film *Fallen Angel*. It would earn her star billing. She also was pleased that Dana Andrews, one of her favorites, would be the leading man. Appearing with them would be a young newcomer, Linda Darnell, who was being groomed by Darryl Zanuck to be his next female darling of the screen.

Having at last achieved her objective of playing a serious role, Alice was a bit apprehensive. She found it calming to have Otto Preminger directing. He worked closely and patiently with her, assuring her that she was doing fine. When the film was wrapped, Alice was certain that she had given a worthy performance.

When editing of the film was completed, Alice arrived early at the screening room and took a deep breath as she awaited the viewing. What she saw stunned her and filled her with a sense of betrayal and anger.

To spotlight his new female star, Darryl Zanuck had eliminated more than a dozen of Alice's scenes. Two more had been drastically cut. Even a scene added specifically for Alice, in which she sang "Slowly" while listening to a radio, ended up on the cutting room floor. The result was a film whose plot was difficult, if not impossible, to follow. It certainly was not one in which Alice's choppy appearances would do her credit.

Alice found it difficult to speak as she rose from her seat and said to Dana Andrews, "I'll never do another picture." She paused on her way to the exit just long enough to scribble a note to Zanuck. What it said was never revealed, but many years later she said that it was unprintable, "even today."

In her chauffeur-driven car, she headed off the lot, but had the driver stop at the security gate. She handed the guard the note and her dressing room keys and asked him to deliver them to Zanuck in the morning.

Darryl Zanuck was furious. He tore up her contract and angrily declared that she would never work in Hollywood again. In fact, once his rage subsided, Zanuck realized that Faye was still a popular draw. For several years he attempted to bring her back, offering her roles in such films as *A Tree Grows in Brooklyn* and *The Razor's Edge*. They were parts that would have enabled her to do some serious acting, with the added incentive that there would be parts for Phil.

Alice refused to take the bait. She had no intention of returning to film work, especially at 20th Century-Fox.

Phil was established as a band leader and a fixture on the Jack Benny show. There was no doubt he could support the family. They had now settled in a home about 110 miles from Los Angeles in the Southern California desert country that Phil loved. It was an easy commute to the NBC studios for rehearsals and shows. He could indulge his love of golf at a growing selection of courses.

As for Alice, no role she had ever played on the screen was more fulfilling than her new role as a stay-at-home mother. In spite of some rough times and hardships, she treasured many memories of happy family times as a child. Now she was free to bask in the satisfying role of homebody and mother to her two cute young girls.

Reminiscing about the transition many years later, Alice said, "I decided to make a new life for myself. A home life. I had been chauffeured to work, made up, dressed, given my meals, and chauffeured back home. There were so many things I hadn't done. I equated independence with seeing daylight during the week and learning to drive a car." With her movie-making days supposedly behind her, she was free to luxuriate in being a stay-at-home housewife and mother.

Then came an offer that was too good to pass up. The folks at the F.W. Fitch Company wanted Phil and Alice, as a team, to star on *The Fitch Bandwagon*. It would give Alice and Phil the opportunity to work together, without requiring a great deal of Alice's time away from her girls. After discussing the offer and agreeing that it was a good one, Phil and Alice accepted and worked out a schedule that would minimize Alice's time away from home.

In 1928, Fred Fitch made history in Iowa by being the state's first manufacturer ever to sponsor a national radio program. The original program went through several format changes. By 1941, it was established as a 30-minute program called The *Fitch Bandwagon*. Heard at 7:30 p.m. on Sundays, immediately following the Jack Benny program, it was a top rated show enjoyed by millions of listeners.

The program featured top bands of the era, including Phil's, as well as those of Cab Calloway, Tommy Dorsey, Guy Lombardo, Ozzie Nelson, Harry James and others. Depending upon which band was providing the music and where they were currently engaged, the program originated from various cities, including New York, Chicago and Los Angeles. The show had a singing commercial that was sung to the tune of a familiar oldie, "Smile for Me." Folks who liked big band music and were regular listeners could sing it as easily as any pop record hit:

Laugh a while,

Let a song be your style,

Use Fitch Shaammm-poooo!

Don't despair,

Use your head, save your hair,

Use Fitch Shaammm-poooo!

In 1944, the show underwent another format revision and began including comedy skits between musical selections. During that year, actor Dick Powell filled the role of host and did a bit of warbling. For awhile in 1945, the program featured Cass Daley.

Phil and Alice took over as co-hosts in September, 1946. Following the format that had evolved, they each usually were featured in at least one musical number. In between, they would partner in short sitcom stories. Audience response was more enthusiastic than they could have hoped.

Fans of Alice Faye were delighted to again hear her warm, pleasing voice singing new tunes and old favorites. Folks who enjoyed Phil's somewhat loco humor could now enjoy a double dose, first as he taunted Jack Benny, then on the Fitch program, and they needn't even turn the dial. To the writers' delight, the audience as a whole seemed especially to enjoy the gentle, tart, husband/wife comedy segments.

Perhaps because it was no longer the same program that it had been, the Fitch people abandoned the show in 1948, in spite of its popularity. The Rexall Drug Company liked what they had been hearing and took over sponsorship.

Based in Boston, Rexall was comprised of a nationwide chain of independent drug stores franchised to use the Rexall name and sell its many branded products. At its zenith in the latter half of the 1900s, more than 10,000 retail druggists were Rexall affiliated.

The Rexall people recognized the potential of radio as an advertising medium. At various times, they were sponsors of Jimmy Durante's show and *Richard Diamond, Private Detective*, starring Dick Powell. From 1950 through 1954, they sponsored one of radio's all-time most popular programs, *Amos and Andy*.

Listeners became accustomed to a familiar Rexall pattern for the beginning of their programs. A bit of theme music and an opening intro by the announcer were followed by said announcer introducing "a few words from your Rexall family druggist."

An actor named Griff Barnett would portray the druggist. Barnett had a calm, soothing voice something like that of radio's Doctor Christian and Doctor Kildare. Speaking quietly and not too fast, he would extol the virtue of various Rexall products and the dependable service and advice you would get from you own neighborhood Rexall druggist. He, of course, represented those druggists to listeners all over America, and he came across as though he were speaking to each of them individually. His message always ended with the familiar catch phrase "Good health to all from Rexall."

With its new sponsor, *The Fitch Bandwagon* of course had to be renamed. The Rexall people decided to keep it simple and focus attention on the stars they were sponsoring. It became *The Phil Harris-Alice Faye Show*.

By then the program had evolved into a full-fledged situation comedy, with spots reserved for the stars to do one number each near the beginning and end of each show. Phil's character had been modified, both here and on the Benny show, when he married Alice. Jack even devoted one program to his amazement that an ego-centric bumbler like Phil could land a lovely, intelligent woman like Alice.

Phil became a happy faithful husband and his supposed taste for spirits was eliminated from his character. Gags about the wild behavior of "the boys" in his band were still grist for the mill though, and while Phil was no longer chasing the ladies, he continued to think himself irresistible. The writers often had him stopping to admire his dimples and/or his wavy hair in a mirror. Listeners could always count on this evoking a pleased self-appraisal: "Oh, you dawwwwg!"

Alice played the loving wife who endured his talent for getting himself into a bind in spite of her efforts to discourage his farfetched schemes. Her patience often was tested to the breaking point, and she could sometimes sidetrack him with a tart zinger. Still, with the help of his pal Frankie Remley, he continually got in over his head and had to be rescued by Alice.

A pretend Remley tagged along with Phil when he branched out from the Jack Benny program, joining an array of supporting players that included Phil and Alice's two daughters. The real Remley had no objection, but after Jack's failed attempt to put him before a microphone, it was clear that an actor would have to portray him. Elliott Lewis was tapped for the role. The real Remley nominated him for the part.

Elliott Lewis was one of the most versatile and prolific people in radio—so much so that he earned the nickname "Mr. Radio." By 1940, he was portraying a variety of characters in twenty-two different programs every week. He later branched out into writing, producing and directing, often wearing two or more hats at the same time. In 1945, he played the male lead and provided narration on a recording of Gordon Jenkins' musical saga "Manhattan Tower." It became a bit of a classic, aired on radio many times in spite of its length. From 1951 to 1954, he was the director of "radio's outstanding theatre of thrills," *Suspense.*

When the flickering images of television began luring radio listeners away, Lewis reluctantly went with the flow. By the early 1960s, he was directing *The Lucille Ball Show* and *Petticoat Junction*. His love for radio never faltered, however, and in the 1980s he was writer, director and actor on *Mutual Radio Theatre*. Although his television work provided a lucrative income, he once commented that the most significant advancement in TV was when the screens got bigger, because "that made it easier for people to see how bad the shows are."

Elliott Lewis was a consummate actor, performing in everything from mystery and romantic dramas to a starring role as Othello. His comedy roles were few, but he enveloped himself in the Remley character with relish. He later told an interviewer that afterward he would not take on another comic part, because nothing could ever be as much fun as portraying Frankie Remley.

Lewis, as Remley, was an amoral, woman-chasing, smart-alecky wise guy who was too dumb to ever be anything but cheerful. In effect, he took over the character that Phil had been before he was mellowed by marriage. Although still the left-handed guitar player in Phil's band, Remley's primary function now was to get his pal "Curly" into trouble, or to help him compound an existing problem.

In one exchange, Remley asks, "What would you do without me, Curly?" To which Phil replies, "The same thing you're doing with me—be a moron!"

When Phil, in spite of multiple unhappy past experiences, would confess a dilemma to him, Remley always had a cockamamie solution. Or, if he could not solve the problem himself, he would voice his trademark phrase: "I know a guy...." Whatever the guy's supposed area of expertise, his advice was certain to be of dubious value. Phil and Remley usually came away shaking their heads and still debating what to do next.

Speaking of his role on the show, Elliott Lewis told Chuck Schaden that the real Frank Remley was a gentle soul who was tickled by the personality he was given on Phil and Alice's show. To illustrate what a lowlife that Remley was, Lewis recalled a script that the cast did with some trepidation as to how the audience would respond.

Alice warns Phil, "Remley doesn't really care about you. He's a vile person who's looking to take advantage of you, and you've got to be very careful." Phil keeps insisting it's not true, but finally says, "All right, I'll tell you what. When Remley comes to the door this morning, tell him I just died of a heart attack. Then you'll see what a friend I've got." So when the doorbell rings, Alice opens the door crying, and Remley asks, "What's the matter, Alice?" Alice sobs, "Phil just died of a heart attack." After a long pause, Remley says, "Alice, will you marry me?"

As Lewis recalled it: "No 'Gee, I'm sorry.' Nothing! Then this explosion of laughter! The studio was shaking. I tell you, we could not stop the people from laughing!" Meanwhile, Ray Singer and Dick Chevillat, who had assured everyone it would work, smiled at each other in the control room.

Then there was Julius Abruzzio, the obnoxious delivery boy from the neighborhood store.

Julius was played by Walter Tetley, who already had perfected a similar role as Leroy Forester, nephew of Throckmorton P. Gildersleeve, on *The Great Gildersleeve*. Leroy was a frisky, wisecracking youngster of indeterminate age who practiced piano lessons grudgingly, whose report card left something to be desired, and who often protested rules or tasks set for him by his uncle with a semi-whiny "Gee whiz, Unc." When he tried Gildy's patience, audiences chuckled to hear the great man lower his voice and say, "Leeeee-roooooy!" Despite his sometimes pesky or mischievous behavior, Leroy respected his elders and was basically a good kid.

For the role of Julius, Tetley and the writers cranked things up a bit. Walter suffered a medical problem as a youth that stunted his growth and left him with a perpetually high-pitched voice that sounded like someone stuck in the early stage of adolescence. He embellished that with a touch of a Brooklyn accent, and the writers frequently gave him lines that included phrases such as "me mudda" or "ya wanna?" Two of his most frequent utterances were "Are you kiddin'?" and "Get outta here!" He came off sounding a lot like Leo Gorcey in his Dead End/East Side Kids movies.

His frequent deliveries to the Harris household were both a joy and a trial to Julius because he had a crush on Alice that he could scarcely conceal. He addressed her as "Miss Faye," and privately lamented that she should be stuck with such a schlemiel as Phil. Although he never came out and said it, he clearly thought that Phil and Frankie did not have a brain between them. When they encountered one another, his greeting was usually something like, "What are youse two geniuses up to today?"

Julius usually showed up about midway into the program, when Phil and Frankie already were in hot water. They would try to brush him off (unless they thought they could utilize him in some fashion), but he always could coax them into fessing up that they had a problem. It was then Julius' joyful mission to say, "Well, if I was youse guys..." and come up with a fix that sounded good to the boys but was sure to raise the water temp.

Audiences knew that there was no love lost between the boys and Julius, about whom Frankie sometimes muttered, "I still think that kid's a midget." They frequently sought to get the better of the little brat with underhanded tricks. On one show, Phil and Frankie debated about whether someone could get caught up in an in-the-wall bed and not suffocate. Julius conveniently made a delivery and they tried to recruit him as a guinea pig.

> Julius: You couldn't get me in that bed for less than a million bucks!
>
> Remley: Well here's two dollars for a down payment. You'll get the rest after you suffocate."

Julius got his revenge in a program wherein he was picked to be honorary mayor for a day during Boys' Week. Phil showed up to settle a traffic ticket and learned to his dismay that he would have to have a hearing before "da mayor." Acting more like a judge than a mayor, Julius pounded a gavel on his desk and began fining Phil fifty dollars each for a variety of comic "offenses."

When Phil tried to get back to the traffic ticket, Julius revoked his driver's license. Then he upped the ante by revoking Phil and Alice's marriage license. As Phil protested, he revoked Phil's birth certificate! Fortunately for Phil, Julius' term as mayor expired at the end of the day, so his fines and judgments were all rescinded.

Some surviving recordings of *The Phil Harris-Alice Faye Show* include a pre-air audience warm-up. Although Walter Tetley was close to forty years old at the time, Phil introduces him as "the kid who steals the show every week."

Although Phil's vain, not-too-bright personality was a carry-over from the character established on the Jack Benny show, he and Alice ostensibly were playing themselves. Most of their fans knew that they had two lovely daughters at home. So writers Ray Singer and Dick Chevillat thought it only natural that their whole family should be part of the show.

The Harrises were agreeable, but they didn't want their youngsters' home and school life disrupted. So two young actresses, Jeanine Roose and Anne Whitfield, came onboard to play "Baby" Alice and Phyllis. The girls were portrayed as young enough to still be cute and old enough to be inquisitive. Both had picked up some of their father's penchant for jivey banter. That was balanced by a youthful version of their mother's cool charm and her ability to detect shenanigans.

In one episode, Frankie did not let friendship prevent him from taking advantage of an opportunity to have Phil bumped from the band and take over as the leader. When confronted by the girls as to how he could stoop so low, he tried to soften them up by saying everything was okay because their dad still had a job with Jack Benny. Which prompted Alice Jr. to snap back, "You know there ain't no money connected with that job!"

Singer and Chevillat went a step further and expanded the Harris habitat by creating a brother for Alice. William, or Willie, was super-educated and supposedly served as a business manager for Alice. That apparently was his sole occupation, and from all indications he roomed and ate with the Harris family free of charge.

Phil had been in New York about a year earlier and seen a fellow named Robert North in a Broadway play. He was impressed with North's performance and tucked the actor's name away for future reference. When the writers broached the idea of the new character, Phil tossed out the name Robert North and they contacted him. North agreed to give it a try and came out to Hollywood to audition. Everyone liked North, he liked the part, and he joined the show.

Given Alice Faye's personality and New York background, Willie was a bit of an incongruous brother. It was assumed that he was a deadbeat, and he came across as a creampuff as well. He spoke in a manner both educated and prissy.

Alice was blind to her brother's shortcomings. Out of love for his wife, Phil endured him, but he groaned each time they met and Willie greeted him: "Gooood morning, Philip." It became a catch phrase anticipated by the audience. Willie's main purpose on the show seemed to be making Phil pull his curly locks, and he did an excellent job of it. In the final season of the show, actor John Hubbard stepped in to replace the departing Robert North. He assumed the role so smoothly that audiences scarcely noticed the difference.

Finally, with the blessing of the sponsor, Singer and Chevillat wrote in a fellow named Mr. Scott, a none-too-genial representative of Rexall. The venerable actor Gale Gordon was recruited to take on the role. Gordon's only starring role had been that of Flash Gordon on the afternoon adventure series for kids. His deep, clear voice was nonetheless familiar to listeners as a supporting player on countless adult dramas.

In the comedy venue, he became Mayor La Trivia on the *Fibber McGee and Molly* program, where every week the McGees would pop his pompous balloon by goading him into a speechless tantrum that left audiences hysterical with laughter. As Principal Osgood Conklin, he created halls of poison ivy for Eve Arden on *Our Miss Brooks,* both on radio and in the 1952 television adaptation.

As Mr. Scott, he played an executive representative of Rexall charged with keeping an eye on Phil, Alice, et al, and looking out for the company's interests. While he admired and had great respect for Alice, he made no bones about his belief that Phil and Frankie were a matched set of nincompoops. Phil's inability to remember the company's trademark colors of blue and orange did nothing to dispel this opinion.

Neither did Phil make any points by suggesting that the company could rake in the bucks if they bottled and sold some of his charm. Frankie's attitude was that the company was trying to cramp their style, and he once asked, "What is a Rexall, anyway?" All of which confirmed Mr. Scott's opinion that these two philistines should be paying Rexall for the privilege of being on the show, rather than the other way around.

Many radio programs used a little humor to incorporate a disguised message from the sponsor at the middle of a program. With the writers' help, Rexall went a step further by having plots in which the boys actually schemed against Mr. Scott, whose pomposity made him an easy target. The real executives at Rexall apparently had a sense of humor (unlike some sponsors, who could be quite touchy) and saw the value of allowing their company to take a little ribbing.

Rexall sponsored Phil and Alice through 1950 before opting out. The show was popular enough that NBC continued to carry it on a sustaining, i.e., unsponsored, basis until it was picked up by RCA Victor. Undeterred, Mr. Scott changed hats and continued to haunt Phil and Frankie as the RCA watchdog.

Speaking of dogs, with the change of sponsorship, the Harris family acquired a new pet, a dog named Nipper. Most listeners recognized this as the name of the Jack Russell Terrier who sits with one ear cocked toward a Victrola phonograph in the famous painting "His Master's Voice." For those who didn't pick up on this, Phil would sometimes admonish the pup when it was being rambunctious by saying, "Sit, boy. Listen to your master's voice."

Throughout the life of the show, running gags included many references to Frankie's taste for the spirits, Phil's vanity and their dunderheaded schemes. Phil would frequently attempt to demonstrate his intellect with comments such as "*The Mikado* might never have been written if Gilbert didn't have faith in Ed Sullivan."

He often was subjected to the humiliation of people recognizing him only as the husband of Alice Faye. That in turn presented opportunities to joke about Alice being the real breadwinner of the family: "I'm only trying to protect the wife of the money I love."

For her part, Alice may have privately considered the show's closing a sort of running gag. Technically, she was still under contract to 20th Century-Fox. So each program ended with announcer Bill Foreman saying, "Alice Faye appears through the courtesy of 20th Century-Fox." She and Darryl Zanuck knew she was not coming back. She may have taken some silent satisfaction in the knowledge that the weekly announcement was certain to irk the great man

In 1949, CBS raided NBC, looking for stars whose programs could bolster their line-up. Jack Benny was one of those who received an offer he couldn't refuse and made the switch. Phil and Alice elected to stay put on NBC, but Phil continued as a staple on the Benny show until he eased himself out in 1952. Bob Crosby, brother of Bing, then took over as orchestra leader.

The two network stations were two blocks apart on Sunset Boulevard. Since Phil and Alice aired right after Jack Benny's show, and Phil was still part of the Benny cast, this presented a problem. Phil said that Jack proved what a great boss he was by directing the writers to make sure Phil's appearance came during the first half of the program. Phil then left and hailed a taxi if possible or jogged to the CBS studio.

References to each other's programs were inserted in both shows whenever a gag opportunity presented itself. Besides the potential laughs, each gag was a plug for the other show to help keep listeners loyal. Sometimes Phil's segment of the Benny show was even used to set up the plot of the Harris/Faye show that was to follow.

After Benny moved to CBS, Phil would sometimes toss out a line that got a good laugh and then say, "I gotta give that one to Jackson. It might bring him back to NBC."

**Alice is not impressed with Phil's effort to improve his mind.
CREDIT: Nostalgia Digest collection**

A constant element of the show was the premise that Alice was always there to rescue her muddleheaded mate even though she was ready to throw up her hands at his misadventures. Underneath the nonsense, listeners heard a genuine love and devotion that was shared by the two. Phil often revised lyrics of his songs to turn them into love songs to Alice.

Compared to film work, Alice found the radio program almost relaxing. Her participation required only Friday and Saturday rehearsals and the Sunday broadcast.

In May, 1951, Alice and Phil did a little extracurricular work, performing together on *Suspense*. It was sort of a family event, because Elliott Lewis was at that time directing the series. In "Death on My Hands" Phil plays Dixie, a touring musician who meets Julia (Alice), a former singer with the band. Later, a young female fan visits Dixie in his dressing room. As he tries to ease her out, she impulsively reaches into his open suitcase to grab a souvenir. A handgun he carries with him in the suitcase accidentally goes off and kills her. The rest of the story involves Julia's efforts to save Dixie from an angry lynch mob.

Suspense writer E. Jack Neuman noted that the show often featured popular film stars, but many of them were prone to flubbing lines or had difficulty emoting when simply standing in front of a microphone. He gave Alice and Phil high marks for their performances and was especially impressed by Phil, saying "…we had him whimpering and crying and begging, and he was a brilliant actor. He could do it!"

With television luring audiences away (and with RCA making a lot of the TV sets), RCA dropped the show at the end of the 1954 season. Alice and Phil could have tagged along with many other radio performers who made the transition to television. They instead made a conscious choice to make family life a priority and limit their show biz involvement. Gerald Nachman, author of *Raised on Radio*, notes that the complexities and pace of television far exceeded the demands of radio, where the Harrises were essentially working part time and could be together with their children most of the time.

At a radio convention gathering, co-writer Ray Singer avowed that his time on *The Phil Harris-Alice Faye Show* was "six of the happiest years of my life. They're wonderful people, and it was a writer's paradise, because Phil was the kind of guy who loved living. (He) didn't want to be bothered with work. He left us alone. We never had to report to him. Dick and I would work out a premise and write the script. Phil and Alice lived in Palm Springs. They'd come in on Fridays and we'd rehearse. We'd do a rewrite on Saturday, do the show on Sunday and they'd go back to Palm Springs. (Phil) never knew what was going to happen... it was left in our hands. It spoiled us for everyone else."

When she found herself retired from both pictures and radio, Alice cheerfully switched roles. As she told it, "The end of Alice Faye, movie star, marked the beginning for Alice Harris, housewife and mother. I segued from one career to another without missing a beat."

In reality, it was not that simple. Alice did treasure the freedom to spend time entertaining her girls, playing with them, even singing to them. Still, the girls had nannies until they were old enough to be sent to choice boarding schools. There always was a housekeeper on the premises.

Alice took up grocery shopping, but she was prone to buying too much of one thing and too little of something else; nor did she hone the typical housewife's skill at bargain hunting and comparison shopping. She gave over the kitchen to Phil. Her cooking skills did not extend much beyond preparing soup. Phil was an accomplished cook from his bachelor days. Daughter Phyllis remembered teasing her by saying, "Mother, why don't you go put the towels in the washing machine." Alice's reply: "Where is it?"

Besides spending time with her children, Alice's routine included cleaning her closet, taking in a matinee movie with friends, or joining them for lunch. She maintained a regular exercise program to keep her trim figure, something she had been doing since her chorus line days . She took up painting and became rather good at it. Frank Sinatra once bought one of her pieces.

Alice's mother had seen her role as looking out for her daughter's welfare long after Alice had become the family's chief breadwinner. In 1959, however, the roles were reversed when Alice the elder took ill. She did not make it through the year.

Phil resumed his musical career, but at his own leisurely pace. During the 1960s and 1970s, he made numerous guest appearances on such TV shows as *Kraft Music Hall* and *The Dean Martin Show*.

In addition to his love of golfing, he was active in a number of other sports. As a result, he appeared on ABC's *The American Sportsman*, which took celebrities on trips around the world to hunt and fish.

When it came to golf, he was involved in as many pro-amateur events as he could work into his schedule. He was a close friend and associate of Bing Crosby and, like Bing, helped promote various golf events and charities. His name on the list assured a large gallery because of his antics and teasing of fellow players. When Bing died in 1977, Phil stepped in to do commentary of the annual telecast of the Bing Crosby Pro-Am Golf Tournament.

In the music realm, Phil scored a hit with his 1950s novelty song "The Thing," about a mystery something in a box that a poor soul found and tried unsuccessfully to give away. During the 1970s and 1980s, he made frequent appearances leading a band in Las Vegas, often on the same bill with Harry James, the legendary swing era band leader.

When not behaving as the vain, inept character that he developed for comedy purposes, Phil was quite a talented musician. His bands and orchestras (whose theme song, by the way, was "Rose Room") played smooth, up-tempo music and had numerous hit recordings.

Even so, his talk/sing novelty songs are probably what fans most remember. Long before "The Thing," he had hits with "Woodman, Spare That Tree," "The Old Master Painter," "Smoke! Smoke! Smoke! (That Cigarette)" and "The Preacher and the Bear." Perhaps to counter that somewhat, Phil in 1972 produced an album for Mega Records called "Southern Comfort: The Best of Phil Harris." During the 1960s, he even branched out into doing some Country and Western.

In 1951, he appeared in the film *Thunder in the Pacific* with Walter Brennan and Forrest Tucker. In 1954, he appeared with none other than John Wayne in *The High and the Mighty*. Both parts were dramatic roles for which he received mostly favorable reviews.

In 1956, Phil made a cameo appearance in the Paramount Pictures remake of Cole Porter's hit stage production *Anything Goes*. Here he basked in the glow of stars Mitzi Gaynor, Bing Crosby and Donald O'Connor.

He found a new outlet for his acting and singing talents when he lent his voice to several Walt Disney animated feature films. In 1970's *The Aristocats*, he supplied the voice of Thomas O'Malley. In 1973, he was the voice of Little John in *Robin Hood*.

By far his most memorable Disney role was Baloo the bear in 1967's *The Jungle Book*. Walt Disney himself suggested Harris for the part after meeting him at a party. Phil improvised much of his dialogue, saying the scripted lines "didn't feel natural." No one objected, and he came across as just the sort of bear the story made Baloo out to be.

In the film's song "I Wanna Be Like You," he gets to do a scat-singing dance routine alongside the monkey king, voiced by the inimitable Louis Prima. But he topped that with his showstopper rendition of the Oscar-nominated song "The Bare Necessities," in which he talks and sings to Mowgli about the merits of a simple life. His Baloo performance won him countless new fans from a generation that grew up with television. In 1989, Phil did a brief reprise, returning to do the Baloo voice for a Disney cartoon series called *Tale Spin*.

Alice did not stay permanently retired. In 1962, with her girls grown, she accepted an offer to return to the big screen with Tom Ewell and Wally Cox in a remake of *State Fair*. Darryl Zanuck was long gone from 20th Century-Fox, and Richard Rodgers was sprucing up this version with several new songs. Any misgivings she may have had were quickly dispelled by the enthusiastic welcome her return prompted from technicians and crew members who had worked with her in the past. One columnist noted that "studio policemen, waitresses and executives came over to greet Alice at her Commissary lunch table."

Alice played the mother of a young Pat Boone. Besides Boone, the film had Ann-Margret, Pamela Tiffin and Bobby Darin to appeal to a young audience. Richard Rodgers inserted the song "Never Say No To a Man" especially for Alice.

Sung to Pamela Tiffin, who is experiencing her first youthful romance, the song is a humorous offering of advice on how to string a man along and let him feel that he's the boss without ever letting him have his way, yet studiously avoiding the word "no." The song has multiple verses, and Alice's light-hearted, conspiratorial delivery is just right for the setting.

Other than that, Alice's only featured number is a duet sung with Tom Ewell, "It's the Little Things in Texas." She also joins, Ewell, Boone and a chorus in a number called "Our State Fair."

Her long-time fans may have been somewhat disappointed, but they weren't the audience the studio was aiming for. The appeal of the younger cast stars was meant to attract the youthful crowd who were increasingly being drawn toward that new musical genre called rock and roll.

Nevertheless, Faye received good reviews; but the film did not do well at the box office. It may simply have lacked the charm of the earlier film with Jeanne Crain, Dana Andrews and Dick Haymes, but the musical as a genre simply was not as popular in this era.

During the 1960s and 1970s, Alice made guest star appearances on numerous television shows. As both actress and songstress, she was seen on the *Perry Como Show, Red Skelton Show, Hollywood Palace, Dean Martin Show, Tonight Show, Mike Douglas Show, Love Boat* and, naturally enough, a Phil Harris special.

In 1973, Alice was offered the female lead in a revival of the play *Good News*. She was at first hesitant, but happily agreed when she learned that her male co-star would be an old friend, John Payne. After decades as a star on screen and on radio, she would at last have a shot at live theatre on Broadway.

The play opened on December 17 in Boston and would tour the country before returning East. Alice forbade her family from attending opening night.

From her early chorus line days, she had always suffered from nerves before performing. Doing films, where retakes were common, lessened the tension but never cured her of an up-tight feeling until she got into the acting. There are no out-takes on stage. She did not want her family to see her blow it on opening night.

Whatever her nervous state when she stepped out on stage, the audience reaction buoyed her. As soon as she appeared, they rose to their feet and cheered with delight at seeing their beloved star. She was among friends.

When the show played near home, Alice gave her family permission to attend. Phil and the girls came together and had front row seats. *Good News* is heavy on poignant moments. The supposedly hardheaded Phil Harris was actually a crier. Armed with a box of tissue, he sniffed and blew through much of the evening. In a scene in which Alice has to throw some object, she tossed it straight at Phil.

The show made its way back to New York and opened at the St. James Theatre on December 23, 1974. New York's sophisticated and probably younger audiences were less enthusiastic about the play and Alice's performance. Their response and the reviews were lukewarm at best. Nevertheless, with Don Ameche replacing John Payne, the play continued through a summer tour, enjoying mostly full houses and a more enthusiastic response from audiences in towns large and small.

Alice was on tour for over a year, doing more than four hundred performances. It was an exhilarating experience and the fulfillment of a girlhood dream: starring in a Broadway show.

Mostly on a lark, she made a cameo appearance in the 1976 film *Won Ton Ton, the Dog Who Saved Hollywood.* It was a good-natured spoof of the popular Rin Tin Tin films of years ago. The most notable thing about the film was that it boasted more than a dozen actors and actresses in starring and featured roles, plus cameos from almost five dozen, ranging from Dorothy Lamour to the Ritz Brothers and Johnny Weissmuller. Fans of Alice Faye who stepped out for a box of popcorn might miss her in her brief scene as a secretary.

Another blow came in 1977, when Alice's brother Sonny died. His arthritis had grown progressively worse and more painful over the years. Alice Jr. remembered that his elbows and knees were horribly swollen. Other than aspirin, there was little in the way of medication, and he sometimes could barely move until mid-morning. Alice had long been a supporter of the Arthritis Foundation. After Sonny's death it became her number one charity.

Alice took on another cameo role in *The Magic of Lassie.* She plays a waitress in the 1978 film, which probably was produced only to take advantage of the famed collie's popularity on television. The cast also included Mickey Rooney and Pernell Roberts (co-star of the popular television series *Bonanza*). The film's only other claim to fame is that it was Lassie's one and only musical, and one of just two musicals featuring James Stewart (who introduced Cole Porter's "Easy to Love" in the 1936 film *Born to Dance*).

Alice got more screen time in another 1978 film, *Every Girl Should Have One*, a comedy in which she starred along with the oft-married Zsa Zsa Gabor. That was to be her last feature film.

From 1984 to 1991, she took on a totally new kind of role as a spokeswoman for Pfizer Pharmaceuticals. In that capacity, she made personal appearances around the country, as well as appearing on television and in a film entitled *"We Still Are."* Her primary function was to promote the virtues of an active senior lifestyle. Assisted by writer Dick Kleiner, she authored a book titled *Growing Older, Staying Young*, in which she extolled the virtues of a healthy lifestyle that included regular exercise and a well-balanced diet.

Remembering his roots, Phil established scholarships for high school students in Linton, Indiana. He performed at the high school and hosted an annual golf tournament bearing his name. He and Alice donated most of their papers and show business memorabilia to the Linton library. Later, after the creation of the Linton Carnegie Arts Centers, these treasures were transferred there.

In Phil's last few years, he and Alice spent much of their time in Palm Springs. He golfed as often as possible, and together they basked in the sun with other Hollywood retirees. One of the fond memories they enjoyed sharing with friends was their "command performance," when they were invited to perform at President Harry S. Truman's inaugural ball in 1949. Dozens of Hollywood stars were on hand, along with Phil Spitalny and his all-girl orchestra. Phil had fun feigning jealousy when Alice sang "I'm Just Wild About Harry" and pretended to be flirting with the president.

In May, 1995, Phil Harris went to Linton, Indiana, to be an honored guest and performer at an annual festival held there. He was in frail health and on dialysis, but had promised to appear and did not want to disappoint. Though he needed to sit in a chair on stage, he sang two songs with much of the old Harris swagger and verve.

On August 11, 1995, in their Palm Springs home, he suffered a heart attack and died. He was ninety-one. Phyllis Harris was with her mother at her father's bedside when he died. Besides Alice, their girls and Phil's son, he was survived by four grandchildren and two great grandchildren. Alice had his body cremated and interred in the mausoleum at Forest Lawn cemetery in Riverside County, California.

Two years before his death, Phil had been inducted into the Indiana Hall of Fame. He also is honored by two stars on the Hollywood Walk of Fame, one at 6651 Hollywood Boulevard and one at 6508 Hollywood Boulevard, for his work in radio and recordings respectively.

After Phil's death, Alice remained at their home in Rancho Mirage, but found time to appear in several television specials and documentaries recalling the glory days of Hollywood's big studios and the many film stars with whom she worked. She also did her best to respond to numerous still-faithful fans who continued to contact her.

In her later years, Alice had contracted arthritis. Although it was never as severe as what her brother Sonny had endured, the ailment eventually led her to give up painting, a hobby that she had found most fulfilling.

She suffered several falls. Not long after Phil's death, one of them resulted in a broken ankle. She was for a time obliged to use a wheelchair. A later fall resulted in a broken wrist that required the insertion of two pins.

Clogged arteries at one point posed the risk of a stroke. Doctors performed vascular surgery to clear the arteries and open her veins. She later had to undergo surgery to remove her spleen. During that operation the doctors discovered a malignant growth. She was diagnosed with stomach cancer. She initially resisted the doctors' urging that she undergo further surgery. In April, 1998, she relented, but it was too late.

Alice Faye died at home on May 9, 1998, with her two daughters nearby. Her ashes are interred beside Phil's at Forest Lawn. She had just turned eighty-three. Because of her youthful fibbing, some death notices listed her as older. Alice doubtless would have had a good chuckle over that.

During their working years, Alice and Phil's time together was sharply curtailed by their respective careers. Phil frequently was on tour with his band or traveling with the Jack Benny program. When he was home, Alice often spent long hours at the studio and returned home late, tired and ready to call it a day.

In later years, when they were semi-retired, Phil took advantage of his free time to indulge in the outdoor activities that he so loved, fishing, hunting and golf. He had a dozen or more show business buddies that he could call on to join him. Bing Crosby was his most regular golfing companion. Alice joked that if she and Phil ever divorced she would name Bing as correspondent.

The separations actually helped to cement their marital bond.

They enjoyed each other's company immensely when they were out together or in gatherings with friends. When they spent too much time together at home they were prone to getting on one another's nerves. That often led to a little lovers' spat, albeit soon resolved.

Whenever they were apart for more than a day, they called each other twice daily, morning and night. They reported on what they were doing and asked about each other's day. The conversation always touched on their missing one another and reassurances of their love.

It may have been an unusual formula for a happy marriage, but for Alice and Phil it worked. There is no question that theirs was a deep-rooted bond. It translated into fifty-four years of mutual respect, love and togetherness.

Alice never let her stardom go to her head. A friend remembered having lunch with her in Beverly Hills in 1979, long after she had forsaken films. Two men eating nearby keep staring, and the friend knew they had recognized Alice. She paid no mind at first, but finally said, "Those men keep looking over here. Are they friends of yours?"

Friends and associates remember that Alice had a personality that was warm, friendly and charming. When called on the phone, she always had time to talk and laugh together with friends, old and new. She would thank them for calling and end the conversation by saying, "Stay in touch." Her callers knew it was not just a phrase; Alice really meant it.

Once, during a trip to London, she was lured into the BBC Television studios. There she was surprised to learn that she was the guest of honor on a British version of *This Is Your Life*. The producers had located and brought to the event one of the nuns who had taught Alice at P.S. 84. The sister told host Eamonn Andrews and his audience, "Alice was an angel from Hell's Kitchen."

In her day, Alice Faye achieved a fame comparable to that of the later stars Doris Day and Barbara Streisand. She radiated a warmth and wholesomeness that drew audiences to her. She was blessed with a pleasantly husky contralto voice and the ability to give a warm and tender rendering of love songs and ballads or a hearty delivery of upbeat and swing tunes.

She was honored for her film work with a star at 6922 Hollywood Boulevard on the Hollywood Walk of Fame. Her many screen appearances won her an army of admirers long before she became a featured star and a regular on radio. Still, that medium reached millions of people who were not regular movie-goers. It surely multiplied the number of her fans, and gave a new stability to her home life.

As for Phil, he considered radio a veritable lifesaver. He once told an interviewer, "If it hadn't been for radio, I would still be a traveling orchestra leader. I played one-night stands for seventeen years, except for a few longer engagements. I slept on buses. I never even voted, because I had no residence. Radio gave me a chance to settle down, to marry, to establish a home and raise a family. It was all fun, everything. I say thanks to God every night that I get a kick out of every day."

Films of Alice Faye

1934 *George White's Scandals* Fox Film Corp.
1934 *Now I'll Tell* Fox Film Corp.
1934 *She Learned About Sailors* Fox Film Corp.
1934 *365 Nights In Hollywood* Fox Film Corp.
1935 *George White's 1935 Scandals* Fox Film Corp.
1935 *Every Night At Eight* Paramount Pictures

1935 *Music Is Magic* 20th Century-Fox
1936 *King Of Burlesque* 20th Century-Fox
1936 *Poor Little Rich Girl* 20th Century-Fox
1936 *Sing, Baby, Sing* 20th Century-Fox
1936 *Stowaway* 20th Century-Fox
1937 *On The Avenue* 20th Century-Fox
1937 *Wake Up And Live* 20th Century-Fox
1937 *You Can't Have Everything* 20th Century-Fox
1937 *You're A Sweetheart* Universal Pictures
1938 *Sally, Irene And Mary* 20th Century-Fox
1938 *In Old Chicago* 20th Century-Fox
1938 *Alexander's Ragtime Band* 20th Century-Fox
1939 *Tail Spin* 20th Century-Fox
1939 *Rose of Washington Square* 20th Century-Fox
1939 *Hollywood Cavalcade* 20th Century-Fox
1939 *Barricade* 20th Century-Fox
1940 *Little Old New York* 20th Century-Fox
1940 *Lillian Russell* 20th Century-Fox
1940 *Tin Pan Alley* 20th Century-Fox
1941 *That Night In Rio* 20th Century-Fox
1941 *The Great American Broadcast* 20th Century-Fox
1941 *Weekend In Havana* 20th Century-Fox
1943 *Hello, Frisco, Hello* 20th Century-Fox
1943 *The Gang's All Here* 20th Century-Fox
1944 *Four Jills In A Jeep* 20th Century-Fox
1945 *Fallen Angel* 20th Century-Fox
1962 *State Fair* 20th Century-Fox
1977 *Won Ton Ton, The Dog Who Saved Hollywood* Paramount Pictures

1977 *Every Girl Should Have One* Robert Fridley Productions
1978 *The Magic Of Lassie* International Picture Show

Short Films

1934 *The Hollywood Gad-about* Educational Films; Fox Films, distributor
1936 *Cinema Circus* Louis Lewyn Productions
1940 *Screen Snapshots: Seeing Hollywood* Columbia Pictures
1948 *Screen Snapshots: Hawaii in Hollywood* Columbia Pictures
1985 *We Still Are* Pfizer Pharmaceuticals promotional film

Films of Phil Harris

1929 *Why Be Good?* Warner Bros.
1933 *Melody Cruise* RKO Pictures
1933 *Double or Nothing* Paramount Pictures
1939 *Man About Town* Paramount Pictures
1940 *Dreaming Out Loud* RKO Pictures
1940 *Buck Benny Rides Again* Paramount Pictures
1945 *I Love a Bandleader* Columbia Pictures
1950 *Wabash Avenue* 20th Century-Fox
1951 *Starlift* Warner Bros.
1951 *Here Comes the Groom* Paramount Pictures
1951 *The Wild Blue Yonder* Republic Pictures
1954 *The High and the Mighty* Warner Bros.
1956 *Anything Goes* Paramount Pictures
1956 *Goodbye, My Lady* Warner Bros.
1963 *The Wheeler Dealers* Metro Goldwyn Mayer

1964 *The Patsy* Paramount Pictures
1967 *The Cool Ones* Warner Bros.
1967 *The Jungle Book* Walt Disney (animated, voice of Baloo the Bear)
1970 *The Aristocats* Walt Disney (animated, voice of Thomas O'Malley)
1971 *The Gatling Gun* Universal Pictures
1973 *Robin Hood* Walt Disney (animated, voice of Little John, a bear)
1991 *Rock-A-Doodle* Samuel Goldwyn Co. (voice of Bassett Hound narrator, Patou)
1991 *Clearcut* Cinexus Capital Corp.

Short Films

1933 *So This is Harris!* RKO Pictures
1936 *Romancing Along* RKO Pictures
1937 *Harris in the Spring* RKO Pictures
1947 *Is Everybody Listening?* RKO Pictures

Songs Introduced by Alice in Films that Became Hit Parade Favorites

"Afraid to Dream" (*You Can't Have Everything*, 1937)

"A Journey to a Star" (*The Gang's All Here*, 1943)

"Blue Lovebird" (*Lillian Russell*, 1940)

"But Definitely" (*Poor Little Rich Girl*, 1936)

"Goodnight, My Love" (*Sing, Baby, Sing*, 1936)

"He Ain't Got Rhythm" (*On The Avenue*, 1937)

"I Feel a Song Comin' On" (*Every Night At Eight*, 1935)

"I'm Shooting High" (*Music Is Magic*, 1935)

"I Never Knew Heaven Could Speak" (*Rose of Washington Square*, 1939)

"I've Got My Love to Keep Me Warm" (*On The Avenue*, 1937)

"Nasty Man" (*George White's Scandals*, 1934)

"Never In a Million Years" (*Wake Up And Live*, 1937)

"No Love, No Nothin'" (*The Gang's All Here*, 1943)

"Now It Can Be Told" (*Alexander's Ragtime Band*, 1938)

"Sing, Baby, Sing" (*Sing, Baby, Sing*, 1936)

"Slumming On Park Avenue" (*On The Avenue*, 1937)

"There's a Lull In My Life" (*Wake Up And Live*, 1937)

"This Year's Kisses" (*On The Avenue*, 1937)

"Wake Up and Live" (*Wake Up and Live*, 1937)

"When I'm With You" (*Poor Little Rich Girl*, 1936)

"You'll Never Know" (*Hello, Frisco, Hello*, 1943)

"You're a Sweetheart" (*You're a Sweetheart*, 1937)

"You Turned the Tables On Me" (*Sing, Baby, Sing*, 1936)

Ozzie and Harriet pose for a CBS promo shot.
CREDIT: Nostalgia Digest collection

Ozzie Nelson and Harriet Hilliard

Although it may be a bit of a cliché, it is not a stretch to say that both Ozzie Nelson and Harriet Hilliard were born to show biz.

Harriet entered the world in Des Moines, Iowa, on July 18, 1909, the daughter of Hazel Dee and Roy Hilliard Snyder. In her initial appearance, she was known as Peggy Lou Snyder.

Her mother, then Hazel MacNutt, had an early yearning to sing and perform. By age fourteen she was doing so in small roles. For over thirty years, as she became better known, she performed in musical and dramatic stock companies, often in starring roles.

Roy Snyder was a well-known dramatic stock company actor. He also doubled as a director. He at times gave direction to people who would go on to silver screen fame, including Clark Gable, Jack Bailey and Ralph Bellamy.

Early in his career, he took on the name Roy E. Hilliard for professional purposes. After he and Hazel were married, she became Hazel Hilliard. As their daughter later began she own career, it seemed only natural to change her name to Harriet Hilliard. Even if no one made the connection with her parents, it had a more pleasing sound than Harriet Snyder.

Harriet's first stage appearance occurred when she was just six weeks old in what the airlines might now call a carry-on role. Her mother carried her on stage for a scene that lasted two or three minutes. Harriet's part did not call for any crying, gurgling or other baby sounds, and she obliged by sleeping through her brief debut.

Her subsequent stage appearances while a youngster were mostly limited to school plays, but by age three she had a key role in *Mrs. Wiggs of the Cabbage Patch.* She reportedly gave a creditable performance, remembering to speak in a loud, clear voice.

Harriet's parents enrolled her at St. Agnes Academy in Kansas City, presumably because she needed an education and they were frequently on the road. During summer vacations, she toured with them and gained valuable experience by being given minor supporting roles.

When she was fifteen, her mother accompanied her to New York, where she took ballet lessons. Ballet was not to be her forte, but the lessons put her in the proverbial right place at the right time. At age sixteen she was chosen to play the title role in a Broadway production called *The Blonde Sinner.*

The show itself was not memorable, but it led to a prolonged tour on the Radio Keith Orpheum (RKO) circuit. From coast to coast, she danced in the Harry Carroll Revue, the first of RKO's vaudeville units to play double shows daily. En route, she had the opportunity to perform along with such folk as Bert Lahr and Ken Murray.

At age twelve, Harriet had taken up smoking, albeit not within sight of her parents. In this new, exciting life, she began to enjoy a relaxing cocktail or two at the end of the day. In later years she would take great pains to conceal these two negative indulgences.

With scarcely a break following the tour, Harriet got herself booked as a specialty dancer at a popular New York City nightspot called the Hollywood Restaurant.

Audience response was enthusiastic, and what was supposed to be a "limited engagement" was extended, and then re-extended. Soon she found herself singing, working in sketches, and acting as mistress of ceremonies. As Harriet aptly put it, she was "doing everything but sweeping out the joint."

No complaints, though. Harriet had signed on for $75 per week. As her popularity led to a combination of singing, acting and hosting, that had been doubled. The Great Depression had begun, and its impact was beginning to spread. Just being employed was as iffy for show people as anyone else. Even the lower figure was enough to make Harriet feel she was one of the fortunate.

Fortune was about to smile upon her again. On New Years Eve, 1931, a popular band was hired to augment the club's celebration. The young band leader was awed by Harriet's personality, versatility and, as he later acknowledged, the fact that she had a pretty face, a bright smile and a great figure.

The night's festivities gave them little opportunity to get acquainted, but he filed her name away for future reference. When the band returned from a road trip a few months later, he asked her out to lunch and offered her a spot as a singer with his group.

Harriet accepted. It was not yet official—indeed, neither of them yet realized it—but the team of Ozzie and Harriet was born that day.

Ozzie Nelson came from a family in which everyone—parents, aunts, uncles and cousins—played an instrument, sang or both.

His parents, Ethel Orr and George Nelson, lived and met in Jersey City in 1902. Back then the city was a sort of Mayberry small town. Folks with various musical talents often gathered in someone's parlor to entertain each other. For lack of a town theater, larger events open to all were held in a town meeting hall or a high school auditorium.

Variety shows featuring many local talents were very popular. Even if they did not feature any blackface performers, they were commonly referred to as minstrel shows in an era before that became socially unacceptable.

George Nelson had a fine singing voice and was a frequent favorite. One evening he was scheduled to do a little song and dance act. As he waited in the wings, a lovely young lady was introduced as "Miss Ethel Orr." He was impressed first by her voice as she accompanied herself on the piano, and then found himself tapping his foot as she demonstrated her keyboard skill with some fine ragtime playing.

After wrangling an introduction, George began dating Ethel. Soon they were performing together as "Nelson and Orr." It was not long before "Love In Bloom" had become their song. The duo wed in 1903. Ethel gave birth to their son Alfred in September, 1904. He was joined by brother Oswald George Nelson on March 20, 1906. A third sibling, Donald, was a late arrival, rounding out the family in 1927.

When not entertaining at local programs, George Nelson had a steady day job at Chase National Bank in New York City. It enabled him to provide a comfortable home for his family, where the various relatives often gathered and entertained one another with their respective singing and/or playing.

Oswald was eight years old when he made his first performance at a local event, singing a duet with Alfred. It was well received by the audience, but made memorable to Oswald primarily by the fact that he had to dress as a girl.

He made no other notable appearance until he was a teen. By the time he was in high school, he had taken to calling himself Ozzie, and he was known by that name to everyone except his teachers.

He was by then playing a mean banjo. He formed an unusual duo with a friend named Frank at Ridgefield High School. Ozzie didn't yet read sheet music, but Frank did. He would call out the chords to Ozzie as they practiced new tunes together. They worked out arrangements and developed an extensive repertoire, but their performances before an audience were limited to school assembly programs.

That changed when a snow storm prevented a small band from getting to a dance planned by the local Women's Club. Someone (Ozzie suspected it was his mother) suggested they be recruited, and they gladly agreed. In between dance numbers, Frank played some classical pieces and Ozzie sang with Frank's piano accompaniment. They were paid five dollars each and discovered at the end of the evening that they had been a big hit.

With only word-of-mouth advertising, the boys soon were regularly playing for parties, not only in Jersey City but in several surrounding towns. On occasion, when they played at dances, they would recruit a friend who played drums and Frank's brother on violin. For those gigs they called themselves the Syncopation Four.

Aware that they had a good thing going, they dared to up their price and began receiving ten dollars apiece. Working almost every weekend, and sometimes midweek, Frank and Ozzie enjoyed a handsome income for a couple of teens in 1920. Ozzie used part of his loot to buy a saxophone. A quick learner, he soon began alternating between playing banjo and sax.

Ozzie was a good student, so his parents never objected that the increasing semi-pro performances were interfering with his schooling. He also enjoyed sports, and managed to get on the school football team. He was the runt of the team, but in 1922, his senior year, he had the thrill of playing quarterback as his team went undefeated for the season.

Brother Alfred had enrolled at Rutgers College in New Brunswick.

Ozzie followed him there with the intent of pursuing a law career. That was not to be.

He completed his four years, and could have gone on to a one-year clerkship that was required before taking the bar exam. But while in college he had put together a small band that played at proms, hotel ballrooms, nightclubs and other venues. For a signature theme, they even used the school's song, "Loyal Sons of Rutgers." The group proved to be as popular as the Syncopation Four had been, and it drew a higher fee. That and something about Ozzie's appearance led to a different career decision.

The advent of radio was proving to be a great boon for dance bands. Rudy Vallee, with his relaxed style and good looks, was one of the most popular singing band leaders. Ozzie looked a bit like Rudy, so he playfully began adapting his singing a bit, learned all of Rudy's songs and added to the effect by acquiring a megaphone. It wasn't long before groups in need of a band began asking for "that guy who sings like Rudy Vallee."

Had he gone forward with his goal of becoming a lawyer, he knew it would put a crimp on his freedom to perform. When he mulled it over, he reasoned that he was already making more than he would make as a starting law clerk. Plus, he was having a great time doing it. The courts would have to get on without him.

Ozzie added a few more band members and the group found steady employment at various venues. One fateful engagement was a 1931 New Year's Eve gala put on by New York's Hollywood Restaurant. In anticipation of a large crowd, the restaurant rented the grand ballroom of the Edison Hotel. It was there that Ozzie was impressed by the talents and good looks of the young female singer who acted as hostess and Mistress of Ceremonies.

In mid-1932, the orchestra snagged a coveted engagement at the Glen Island Casino, where the likes of Glen Gray, Claude Thornhill, Glenn Miller and other greats were regulars. For the first time, Ozzie's ensemble was heard coast to coast, broadcasting nightly over CBS radio. Before their first week was over, they had signed to do some recording for the Brunswick label.

Ozzie had been toying with the idea of hiring a female singer to do solos and also duets with him. He hadn't forgotten the name of that good looking singer/hostess, Harriet Hilliard, who had made such an impression on him. With some friends, he visited the Hollywood as a patron and a talent scout. Her performance confirmed what he'd been thinking. She was the gal for the job.

When he was able to speak to her during a break, he invited her to lunch at Sardi's and she accepted. He later confessed that he'd never before been to Sardi's, but selected one of New York's most prestigious restaurants to impress her. Whether she was impressed or not, they hit it off well. When Ozzie made his offer of a job, Harriet needed only a minute or two to think it over. She allowed the Hollywood management time to find a replacement M.C., and then joined Ozzie's group in time for a long road trip.

There was an immediate on-stage rapport between Harriet and Ozzie that may have been a precursor to their later romance. They developed a routine of singing back and forth to one another. They exchanged banter during and between songs. Ozzie even created some short, comic, boy/girl skits that they did between numbers. It all became part of a unique onstage signature. Audiences accepted it and showed that they enjoyed it by their applause.

In the economic throes of the Great Depression, many smaller nightspots were operating on tight budgets. During the tour, Ozzie and his crew sometimes almost had to strong-arm managers to get paid at the end of the night. The next morning they would be on the road before the bank opened. So they often carried a lot of cash in a satchel. After an "I thought you had the satchel" mishap, they began taking a leisurely breakfast and stopping at the local bank before leaving town.

Almost from the start, there was a strong attraction between Harriet and Ozzie. They mostly kept it under wraps, lest it become a distraction for the band members or themselves. But they occasionally were able to have a private lunch or early supper together. Their mutual attraction was no secret to the musicians.

As more and more Americans felt the pinch of the Depression, radio was becoming a prime source of entertainment. Ozzie and crew climbed aboard in the fall of 1933 when they were signed to do a weekly show called *The Bakers' Broadcast,* sponsored by Standard Brands. Initially, the show's star was Joe Penner, a comic best known for the catch phrase "You wanna buy a duck?" Like many vaudeville stars, Joe was attempting to make a transition to radio, but his comedy style didn't play well in that venue. He lasted two seasons, and then was replaced by Robert L. Ripley.

Ripley was a newspaper correspondent famed for his cartoon presentations of stories that seemed incredible but were, he claimed, completely true. That may seem a strange qualification for a radio host job, but as his cartoon title declared: "Believe It Or Not."

During Ripley's two years on the show, the producer was Ed Gardner. Ed later wrote and starred as "Archie, the Manager" in the popular radio program *Duffy's Tavern.* The program began every week with the telephone ringing and Ed picking up to say, "Duffy's Tavern, where the elite meet to eat. Archie, the Manager, speakin'. Duffy ain't here." A pause, then, "Oh, hello, Duffy," followed by a brief exchange in which Archie told the boss (and the audience) what guest was expected at the tavern that evening.

As the *Bakers' Broadcast* radio show evolved, so did the Nelson orchestra. A few more musicians were added and the group developed a distinctive relaxed style. On the air, Harriet and Ozzie usually each got to do a solo number, and when possible they began incorporating duets that were either comic or boy/girl romantic.

The show undoubtedly added to their following. It was on only once a week, required little rehearsal, and took a summer break. That left ample opportunity for the orchestra to perform at various local spots or take short road trips. Their popularity also enabled Ozzie to negotiate more generous fees.

In August, 1935, the band was on a tour that would include some time in California. To make the most of it, various members were carpooling so that they'd be able to get around more in their free time. After a ballroom date in Henderson, Texas, they were on the road nearing Dallas. A fellow named Harold Lane was driving Ozzie's car while Harriet and Ozzie, sitting in the back, took in the passing scenery.

After mentally reviewing his finances, Ozzie turned to Harriett and said, "I think we have enough money saved. Why don't we get married?"

Harriet tapped Harold on the shoulder and said, "Hey, Harold. Ozzie just proposed. We're going to get married."

Harold turned just long enough to roll his eyes and say, "I thought he'd never ask."

In 1932, Harriet had made her break into films. Thanks to Vitaphone having studios in New York, she was able to play a supporting role in *The Campus Mystery*, a short film based on an S. S. Van Dine story. The other stars of the film were Neil Hamilton (as Inspector Carr) and Harry Davenport. Anybody remember them?

Probably as a result of this venture, she had made a screen test for Metro Goldwyn Mayer, and even engaged an agent named Leo Morrison in case anything came of it. Something did.

While Ozzie and crew were appearing at the Cocoanut Grove, Leo got wind of a part at RKO Pictures that he thought was perfect for Harriet. He persuaded an RKO executive to sit with him and watch her screen test, and the exec agreed. Leo proudly came to Harriet with an offer to play the part for a salary of $750 per week.

To his shock and amazement, Harriet turned him down. It was a tempting offer, she said, but she was soon to be married and she hoped to be able to settle down to a "normal life," having a home, raising kids, etc. She might even give up her singing career.

Leo was close to tears when he reported to RKO, but he had done a better selling job there than with Harriet. The exec sent Leo back with a new offer of $1,000 a week. It didn't persuade Harriet, nor did a subsequent offer of $1,500. In desperation, Leo appealed to Ozzie to reason with his intended.

Ozzie told Leo that it had to be Harriet's decision, but he would speak to her. He did, and he came up with an excellent argument. He told Harriet that he did not want her to some day look at him across the breakfast table, see a worn-out, balding band leader and say to herself, "Yes, and I once had a chance to be a Hollywood star."

Harriet relented, but with a big "But!" She said, "Okay, but just this one picture. Then I'm going back home and we're going to start raising a family."

Harriet and Ozzie were married October 8, 1935. His father had died and his mother now lived in a fairly large apartment in

Hackensack, New Jersey. The wedding was conducted there, with brother Alfred and his wife as best man and maid of honor.

There was no time for a traditional honeymoon. On the Sunday before the wedding, they began the new season of *The Baker's Broadcast*, with Robert Ripley making his first appearance as host. The orchestra also had an opening the following Friday at the Lexington Hotel. Just a week after their marriage, Harriet boarded a plane, accompanied by her mother, and headed for Hollywood. It was to be another of those fateful occasions.

The film in which Harriet was to appear was a low budget drama called *Two O'clock Courage*. At the same time, RKO's top director, Mark Sandrich was about to film a new Fred Astaire/Ginger Rogers film, with music by Irving Berlin. Randolph Scott and Irene Dunne would be a second romantic duo. Unfortunately, just as production was about to start, Miss Dunne became unavailable.

Sandrich nixed about a dozen other actresses who might have sufficed. Then he happened to be in the room as an assistant director screened Harriet's test for the benefit of her wardrobe and make-up people. He watched intently, then asked who she was. Told that Harriet was a newcomer who would be in *Two O'clock Courage,* Sandrich said, "Find someone else. This lady is going to play Irene Dunne's role in *Follow the Fleet*."

And so it was. *Follow the Fleet* opened in February at Radio City Music Hall. Rogers and Astaire were for sure the stars of the picture, but Harriet got glowing reviews for both her acting and her singing of two torch songs, "Get Thee Behind Me, Satan" and "Here I Am, But Where Are You?" One reviewer said that she all but stole the show. Another said, "If you've seen *Follow the Fleet,* you know there's a new star on the Hollywood horizon."

A bonus for Harriet was that she and Ginger Rogers hit it off beautifully. Ginger took Harriet under her wing, offering advice and coaching her. The two developed a friendship that lasted a lifetime.

Harriet's great showing in the film led RKO and Sandrich to propose a five-year contract. Harriet reiterated that she'd just gotten married and that her next production was going to be a baby. Sandrich asked Ozzie to try his influence. Ozzie interceded with an alternative suggestion for an open-ended contract that required no more than three pictures per year. RKO agreed, and Harriet signed.

The change of plans in Hollywood extended Harriet's stay from an anticipated six weeks to thirteen. The separated newlyweds called each other daily with long reports of their activities and how much they missed one another. At a time when long distance calls were not cheap, gossip columnist Louella Parsons reported that the two were helping to keep Ma Bell profitable.

When she returned and resumed her new role as Mrs. Nelson, Harriet slipped back quickly into what was a busy year for the band, with dates throughout the East and along the East Coast. Whether the separation was a factor or not is uncertain, but she also fulfilled her goal of becoming pregnant.

That didn't stop her from traveling and singing with the group. As her condition began to show, Ozzie arranged that spotlights on her should be focused about shoulder high. Late in the game Harriet had to resist flinching as she got kicked during her number. "If he has to kick me," she joked, "I wish he'd at least keep time with the music."

On the morning of October 24, 1936, Ozzie was awakened by a poke in the ribs, and Harriet informed him, "This is it." They called for a cab and then phoned Harriet's mother, who met them at the hospital. As Hazel and Ozzie paced the coffee shop and took turns checking the time, Harriet gave birth to a healthy baby boy who was named David Oswald Nelson.

The Nelsons had a comfortable, roomy apartment and could afford to hire some help for Harriet. A lady named Geneva came in days to clean and cook. At the hospital, Harriet befriended Miss Elizabeth Jones, a nurse, and Ozzie persuaded her to come home with Harriet and David for three or four weeks. A British import, "Jonesie" put on a bit of a formal front, but it couldn't subdue her warm and loving nature. Her tenure ended up stretching to six months.

Early in October, Ozzie and the band had returned to the air with Robert Ripley and opened for a second season at the Lexington Hotel. A talented blues singer named Shirley Lloyd had joined them to fill in for Harriet.

Harriet rejoined the group briefly in mid-December, but she already had had a call from RKO to start filming two musicals in January. Reluctantly, she left Ozzie and Jonesie in charge of caring for little David as she flew back to Hollywood.

Although his career was winding down, Joe Penner starred in both of Harriet's two films. In *New Faces of 1937*, he and Harriet were joined by comics Milton Berle, Parkyakarkus and Bert Gordon, another former vaudevillian, known as "the mad Russian." He later became a frequent guest character on radio for Eddie Cantor, and occasionally popped up on the Jack Benny show and others. He was best known for his deep-voiced opening line: "How doooo you do!"

In *New Faces*, Harriet did two duets with William Brady: "If I Didn't Have You" and "Our Penthouse on Third Avenue." In the latter, she provided the piano accompaniment. Brady also sang "Love Is Never Out of Season" while Harriet danced with a male chorus.

In *Life of the Party*, Penner and Harriet were joined by Victor Moore, Billy Gilbert and Ann Miller, who would go on to fame in such MGM musicals as *Easter Parade, On the Town* and *Kiss Me Kate*. She was just fourteen at the time, having fibbed about her age when signing with RKO Pictures. (There was a lot of that going on back then. See the preceding section about Alice Faye.)

Neither picture received rave reviews. *New Faces* did reasonably well at the box office, probably drawing patrons who had heard of the popular Broadway show that inspired it. Regardless, Harriet undoubtedly gained additional name recognition that would benefit her return to singing with the orchestra.

The radio show would soon begin its 1937-38 season, again with a new star, a fellow named Frederic "Feg" Murray. Murray was a *Los Angeles Times* sport cartoonist and columnist who found his niche with a cartoon series called "Seein' Stars." It was Louella Parsons movie star trivia done in cartoon form. Syndicated by King Features, it appeared in hundreds of newspapers and was immensely popular. Murray then parlayed his "stargazer" reputation into a radio career as he assumed the role of host on the *Baker's Broadcast*.

Because Standard Brands was located in California, the show's sponsor wanted to move the broadcast there. There were then few clubs in California that would afford the orchestra extended engagements. Ozzie did some figuring to calculate what it would take to support all concerned if they relied solely on their radio checks. He presented a figure to the sponsor and, much to his relief, it was accepted without dickering. They also offered to assist the Nelsons and all the orchestra members in relocating.

The Nelsons found a suitable house that they were able to rent. It was a pleasant English Tudor style located on Toluca Lake and near Lakeside

Golf Club, where Ozzie became a member. Anticipating that they eventually would return to New York, they sublet their apartment there.

When Frederic Murray took over the program, *The Baker's Broadcast* became subtitled *Seein' Stars in Hollywood*. Murray presented behind-the-scenes Hollywood stories and interviewed many of the screen's current favorites. In an informal format, the Nelsons sometimes sat in to help move the interviews along. In a memorable broadcast on March 13, 1938, Murray juxtaposed Ozzie and Harriet with the horror films stars Bela Lugosi and Boris Karloff. The show's relaxed atmosphere made it fun to do and did not put any strain on Ozzie, Harriet or the orchestra.

At the end of the 1937-38 season, the sponsors decided that the show had about run its course, and it was not renewed. When their sublease was up, the Nelsons returned to their New York apartment. By September of 1938, the band was playing at New York's Strand Theatre. After that they were soon back on another road tour.

True to her earlier intent, Harriet devoted most of her time to being a mom. A new "Nana" was on board to watch over David. Now two years old, he was a bundle of energy, so Harriet took over whenever possible. As she told an interviewer, "Ozzie handles the business, and I handle the domestic problems."

Although Harriet, Nana and David traveled with the band, Harriet limited her involvement to special "guest" appearances. To fill the gap, Ozzie was able to hire several female singers for short stints along the tour route.

Harriet did find time to film 1938's *Cocoanut Grove*. Appearing opposite Fred MacMurray, she sang just one song, a Frank Loesser tune called "Says My Heart."

After an engagement at the Gold Coast Room of Chicago's Drake Hotel, it was back to New York in time for the holidays. When their lease expired, the Nelsons opted not to renew. Instead they rented an apartment in the building next to Harriet's mother, Hazel, and just blocks away from Ozzie's mother, Ethel. They felt fortunate to be so close, because Harriet expected to soon make Hazel and Ethel grandmothers again.

Harriet remained at home as the orchestra headed to Chicago in February, 1940, to begin a ten-week engagement at the Blackhawk Restaurant. A plus of that gig was that it was aired over radio station WGN, heard throughout the Midwest. While there, they recorded three numbers that were among their best-selling hits, including a Count Basie instrumental called "Riff Interlude."

Harriet was due in late April. Ozzie called nightly to check, but kept getting a "not yet" report. On May 1, the band opened for a stay at the Riverside Theatre in Milwaukee. The afternoon show had just ended on May 8 when the phone rang in Ozzie's dressing room. Brother Al was on the line to report that David had a new baby brother. Ozzie called the hospital to check on Harriet, who was doing fine. They decided that the newest member of the family would be named Eric Hilliard Nelson.

With a few free days between Milwaukee and the next stop on tour, Ozzie flew home for a quick visit. He took David with him to the hospital and together they had their first look at little Eric. Almost from Day One, the newcomer was referred to as Ricky.

The Nelsons decided it was time they had a home of their own. In their free time during the summer, they looked around and selected an almost-new house on the edge of a lovely wooded area in Tenafly, New Jersey. With what was left of their nest egg, they bought a small remodeled farmhouse just down the road for Ethel and Ozzie's brother Donald, who was then thirteen.

Christmas was an especially joyful one that year, as all the family gathered at the Nelsons' new domical. The evening was capped by carolers singing at the front steps. When they opened the door to listen, it turned out to be the King Sisters, who had just wrapped up a holiday show nearby. They were, of course, invited inside, and an evening of group singing ensued.

A six-week stay at the Strand had facilitated time at the new home for the holidays. In February, 1941, the band began a New Orleans engagement that would take them through the Marti Gras season. Harriet and David both came along. Ricky stayed home with his two grandmothers and a new nurse.

Next stop was San Francisco. Ozzie had wanted to work there for some time, but there were only three hotels that booked orchestras for extended stays. When the band was booked at the Palace Hotel, Harriet found a nice rental house atop a mountain in San Rafael. Being in California coincided with Harriet being given roles in two more films, this time at the Columba Pictures studios.

She had non-singing roles in both pictures. *Confessions of Boston Blackie* starred Chester Morris in the second of fourteen films about the reformed crook who now spent much of his time outsmarting those who had not yet wised up. Morris also got top billing in *Canal Zone*, but the cast included several names that would eventually appear on theater marquees: Larry Parks, Forrest Tucker and Lloyd Bridges.

The Blackie film was directed by Edward Dmytryk, who later was charged with contempt of Congress and spent time in prison for refusing to testify during the infamous anti-Communist investigations conducted by the House Committee on Un-American Activities. His early films included *Murder, My Sweet*, an adaptation of Raymond Chandler's Phillip Marlowe crime novel *Farewell, My Lovely*. He later directed *The Caine Mutiny, Raintree County, The Left Hand of God* and other acclaimed films.

While in California, the Nelsons also had the opportunity to do their first film together. Utilizing a typical Hollywood ploy, *Sweetheart of the Campus* was a lightweight romance designed as background for a lot of music.

A college with a dwindling student body is in financial trouble until an entire band decides to enroll. Their popularity draws the crowds and results in an overflow of applicants. Ruby Keeler, better known for her dancing, plays the band's lead vocalist. Harriet did some singing, but rather than being part of the band, she played a cute co-ed. Ozzie did his best with some numbers specially written for the band, although he found them rather unexciting.

Not long after closing at the Palace, Ozzie had a visit from Ed Fishman of the William Morris agency. The Brown and Williamson Tobacco Company was planning to sponsor a new radio program in the fall that would star the popular comic Red Skelton. They wanted Ozzie and Harriet to provide the music.

Coming up from a circus and vaudeville background, Richard "Red" Skelton made his screen debut with a supporting role in 1937's *Having Wonderful Time*, then provided comic support in the Dr. Kildare film series. The Nelsons had seen him on the screen and performed with him at a number of special benefit shows. They knew he was a coming star, and had no hesitation agreeing to join him on the radio show.

On October 7, the deep, dignified voice of Truman Bradley proclaimed the opening of "*The Raleigh Cigarette Program*, starring Red

Skelton!" After a bit of opening theme, Red was introduced and the fun began. A string of topical gags would be exchanged between Skelton, Bradley and the Nelsons. Red got most of the gag lines, but the others also had a few, usually at his expense. Harriet was billed on the show as Harriet Hilliard.

The mid-point of the show would be a musical number. Sometimes it was just the band, sometimes a song by Harriet, but most often it was a duet specially arranged for the two Nelsons. These were usually humorous pieces, and Red would be in the wings laughing along with the studio audience.

The rest of the show was a rotating series of comic sketches in which Red portrayed half a dozen or more recurring characters. In these, Harriet's years of vaudeville were a great asset. She originated a number of supporting characters, including the gal friends of Red's Dead Eye and Clem Kadiddlehopper. ("Whoa, hoss, whoa. Aw, come on hoss, whoa!")

Perhaps Red's best remembered and most popular character was Junior, "the mean widdle kid." Old time radio fans usually remember the versatile character actress Verna Felton as his Grandma. She did take over the role, and made it a staple of the Junior skits, but it was created and originally played by Harriet Hilliard.

The Skelton show was a hit from the start. Its choice spot in the NBC Tuesday night lineup was certainly a plus. Jim and Marian Jordan, a.k.a. Fibber McGee and Molly, were followed by Bob Hope, followed by Red Skelton. Listeners enjoying one program were inclined to stay tuned long enough to at least hear what was coming next if they didn't have the schedule memorized. As Blondie's announcer used to caution listeners: "Uh, uh, don't touch that dial."

Convinced they had latched onto a good thing, the Nelsons decided to start thinking long term. Roaming around the Hollywood

Hills, they spied a white colonial style house with green shutters and a "For Sale" sign out front. The large front lawn and several vacant lots behind looked as though they would provide an ample playground for two young boys. After one walk-through with the owners, they agreed it was just what they needed.

In November, 1941, they moved in. While their furniture was being shipped from New Jersey, they slept on mattresses in front of a large fireplace. A lady named Grace Johnson became their housekeeper and stayed with them for thirteen years. David soon was enrolled in kindergarten at nearby Gardner Street Public School.

Apart from minimal rehearsal times, the Skelton show left them free most of the week. Harriet took part in a Universal Pictures musical called *Juke Box Jenny*, along with Ken Murray and the Charlie Barnett orchestra. Ozzie's group appeared in a musical called *Strictly in the Groove*, as well as the Paramount Pictures film *Big Street*, starring Henry Fonda and Lucille Ball.

The band was able to arrange a series of bookings and found time to cut three recordings. Thanks in part to their radio exposure, all three enjoyed a lot of air play by the disc jockeys who were beginning to populate the airwaves.

With America's entry into World War II, band members were one by one drafted or enlisted in the armed services. By the time the band opened at San Francisco's Golden Gate Theatre, it included only two of the original troupe.

Ozzie augmented the band's shows with various other entertainers, such as a juggler and a fellow who sang funny Swedish-dialect songs. Harriet would not be listed on the bill, but would surprise the audience by coming out for a song at closing. Then she and Ozzie would do one or two of their special material duets. The popularity gained by their radio work with Skelton was apparent in both the audience enthusiasm and its size.

During the early 1940s, America craved entertainment to take its mind off the war. The next couple of years were busy, prosperous and fun. During the summer of 1943, Ozzie brought his "kid brother," Don, out to the coast to work with the group as a prop man.

Red Skelton's show was still getting high ratings when he was drafted in the Spring of 1944. His departure was a turning point for the Nelsons. It was possible the sponsor might hire another comic or create a similar show on which they could be part of the cast. However, they felt that they had had sufficient experience and exposure to ready them for a show of their own.

A purely musical program might work, but there was an abundance of those already. They bounced ideas back and forth for weeks. Finally they agreed upon a situation comedy in which they would be musicians who inherit a small town's general store. Tired of cross-country tours, they decide to have a go at actually running the store. There would be a series of customers coming in to facilitate comedy bits. It was simple, homey and left open the possibility for some musical interludes.

Ozzie had pitched in on a lot of the scripting of Red's show, and he and Harriet had worked out numerous little comic skits to spice up their stage shows. Rather than seeking a professional writer, he sat down to give it a shot. It was hard work, especially the part about trying to be funny. When he had a finished script, he held his breath as Harriet critiqued it. To his relief, she rated it good. Not great, but good.

The next step was to line up some radio performers and rent out a studio at NBC in which to record the program. As the audience filtered in and found seats, the Nelsons watched from the wings and chewed their nails. Harriet said aloud what they both were thinking: "What if they just sit there and stare at us?"

The program began, and the first big laugh came where expected. The Nelsons felt their tension easing. No one made any serious flubs, and more laughs came in the right places. Taking final bows to warm applause, Ozzie told Harriet, "I think we've got something here."

The next step was to play the recording for Wally Jordan, a sharp young fellow from the William Morris agency, who was head of the West Coast radio department. His reaction was a treat to their ears. "This is great!" he declared.

Morris took the recording to New York to shop it around. Ten days later he called the Nelsons to inform them he had sold the show to the International Silver Company. With high spirits, the Nelsons set off on what would be the band's last tour in the summer of 1944. Brother Don joined them again, this time as a band member, playing tenor sax. At the end of the tour, the band returned to the coast. Ozzie and Harriet went to New York. There they met with their sponsors to plan promotional activities for the first season of their show.

All went well, but once back home Ozzie grew anxious. The more he thought about it, the more uncomfortable he was with the concept of the store as a backdrop for the show.

Joe Moran, the Young and Rubicon advertising rep who handled the International Silver account, was an old friend of the Nelsons. He was coming for dinner the next week. Ozzie determined to voice his concern and ask if Joe could convince the sponsor to allow a format change to eliminate that aspect.

As soon as Ozzie began to expound, Joe's face broke out in a grin. "Mr. Stevens (the company's president) called me the other day," Joe said. Stevens said that he and his people didn't want to tell Ozzie how to run the show, but they all felt that the store idea didn't seem right. He wondered if Joe could convince Ozzie to change it.

Laughing, Joe told Ozzie, "I'll call him tomorrow and tell him it was a tough sell, but I was finally able to convince you."

In Ozzie's revised version of the show, the village store was out. He and Harriet would use their own names and play comical versions of themselves. As musical professionals, married, their light-hearted weekly "adventures" would involve trying to resolve various mishaps that created humorous bumps in their efforts to live a reasonably normal home life.

October 8, 1944, was the Nelsons' ninth wedding anniversary. They celebrated a day early because it also was the evening when Jack Bailey stepped up to a CBS microphone and announced: "From Hollywood, International Silver Company presents *The Adventures of Ozzie and Harriet.*"

After a bit of theme music, Bailey set the scene by explaining that the Nelsons had finished a summer tour and were learning their way around their new home at 1847 Rogers Road. The address, mentioned in every episode, was a tie-in to 1847 Rogers Silver, one of the sponsor's most popular lines.

On early broadcasts, Harriet and Ozzie were introduced in the opening credits as "America's favorite young couple." That delineation was still being used when the Nelsons were in their forties, but it later was modified to "America's favorite young family."

Hoping to avoid being perceived as just another sit-com couple, they sought to establish early on that they were a happily married couple who just happened to be in show business. That first program, which found the Nelsons moving into their new home, focused on presenting them as regular folks trying to get settled into a more normal life.

Ozzie: It's wonderful to be living like regular human beings again.

Harriet: Yes, it is. So try to remember that this is our own home, and stop putting the towels in your suitcase.

The initial format acknowledged its stars' musical background, with story lines that involved the tribulations of trying to maintain a normal family life when Pop, and sometimes Mom, were frequently on road tours. Comedy sketches were separated by musical numbers, but to establish that the program was primarily a comedy rather than a musical/variety show, neither Harriet nor Ozzie sang. In later episodes, one or both of them would sing if the song chosen could serve as a natural interlude, as in film and theater musicals.

It was unrealistic to suppose that Ozzie could crank out a program a week, so they had hired two seasoned writers, both well known to them. John Medbury was noted for his sketch writing. Jack Douglas had been a key person on Red Skelton's writing staff. Prior to that he had worked for Eddie Cantor and Bob Hope.

The weekly demands of rehearsals and actual broadcasts of course required some of the couple's time. Ozzie also spent many late evenings fine-tuning scripts. Still, the end of touring gave them much more time to do things together and with the boys. The home began to feel more like it was really theirs as they made alterations, added furniture and had a swimming pool built out back.

The contract with the sponsor called for a minimum eleven-piece orchestra. Ozzie actually had four rhythm pieces, seven brass and five woodwinds. Still, to achieve some desired effects, he added a viola, cello, harp and three violins.

He was indeed fortunate to have brought in trumpeter Billy May just before the Skelton program ended. Billy was a superb arranger who later went on to leading his own orchestra and providing back-up and/or arrangements for such top vocalists as Frank Sinatra, Peggy Lee, Nat King Cole and Bobby Darin.

The King Sisters came on board to provide a musical interlude. This minimized the songs by the Nelsons and emphasized the fact that the program was meant to be a sit-com rather than a musical/variety show.

In early episodes of the show, the cast was almost exclusively Ozzie and Harriet. Most listeners knew that they had children, and they would work in references to the boys via discussions of amusing comments they made, tricky questions they asked, or issues that their parents (like parents listening in) sometimes had to deal with. Initially, however, David and Ricky were off-stage characters. When they began being written into the scripts, they were at first played by two young actors.

As the show became established and story lines broadened somewhat, various neighbors and other characters began to appear. Several supporting players, all folk who were heard in many radio roles, joined the cast in regular or recurring roles.

Harriet's mother, Hazel, was living just a few blocks away. It seemed natural to work her into some of the situations. Lurene Tuttle was brought in to play Hazel, albeit a comical version of her. From a career that began in vaudeville, Lurene Tuttle moved smoothly into the world of radio. She was Sam Spade's secretary, Effie Perrine, and played almost every female role on that show. On the Red Skelton program, she was Junior's mother and Daisy June in the Clem Kadiddlehopper skits. She had supporting roles in several Hollywood films. As television became the nation's primary parlor entertainment, she appeared in literally hundreds of roles on programs that spanned every genre.

John Brown's voice was familiar to radio listeners from a multitude of supporting roles and guest appearances, as well as his starring role on *The Damon Runyon Theatre*. He also played Irma's conniving, ne'er-do-well boy friend Al on *My Friend Irma*. On *The Life of Riley*, he was Chester A. Riley's friend "Digger," a.k.a. Digby O'Dell, "your friendly undertaker." In their frequent meetings, he would invariably remark, "You're looking fine, Riley. Verrrry natural."

Brown became the Nelsons' next door neighbor, Syd Thornberry, affectionately known to Ozzie as "Thorny." When he came calling on the Nelsons, his arrival was announced by a "rat-tat-a-tat-tat" knock on the door in the rhythm of the chant "shave-and-a-haircut." The double knock of "two-bits," however, was omitted. Listeners came to know who was about to show up before Ozzie informed Harriet, "Oh, there's Thorny at the door."

In conversations over the back yard fence, Thorny frequently acted as a sounding board for Ozzie (whom he almost always called Oz) when he was mulling over a problem or decision of some kind. Always sympathetic, Thorny was prone to offering Ozzie advise that was well-intended but ill-advised. Ozzie later confessed that some of Thorny's personality was borrowed from a real neighbor.

The incredibly versatile Bea Benadaret played the Nelsons' first maid, Gloria, a bit of a sad sack.

Gloria: I'll need some time off for my sister's wedding. She marrying a soldier.

Ozzie: Ah. Is he an officer?

Gloria: Yes. He's a second lieutenant.

Ozzie: A second lieutenant?

Gloria: Yes. The first one got away.

In addition to other roles, Bea Benadaret's voice was familiar as the snippy telephone operator who frequently frustrated and annoyed

Jack Benny when he needed assistance making a call. On *Fibber McGee and Molly*, she played the wealthy and uppity Millicent Carstairs. She later made a smooth transition to television and starred on the popular show *Petticoat Junction*.

A character who became a favorite of everyone, cast and listeners alike, was the almost breathless fourteen-year-old neighbor, Emmy Lou. The quintessential, swooning, overly dramatic teenager was played by the lovely Janet Waldo, who at the same time was starring in her own series, *Meet Corliss Archer*. Like Thorny, Emmy Lou was happy to offer Ozzie her teen-aged perspective on all situations, especially if they involved the boys. Another trait she shared with Thorny was that any advise she gave Ozzie only tended to compound his current problem.

In almost all of her encounters with Ozzie, something in the conversation would provoke one of her excited, gushing exclamations of delight. It was a sort of high-pitched squeal that rode up the scale and back down again: "OooooEEEEEEooooo!" It became a trademark of her giddy teenage character that audiences anticipated whenever she and Ozzie met.

Janet once was a guest on Bing Crosby's program. When she agreed to appear, Bing sent a tongue-in-cheek note to Ozzie asking if her squeal was copyrighted and, if so, could he have permission to have her use it on his show. Ozzie responded in kind with a note saying that it was okay for Janet to do her thing as long as the show's closing announcements included a statement that "Janet Waldo's squeal was heard through the courtesy of Ozzie and Harriet."

In 1952, when she was twenty-eight, Janet portrayed (believably) a lovesick teen smitten with Ricky Ricardo on the *I Love Lucy* television show. She also reappeared as Emmy Lou on a few early television episodes of *The Adventures of Ozzie and Harriet*.

For a new show establishing its pitch and pace, the program went well. Listener response was positive, even though the show didn't gain a top rating. At the end of the last episode of the season, there was no doubt that the show would return in the Fall.

As the 1945 season began, Ozzie persuaded Billy May to take over conducting the orchestra. Until then, Ozzie had been obliged to hold a script in one hand and a baton in the other, dividing his attention between acting and conducting background music and bridges.

The scripting process also changed, as John Medbury and Jack Douglas moved on. Now there were five writers who gathered at the Nelson home on Monday nights. They hashed out a story line, were rewarded with ice cream sundaes, and went home.

At the next meeting they each presented a complete script based on the story idea. Ozzie read them all and took what he felt were the best scenes or individual lines to patch together a final version. It was a bit time-consuming for Ozzie, but the end result was what he and Harriet felt were a steady series of quality scripts in which they came across as real people.

Although most of their listeners knew that the Nelsons had children, they had kept the boys mostly off stage during the first season. A lad named Joel Davis occasionally had played David with just a few gag lines that did not make him essential to the story. This season, Tommy Bernard and Henry Blair joined the cast to portray David and Ricky respectively. The activities of the boys were incorporated into story lines and sometimes became the main focus.

In the 1946 season, the musical interludes were dropped, establishing thence forward that the show was a pure sit-com. Listeners familiar with the Nelsons from their years of performing on stage and radio took that in stride as a mere format change. However, some listeners, especially newer ones, were unaware of their musical background. That created a grey area that was to hover over their show both on radio and, later, on television.

As the program evolved, there were no more mentions of Ozzie and Harriet's profession or their tours. The Nelsons became a typical middle class family, except for the fact that Ozzie seemed to be a stay-at-home dad.

There was never a scene in which Ozzie returned from the office or wherever and called out, "Hi. Honey! I'm home." Indeed, most of the time he already was wandering about the house or talking with Harriet as stories began. Having opted not to use the grocery store idea, and making no mention of his orchestra-leading status, Ozzie was without any visible source of income.

Given lifestyles of the era, Ozzie was assumed to be the breadwinner. Yet listeners who came late to the program had no idea how he supported his family. Throughout the radio and television series, listeners and viewers were left wondering about his occupation.

Choosing simply not to address that question, Ozzie molded scripts in such a way that it appeared the action was taking place on a weekend, when he would be expected to be at home with his family. The boys were pointedly never in school when Ozzie was at home with Harriet. Nevertheless, the pundits, reviewers and comics over the years often got a chuckle by wondering, "What does Ozzie do for a living?"

Although asked jokingly, the question came up frequently when Ozzie met fans. If pressed, he would sometimes say that his on-air character was a lawyer. He and Harriet actually had a bit of fun with the issue when appearing on *The Tonight Show*. They did a skit in which Harriet asks, "What *do* you do for a living?"

During the *Baker's Broadcast* years, and after launching their own show, Harriet and Ozzie built up their radio presence and recognition with numerous guest appearances, together and individually. Visits to comedy shows such as *The Fred Allen Show* were most common. But in December, 1947, they demonstrated their dramatic skills on *Suspense* in a thriller called "Too Little To Live On." They subsequently were invited back to perform in two other dramas on "radio's outstanding theatre of thrills."

During the 1947-48 season, the Nelsons made a guest appearance on Bing Crosby's radio program. Bing was pleased with the way the show came off. He told the Nelsons if they could come up with a story idea, he'd be happy to return the favor and appear on their show some time and bring along his son Lindsay. The Nelsons loved the idea. Ozzie got the writers working on it and an appropriate script was soon ready.

David and Ricky often played tennis with the Crosby boys. When they heard about the planned program, they dashed home and wanted to know why they couldn't play themselves on the show.

Harriet and Oz weren't entirely opposed to the idea. They had anticipated that the question would come up sometime, but just not so soon. They explained to the boys that show business was not all fun and games. The pressures and headaches could be daunting, and a blown line could disrupt a show and cause problems for all their fellow performers.

David and Ricky assured their parents that they understood that, but they believed they were up to the challenge. David said that he and Ricky had often discussed it, and had long felt that they would one day be a part of the show. Opting to proceed with caution, their parents compromised. They agreed to let the boys play themselves in a preview performance of the show. The preview was a rehearsal of the entire program that was performed before a live audience, but did not go out over the air.

**The Nelson family at about the time that Ricky (at left) and David joined the cast.
CREDIT: Nostalgia Digest collection**

In December of 1948, the boys had their shot. Within a few minutes into the show, they demonstrated their readiness. Both boys were quick studies and seemed to possess an instinctive comedy timing. The laughs came where expected as they read their lines like seasoned veterans, never missing a cue. In February of 1949, when Bing and Lindsay made their guest appearances, the studio billboard read "THE ADVENTURES OF OZZIE AND HARRIET, starring the entire Nelson family, Ozzie, Harriet, David and Ricky."

During the boys' early appearances on the show, Ricky was too small to reach the regular microphones. He sat at a small table and had his own goose-necked microphone. As the program began and he took his place, the first thing he did was to kick off his shoes. That always got a chuckle from the studio audience.

Ricky's reading skill was still at the beginner's level, but with David's coaching, he memorized his lines, and the cue lines that would prompt them. Sitting at his table, he held a script in his hands as though reading, and glanced frequently at the other cast members. When they turned a page, he did likewise.

For the most part he kept up with the story's progress and piped up where expected. On one occasion, however, he jumped his cue. That prompted Harriet to cut him off, saying, "Not now, Ricky!"

The boys' addition to the cast proved to be well timed. Prior to 1949, all three major networks had insisted upon only "live" broadcasts; i.e., no recordings. With the advent of tape, many performers began pressuring the networks to relent. Bing Crosby, whose popularity made him hard to refuse, was especially influential in bringing about a change of policy.

For the Nelsons, taping the program relieved a strain on their household routine now that the boys were part of the cast. It made possible some flexibility for recreational activities or special events. More importantly, they could record their shows at a time that did not interfere with the boys' school days or the time they needed for homework. That was a plus, because neither boy was especially inclined toward scholarly efforts. On one occasion, Harriett was encouraging Ricky to focus on his homework. His response was, "Gee, Mom, I'm probably going to be a radio actor all my life, and I can already read the scripts, so why do I even need to go to school?"

From a performance point of view, taping also allowed for retakes and editing to improve the end product that went out over the airwaves. In the years that followed, many prime time radio programs began with the announcement: "The following program has been electronically transcribed."

Around this time, Ozzie's baby brother Donald joined the writing staff. With his own boyhood not far behind him, Don was especially adept at writing for the boys, with whom he'd spent a lot of time. It was he who came up with the line that became a catch phrase for Ricky: "I don't mess around, boy!" As many times as Ricky uttered it, the line always got a hearty laugh from audiences.

Always intent on getting scripts fine-tuned, Ozzie found it helpful to now have the boys part of the troupe. Casting a critical eye at lines that were to be read by one of the boys, he sometimes found them stilted or not phrased properly for their respective ages. He then would simply ask, "Is this the way you would say this?"

Though their respective personalities may have been magnified for dramatic and comic effect on the program, the siblings were cast pretty much as themselves. David was capable of some mischief and snappy lines in real life. Some of this found its way into scripts. But for the most part he was the more mature (for his age) older brother, who gave Ricky wise counsel and tried to restrain his sometimes rambunctious impulses.

Ricky was a well behaved kid at home, but still young enough to be testing the limits of adult authority and questioning their wisdom. This was played up in scripts, and he came off on the air as a basically good kid with a knack for snappy come-backs. Often these came across as youthfully wise observations about comic situations that were being played out.

As a result of their on-air personas, David was accepted as the more rational and protective older brother, while Ricky became the darling of audiences, who looked forward to his antics and smart-alecky comments. David took it in stride and never begrudged Rick the larger share of the spotlight. He noted that because of their age difference (about three and a half years) he never felt any sense of competition, and he was genuinely proud of his brother's accomplishments. He once quipped that Rick had to answer three times as much fan mail, but they both received the same salary as cast members.

For his part, Ricky never allowed his popularity to give him a swelled head or cause a fissure in the close relationship that he and David enjoyed. Even when he later became a rock and roll recording star with his band, he accepted the status as simply a part of the show business career into which he felt he'd been born.

During a visit to *The Tonight Show*, Johnny Carson asked how he coped with being a "teenage idol." Rick mused that it was rather weird doing one-nighters where girls were screaming, fainting and trying to tear his clothes off. Then, he added with a wry grin, his real status was made clear when he got home and his mother would yell, "Ricky! Come back upstairs and pick up this wet towel!"

Much of the appeal of *The Adventures of Ozzie and Harriet* was that it did not come across as just another sit-com program. In spite of the often nonsensical situations, usually created by Ozzie, listeners perceived the Nelson family as real people. Unlike *Henry Aldrich, Date with Judy, Life of Riley* and other programs in which the family members were all actors, the Nelsons actually were a family.

Although they truly were not a typical American family, Ozzie took pains to see that they came across that way. Scripts were designed to create humor out of real life situations, if somewhat exaggerated, that were familiar to most families. Plots often involved little misunderstandings that mushroomed: a Christmas Card mistaken for a traffic ticket; a set of mistakenly delivered chairs.

Ozzie drew heavily on little incidents in the lives of Ricky and David, often going over a plot idea with them to be sure he wasn't overdoing the comic aspects. As the boys got bigger and progressed in school, more possible story ideas frequently arose.

Ozzie also was adept at seeing the humor in activities and discussions that took place around the home. In one 1949 episode he spends the entire half hour working on their income tax return, struggling to make heads or tails out of the instructions, and trying to find every possible deduction, while being interrupted repeatedly by Harriet and the boys.

At the end of the 1948-49 season, Ozzie met with the sponsor's representatives for a contract negotiation. Year-to-year contracts were the norm, and International Silver was quite willing to sign the Nelsons for another year. However, with a yearning to provide a bit more security for his family, Ozzie proposed a five-year contract. The folks at International Silver were not comfortable with that, and so there was an amiable parting of the ways.

To pursue his goal, Ozzie went to New York and signed up with Music Corporation of America as the family's new agency. He had the good fortune of being able to have the account assigned to a fellow named Sonny Werblin. In addition to being an old friend, Sonny had the reputation of being one of MCA's best agents.

Ozzie explained that, in addition to the security issue, he felt he could do a better job of coordinating and creativity if he was relieved of the annual pressure to renegotiate. Sonny thought that it was a great idea and added, "While we're at it, let's go all the way and make it for ten years!"

Rather than seek an individual sponsor brave enough to go along, Werblin went directly to the executives at the American Broadcasting Company. ABC lacked the financial stability of rivals NBC and CBS, where much of radio's top talent drew large audiences. On the lookout for programs that could compete with the highly rated shows on the other networks, ABC executives agreed that Ozzie and Harriet's program had the potential.

Living up to his reputation, Werblin negotiated a contact that delighted the Nelsons and was signed in July, 1949. A ten-year non-cancellable contract (the first of its kind in the business), it covered all four Nelsons. It would provide a basic salary whether the program aired or not. ABC would have the right to put the Nelsons on television after the first year, with salaries to be renegotiated. Since the boys were minors, it was stipulated that either of them could opt out of the program at any time should they so choose.

It would be up to ABC to find a sponsor or sponsors for the program, or if they chose, to carry it as "sustaining" (no sponsor). One stipulation that Ozzie especially appreciated was that he would have complete artistic control. Thus, whether on radio or television, the continuity or characterizations could not be influenced by sponsor whims.

That never became an issue, according to Ozzie. Over the next few years the Nelsons had a happy working relationship with such sponsors as Hotpoint, Heinz Foods, Eastman Kodak, Quaker Oats and American Dairy.

From the standpoint of ABC, the contract was a solid investment worth sticking its corporate neck out for. The network struggled to attract and hold listeners as it competed with the programming and big-name talents of NBC and CBS. Though not one of the top ranked programs, *The Adventures of Ozzie and Harriet* enjoyed consistently high ratings and a loyal listening audience.

To celebrate the signing of a contract that guaranteed a steady income for ten years, the Nelsons bought a large Mediterranean-style beach house in South Laguna. It became a regular weekend retreat to which they headed every Friday night after taping the next week's program. All of the Nelsons were good swimmers and loved the water, so almost every weekend included a visit to the public beach, complete with a picnic lunch. David later professed that some of his happiest youthful memories were their weekly drives to the beach as they told jokes and sang together, all anticipating the prospect of a relaxed family weekend ahead.

Given the popularity of television and the clause in their contract, the Nelsons knew that they would soon be appearing on the small screen. Concerned about how the show would carry over into the new medium, Ozzie approached MCA with the idea of a Hollywood film to get audience reaction. After some negotiation with Universal Pictures, a deal was worked out for a film to be called *Here Come the Nelsons*.

Scripted by Ozzie, brother Bob and one of the regular team writers, the screenplay naturally focused on the Nelson family. No doubt adding to its appeal, the supporting cast featured a number of radio folk, including Gale Gordon, Jim Backus, Sheldon Leonard, Barbara Lawrence and Frank Nelson. Though their faces may not have been familiar to the film's audiences, their voices certainly were. The film also was one of the first for a fellow named Roy Fitzgerald, a handsome young leading man who only recently had changed his screen name to Rock Hudson.

It was a low budget film, but benefited from the direction of Fred de Cordova, who later was a long-time producer of *The Tonight Show* with Johnny Carson. The favorable audience response allayed any anxiety Ozzie harbored about the eventual move to television.

The decision by ABC to make that move was soon forthcoming. Once again Ozzie took charge. He enlisted brother Don and two other associates, Bill Davenport and Ben Gershman, to crank out the shows under the Five Star Productions banner.

Filming began in August of 1952, and the first season was a hectic one. To help minimize production costs, Harriet took on the responsibility of set decorating and became the boys' wardrobe supervisor. For his part, much as on the radio series, Ozzie doubled as producer, director, story editor and head writer.

One aspect that made things a bit easier was the location of the studios, near Santa Monica Boulevard in Hollywood. It was about ten minutes from the Nelsons' home and the boys' respective schools.

To lend a sense of authenticity for the Nelsons, if not for the viewers, occasional footage of their actual home was inserted when outdoor scenes occurred. Harriet worked with stage crews to design sets that were near-perfect replicas of rooms inside the house.

The practice of product placement that was common in filmmaking became equally as prevalent on television, where an even wider audience was possible. When Hotpoint was for awhile a sponsor, sharp-eyed viewers could spot the Hotpoint emblem on the Nelsons' refrigerator and kitchen range. The Nelsons had no objection, since Hotpoint also installed identical appliances in their real home.

However, Ozzie nixed any suggestion of scenes in which family members would be seen gargling with Listerine or eating Quaker Oats at supper. That clause in the contract which gave him final approval also enabled he and Harriet to become the first—and for many years the only—television couple who slept together in a double bed.

The first telecast of *The Adventures of Ozzie and Harriet* was on October 3, 1952. The show was well received, probably picking up viewers who were new TV set owners in addition to those who had long been radio listeners.

Producing two shows every week, one on radio and one on television, required some strategic scheduling, especially with the younger Nelsons still in school. Ozzie's team focused on recording or filming parts of the scripts that included the boys at times that did not interfere with their school attendance or other activities. Both boys were active and competitive players in several sports.

Ricky proved to have the drive and a natural talent for tennis, playing in young people's tournaments and in interscholastic matches at Hollywood High School. He soon began to fill his room with trophies. In his junior year he ranked fifth in Southern California's 15-and-under division.

David's favorite sports was football. While in high school he played in a touch football league. In 1950, he played quarterback on an All-Star team. When he entered USC in the fall of 1955, he tried out for the football team. At 170 pounds, he was a runt compared to the other players (all of whom were there on athletic scholarships). Nevertheless, he was accepted and appreciated on the team because he had a good eye and a great arm for passing.

In one game against Stanford at the Coliseum, his parents and Ricky cheered as he threw a game-winning touchdown. Then they were crestfallen as the referees declared it no good because of an offside penalty by a teammate. Their only consolation was that the game ended in a tie.

Although many story ideas were used on both shows, the week's radio story never was repeated on that week's television program. That made for some extra work for script writers and more rehearsal by the cast. But it avoided the problem of trying to reproduce on television some scenes that came off more easily when left to the imagination of the radio listener. It also meant that television viewers would not skip the program, thinking they'd already heard the story on radio.

Another new wrinkle on television was the laugh track. Most comedy programs on radio were performed before a live studio audience. The gags either got laughs or they didn't. As a frustrated Milton Berle sometimes lamented, "These are the jokes, folks." Television shows like the Nelsons' were mostly filmed in a studio and, like a movie, often had scenes filmed out of sequence and then patched together in final editing. Thus there were no audience laughs, because there was no audience.

In the minds of television executives, many viewers were not smart enough to know which lines were funny. So "canned" (i.e., recorded) laughter was patched into the film soundtrack at what were deemed appropriate spots. This supposedly would prompt the at-home viewers to join in with their own laughter. Many television critics derided the practice, noting that laughter often was inserted for lines or scenes that weren't really funny, or a gag worthy of a chuckle was rewarded with an outburst of hilarious laughter.

Ever the perfectionist, Ozzie would have none of that. Knowing it would be a lost cause to insist on no laugh track at all, he utilized the clause in their contract that made him essentially the quality control manager for the program. Every week he screened the television show for three separate preview audiences. He made notes as to where the laughs came and whether it was mild laughter or a real outburst. Armed with this information, he had appropriate laugh tracks inserted at spots that had earned them.

Another quality issue in early recorded television was the use of kinescope filming. The name Kinescope referred both to the method of filming and the finished product. It involved mounting a 16mm or 35mm movie camera in front of a video monitor. The resulting filmed program had a quality level that was noticeably inferior to live telecasts or theater films. Even untutored audiences at home could tell the difference.

In 1951, Lucille Ball and Desi Arnaz decided that their *I Love Lucy* show would be shot directly with 35mm film, using a three-camera system that allowed for capturing scenes from various angles and selecting the best shot during editing.

Given his insistence on quality, Ozzie took note of the difference. When *The Adventures of Ozzie and Harriet* took the leap to television, he insisted that it be filmed the same way. As a result, late-night reruns of the *Lucy* show and the Nelson family adventures are noticeably clearer and sharper than most other reruns from early television.

As they had on the radio program, the Nelsons expanded the story line potential by populating the cast with additional characters. Some familiar faces and some new ones appeared on the television version of the Nelsons' adventures. Screen actor Don DeFore stepped in to take over the role of Mr. Thornberry. The next door neighbor's laid back, easy-going persona probably was a role that came naturally for him.

DeFore became a fixture of the cast who appeared, at least briefly, in almost every week's story. In 1955, he was nominated for an Emmy Award as Best Supporting Actor in a Regular Series. At the end of the 1955-1956 season, he opted to bow out in order to more actively pursue his movie career. He may later have had second thoughts.

During the 1940s and 1950s, DeFore enjoyed featured supporting roles in at least twenty films, including the acclaimed *Thirty Seconds Over*

Tokyo, starring Spencer Tracy. But his last film appearance was in 1960 in *The Facts of Life*. Not long after, he returned to television, co-starring as George Baxter on the show *Hazel*, which ran from 1961 to 1965. Based on a popular cartoon character, it also starred Shirley Booth as Hazel, a housekeeper not reluctant to put in her two cents worth on the family's activities, and regularly helping to resolve their problems.

To fill in the void when Don Defore left the show, the Nelsons acquired two new neighbors, Joe and Clara Randolph. Joe was an apt replacement for Thorny, a similarly easy-going fellow. His wife, Clara, while likeable, could be a bit nosy and outspoken.

Joe Randolph was played by Lyle Talbot, whose acting career began on the stage. In 1931, he gravitated to the silver screen and appeared in a host of films until 1960. Although never one of Hollywood's top rated stars, he was a suave and very handsome leading man in some lesser films. In others, he played opposite such stars as Humphrey Bogart, Barbara Stanwyck, Mae West, Spencer Tracy and Carole Lombard.

His union activism caused him to fall out of the good graces of the major studios. In the 1940s and 1950s, he was relegated to supporting roles. He later proudly claimed that he never rejected any of them, giving his best even in low-budget science fiction films, Three Stooges comedies and as Commissioner Gordon in a 1949 Batman and Robin serial. His last film role was in 1960 in *Sunrise at Campobello*, a Franklin D. Roosevelt biography starring Ralph Bellamy.

Talbot had already made the switch to television in 1951. Until well into his eighties, he continued appearing in incidental or recurring roles on virtually dozens of shows. He also found the time and energy to return to the stage in the 1960s and 1970s, starring in road company presentations of various stage favorites.

A lovely actress named Mary Jane Croft played the ebullient Clara Randolph. Her face probably was unfamiliar to most viewers. Yet many may have thought that they knew her, thanks to having heard her voice on a number of popular radio programs. Her credits included roles on *Suspense, One Man's Family, The Mel Blanc Show, Broadway Is My Beat, Blondie, The Adventures of Sam Spade* and *Our Miss Brooks*.

She perhaps became best known to television viewers when she began appearing as Betty Ramsey on *I Love Lucy*. Later, in the revamped series called *The Lucy Show*, she played Mary Jane Lewis, a name that came naturally to her, since she was at the time married to actor/producer Elliott Lewis.

At the end of the 1953-1954 season, ABC decided to discontinue airing the radio version of the Nelson's adventures and put all their eggs in the television basket. Radio was increasingly losing ground to the video medium, so the Nelsons had no objection. The change actually made for a slightly less hectic schedule and allowed more time for them to be a real family when not portraying the somewhat idealized TV family.

As David and Ricky entered their teen years, more stories revolved around their activities with friends and at school. Aiming to keep the hominess of the show as natural as possible, Ozzie mostly steered away from hiring young aspiring actors and actresses. Instead, he had the boys recruit actual friends that they felt could carry small parts in a believable manner.

Their family names, if they came up in a script, would be fictitious, but Ozzie usually allowed them to retain their real first names. That made it less likely that they would miss a cue when someone else in the cast spoke to them and they had a line in response. The boys' friends usually came through nicely.

On one occasion, the script called for a chubby fellow who looked as though he liked to eat. They found him in the person of a young man who was using the stage name Skip Young and doing some summer stock performing. His real name was Plumstead, so the Nelsons named him Wally Plumstead. The audience took a liking to him and he was written into many subsequent scripts. He went on to become a successful comic actor as well as a friend of the entire Nelson family.

One of the milestone episodes of the Nelson family's television series came about as a result of another real life incident. Ricky was dating a girl who was crazy about Elvis Presley. Rick bragged to her that he could perform just as well as Elvis (who had not yet been elevated to king status). He then turned to his father to help him prove it.

On April 10, 1957, the show aired an episode called "Ricky the Drummer," in which Ricky played and sang a version of the popular Fats Waller hit "I'm Walkin.'" Viewers, especially the young ones, loved it.

Once again, Ozzie drew upon his lawyerly knowledge and sharp business sense. Shows were filmed about six weeks before they aired. As soon as this one was in the can, Ozzie had MCA shop it around to the leading record companies, promoting Ricky as a new talent. Several companies offered standard contracts with a minimum guarantee and yearly options. The Nelsons all were convinced that Ricky could do better. So Oz and Ricky negotiated with Verve for a single-record release of "I'm Walkin'" and waited to see what would happen.

The record was released a few weeks after the television show aired. It almost immediately hit the top of the charts and sold a million copies in the first week. That enabled MCA to do some renegotiating, which resulted in a five-year contract with Imperial Records. In addition to royalties and a $1,000-a-week guarantee, Ricky (through his managers, Ozzie and MCA) would have total control of what he recorded and in what style. Overnight the young Ricky Nelson was a rock 'n' roll star.

Ozzie quickly put this new wrinkle to use on the show. Scripts were shortened just enough so that each show could end with a totally unrelated scene in which Ricky and his band performed at what appeared to be a nightclub or theater, with adorning fans gathered near the stage to dance, applaud and cheer.

Ricky soon was making personal appearances, which had to be carefully scheduled so as to enable his continued participation in the weekly television filmings. Over the next half dozen years, he was continually at or near the top of various pop music charts with such hits as "Hello, Mary Lou," "Travelin' Man" and "Fools Rush In."

The popularity of both boys resulted in several movie roles for each of them. In 1957, David risked seeming out of character by taking a role in *Peyton Place*. Based on the novel by Grace Metalious, it dealt in a then bold manner with the sexual activities of adults and teens in a small town. In 1959, he appeared in three films: *Day of the Outlaw* (with Robert Ryan and Burl Ives), *The Remarkable Mr. Pennypacker* (with Clifton Webb in the title role) and *The Big Circus*. In the latter film, he got to perform on the trapeze, a skill in which both he and Ricky had been trained when they were in their teens.

Ricky's first and most memorable film was the 1959 Howard Hawks western classic *Rio Bravo,* in which he had almost equal star status with John Wayne, Dean Martin and Walter Brennan. As a quick-draw sharpshooter with a traveling circus, he joins forces with the sheriff and his deputies against the baddies who have taken over the town. His presence in the film no doubt resulted in ticket sales to a lot of teens, especially females, who might otherwise have skipped a John Wayne western.

In 1960, Ricky appeared in *The Wackiest Ship In the Army,* starring Jack Lemmon. *Love and Kisses,* admittedly a "B" picture, provided him with a starring role in 1965 as a middle-class youth hoping to escape his domineering parents by getting married. Adapted from a stage play, the film version was written, produced and directed by Ozzie Nelson.

The cast included Jerry Van Dyke (brother of Dick) and Jack Kelly (who rose to stardom as one of the Maverick brothers on the popular television series). Ricky was married by then, and his real life wife, Kristin, played his screen bride. One of the supporting roles was played by long-time radio actor Howard McNear. If his face was unfamiliar, audiences no doubt recognized the voice of Doc Adams on *Gunsmoke.* He later played barber Floyd Lawson on television's *Andy Griffin Show.*

On October 24, 1957, the Nelsons held a dual-purpose celebration at their home. It was David's twenty-first birthday, and a representative from Imperial Records also dropped in to present Ricky with his first gold record award for his recording of "Be-Bop Baby."

The Nelsons continued to create story plots drawn from simple little incidents in their daily lives. One episode had Ozzie and Harriet walking to the town ice cream parlor to satisfy her craving for some tutti-frutti ice cream. After the show aired, ice cream parlors large and small were besieged with requests for tutti-frutti. Dozens of ice cream companies wrote in asking to be alerted in advance if they ever repeated that episode.

In December, 1959, the Los Angeles Times announced its "Women of the Year" awards, and Harriet won the title in the entertainment category. A few months later, the Radio and Television

Women of Southern California announced the first of their "Genii" awards, and Harriet was their choice. At a testimonial dinner, the presentation was made by none other than Jack Benny.

Viewers who remembered the boys from their early radio days got to see David and Ricky grow up before their eyes. David was actually twenty-three and still attending college when the script had him graduated and taking a job as a law clerk while going to law school.

In real life, the boys moved out in 1960 and began sharing a small house not far away. They visited several times a week, however, to enjoy Mom's home cooking. Those were, they admitted, among the few square meals they partook.

On June 20, 1961, David married June Blair, an attractive actress who had been an incidental cast member. The marriage and the new Mrs. David Nelson were soon written into subsequent scripts.

In August of 1962, David and June welcomed their firstborn, a boy, whom they named Daniel Blair Nelson. Ozzie and Harriet were now grandparents!

Meanwhile, Ricky had begun dating a girl named Kris Harmon, whom he had known since she was a cute little thirteen-year-old. Kris was the daughter of sportscaster and former football star Tom Harmon and actress Elyse Knox, and the sister of actor Mark Harmon. The Harmons and the Nelsons were good friends. When Kris was prom queen at her high school in Bel Air, Ricky had been her escort. Their rekindled romance led to an announcement in December of 1962 that they planned to wed.

Because the Harmon family were devote Roman Catholics, they insisted that Ricky receive instruction in Catholicism and sign a pledge to have any children baptized and raised in the Catholic faith. Being part of a nominal Protestant family that rarely attended church, Ricky had no objection. He readily agreed.

As his personal fame grew, Ricky had strayed from the moral standards that his parents had sought to instill, and he was intimate with numerous young women. When he and Kris wed on April 20, 1963, she was already pregnant. Thus, when she gave birth, the family announcements were subdued and there were no official press releases. The marriage became stormy over time and ended in 1982, but in the meantime it produced four children: daughter Tracy Kristine, twin sons Gunnar Eric and Matthew Gray, and a third son, Sam Hilliard.

Ricky's and Kris' marriage was, of course, happy at first, and she became a regular cast member of the show in 1963. Little Tracy, and David and June's Daniel, were seldom seen but often mentioned in the scripts. The presence or reference to grandchildren gave an additional hominess to the show's family atmosphere. At the end of the 1963-1964 season, the program was enjoying its highest Neilson rating ever, having made it into the top 30 programs. That enabled Ozzie to negotiate another long-term contract, this one for five years.

With advances in the technology, many special programs and regular series were being broadcast in color. The NBC peacock spreading its colored feathers was becoming a familiar network icon. Color television sets were slowly becoming more affordable, providing manufacturers and dealers with a great boost in sales as people upgraded from their black-and-white sets.

The Adventures of Ozzie and Harriet joined the trend and began airing in color for the 1965-1966 season. As always, Ozzie insisted on using a high quality film that would produce consistent and true colors when the show aired.

Despite the upgrade, however, the program's ratings began to falter. It may be that the show had outlived or outgrown its original family appeal. It's also likely that viewers' tastes were changing with the times.

The nuclear family was becoming less the norm, and networks were experimenting with new concepts in both serious and comedy offerings.

Whatever the cause, Ozzie received a call from the president of ABC at the end of the season and was told that the show would not be included in the program schedule for the coming Fall. It came as a surprise, as there had been no warning. Yet, after they had had time to absorb the impact, both he and Harriet agreed that it might be a good thing to finally be free from their rigorous routine. They could look for other less demanding work or just kick back for awhile to relax and enjoy.

For the next few years, they took the latter option. They did some traveling and were able to spend more time with their growing family. They entertained and visited with friends. Ozzie was able to get out on the course more often with some of his golfing pals.

With a bit of the workaholic in his nature, however, Ozzie did not decline an occasional offer to make a cameo appearance on various television series. Over a period of years, he was seen on *The Bob Cummings Show*, *The Mothers-in-Law*, *Adam 12*, *Night Gallery*, *Love American Style* and others.

For her part, Harriet immersed herself in the role she loved best, being a housewife, mother and grandmother. In an interview years later with old time radio historian Chuck Schaden, she noted that Ozzie handled all of the scripting, production and business details right from the early radio days. "That wasn't my cup of tea," she said. "I can't sit still too long. Ozzie would ask my opinion. But I took care of the house and the boys (while Ozzie took care of business). We had," she reflected, "a wonderful working relationship, besides the other relationship."

While the older Nelsons were enjoying their new freedom, the boys were getting on with their careers. Upon turning 21 in 1961, Ricky had his name officially changed to Rick, hoping fans would begin thinking of him less as a cute kid and more as a serious musician. He was blessed with a voice that enabled him to perform equally well on ballads, up-tempo rock songs and rockabilly.

Between 1957 and 1962, thirty of Rick's singles were Top 40 hits, more than any other artist except Elvis Presley (53) or Pat Boone (38). His last Top 40 hit was "Garden Party" in 1972. His star status waned during the 1970s, but his recordings still sold and he still drew crowds at nightclubs and one-night stands. In the late 1970s, he became a popular favorite at theme parks such as Disneyland and Knott's Berry Farm.

The quieter and more studious David had entered USC with ambitions of following the lawyer path that his father had pursued, then abandoned. He got off to a rather bad start. He joined a fraternity, which entailed a lot of late night parties. Although he had a more than adequate income, he took a part-time job waiting tables at a sorority because it was a great way to meet girls. At the end of the Spring semester he paid the price for his extracurricular activities. He flunked out.

That proved to be the end of one potential career and the beginning of another. Upon returning home, with head bowed, he gravitated into a behind-the-scenes area of show biz.

During the last year of the television series, David had tried his hand at directing. Ozzie the workhorse was showing signs of tiring and slowing down. To reduce the pressure on his father, David offered to step in as director.

Ozzie appreciated the offer, but hesitated. He took cameraman Bobby Marino aside and asked if he thought David could handle it. Bobby said, "Absolutely! We're all here, so there's nothing David can do that's going to be wrong." Then he added, "But there's one condition."

"What's that?" Ozzie asked.

Bobby said, "You can't come on the sound stage!"

Ozzie got the point. Don't be looking over the kid's shoulder. He agreed.

David took over directing, and things went well. Ozzie kept his promise and stayed away, except to work on scripts offstage and view dailies with the crew.

On the third day of filming, Bobby said to David, "Come here. I want to show you something."

They walked to the stage door and Bobby cracked it open just a bit. David looked out and saw Ozzie pacing back and forth in the alleyway of Stage 5.

For his freshman effort, David was given high marks by the production staff and, most importantly, by his producer/director/scriptwriter father. When the series ended, he opened his own little television production company. While getting established and trying to overcome the perception of clients that he was still one of the Nelson "boys," he branched into doing promotional and industrial films. One pleasant project in that field took him to Germany to direct a series of films for Volkswagon.

The elder Nelsons did not completely metamorphose into retired show biz folk after their television show ended. In 1968, Ozzie agreed to co-star with David Niven and Lola Albright in a film version of the play *The Impossible Years*. With Niven playing a psychiatrist, Ozzie got to play a neighbor who is a hypochondriac.

The Nelsons had seen the stage version of the play and greatly enjoyed it. That, and Ozzie's casting in the film version, led them to take on leading roles as the psychiatrist and his wife in a series of West Coast stage productions and at Chicago's Drury Lane Theatre.

When he was certain that ABC would not reconsider continuing their television show, Ozzie began editing the films for syndication. Several minutes had to be eliminated from each show to fit the syndicated time frame.

Because he felt that some of the music used in bridges between scenes was outdated, he patched in some substitute music. Then, because he believed the show always came across better in black and white, he had each color show that he worked on transferred to black and white film. Painstakingly sifting through a total of 435 episodes, Ozzie selected and edited 200.

In an interview years later, David observed that, for him, watching any of the edited episodes was like seeing a classic Rolls Royce on which someone had mounted new fenders.

In 1969, Harriet and Ozzie agreed to co-star in a stage production of the Richard Rodgers/Oscar Hammerstein musical *State Fair*. Originally a play adapted from a book, the musical version had first been created for the screen in 1945, and boasted such stars as Jeanne Crain, Dana Andrews, Vivian Blaine and Dick Haymes.

The world stage premiere, with the Nelsons as Ma and Pa Frack, was at the Muny Theatre in St. Louis. The music included four tunes that had not been in the film. With a capable supporting cast and the audience's fondness for its stars, the show was well received. It was directed by James Hammerstein (the son of Oscar) and supervised by Richard Rodgers.

During 1970 and 1971, when the extended contract with ABC had run out, the Nelsons fielded numerous ideas that were submitted to them for possible television series. Some were interesting, but none really captured their fancy. Moreover, they wondered if audiences could relate to them playing in a series as other than themselves.

There also were offers of various specials, but these always presupposed that all four Nelsons would participate. Rick and David were now grown and launched on their own careers. Their parents were reluctant to draw them back into the fold, as it were, for the sake of a one-time special that would be a sort of nostalgic family reunion. More than anything, perhaps, they were enjoying their pseudo retirement, in spite of Ozzie's natural restlessness.

That restlessness kept Ozzie coming up with ideas for new series. Many of these he quickly discarded as not doable or simply not funny enough to sustain. Others he played with and tried to work out kinks, but eventually put aside.

Then, in 1971, he had an inspiration. The boys having grown up, married and moved out, the premise would be that he and Harriett would rent out their room. The renters would be two college girls, one white, one black. The comic situations would mostly center on the girls, and the Nelsons would serve as pseudo parents, always offering help and advice. The show's title would be simply *Ozzie's Girls*.

Ozzie ran the idea past their friend Al Smith, a television exec at Filmways, who was enthusiastic. Al arranged for a meeting with NBC's West Coast program director. The result was an agreement for Ozzie to produce a pilot that would be jointly financed by NBC and Filmways.

A search ensured for two suitable women to play the young co-eds. It resulted in the selection of two talented and attractive actresses named Brenda Sykes and Susan Sennett. For good measure, Ozzie wrote in another next door neighbor. Unlike the laid-back and likeable Thorny and Joe Randolph, Mr. Darby was a kind of nosey fellow.

That role was filled by an old friend of the Nelsons named Parley Baer. In a long radio career, his voice was well known to listeners from numerous dramatic series, as well as a few comedies. Most memorable was his role as Chester, deputy to William Conrad's Marshall Matt Dillon on *Gunsmoke*. After making the move to television, he became best known as the rather cranky Mayor Stoner on *The Andy Griffith Show*.

Filming was completed in December, and the pilot was submitted to NBC to be considered for the next year's line-up. But in March, 1972, when NBC announced its Fall schedule, *Ozzie's Girls* was not included.

The Nelsons had mixed emotions. Disappointment, yes. But also relief to a degree, as they slowly came to appreciate the freedom from pressures involved with producing a weekly program.

In April, the Nelsons' theater agent called and asked if they would be interested in a five-week dinner theater engagement in Tampa, Florida in June. Ozzie hesitated, thinking Harriet would prefer to return to her homemaking role. She surprised him with her enthusiasm over the idea of again performing live on stage.

The play was *Marriage-Go-Round,* with Ozzie and Harriet playing a college professor and his wife whose Swedish house guest makes it clear that she would like the professor to help her have a baby. A plus for the Nelsons was the discovery that their old friend Lyle Talbot was included in the cast as a fellow professor.

The part of the house guest was played by Liv Lindeland, who could be described as a budding young actress, except that her statuesque figure had already earned her the title of "Playmate of the Year" in *Playboy* magazine. Given the Nelsons' conservative family image from radio and television, there was a heightened note of hilarity to scenes in which the sexy young house guest attempts to seduce the professor, Ozzie. Audiences gave a warm response at each performance and the entire engagement was sold out, including matinees.

In September, without any advance notice to the Nelsons, NBC chose to air the *Ozzie's Girls* pilot as a one-time special. It got good reviews, earned a more than respectable viewer rating, and generated a mountain of mail. In spite of that, NBC did not elect to follow up with a request for a series. So Ozzie once again leaped back into the fray, deciding to produce a series on speculation and put it out for syndication.

No longer the work horse he had been, Ozzie decided to give himself a break and cut back on the multitasking. He recruited a team of writers and limited his input to offering ideas and having final say on script editing. Producing and directing were high energy tasks, and he saw no reason to exert himself when there was capable help in the family. David was already running his little production company. He came on board to fill both positions. During 1973, a year's worth of episodes were filmed.

In March of that year, Harriet and Ozzie took time off for a nostalgic trip back to Cedar Grove, New Jersey, and the Meadowbrook. In their early days together, it had been a ballroom and they had performed there as "Ozzie Nelson and his orchestra with Harriet Hilliard." Now it was the Meadowbrook Dinner Theatre and they were engaged for a five-week performance in *Marriage-Go-Round*.

Because they would be gone on Ozzie's birthday, March 20, the boys and their families threw a surprise early party for him. In addition to balloons, paper hats, presents and a huge cake, there was tutti-frutti ice cream. As they prepared for bed that night, Ozzie mused, "You know, Harriet, *The Adventures of Ozzie and Harriet* hasn't been cancelled. It's just not on television any more."

When the *Ozzie's Girls* films were packaged and ready to market, Ozzie and David negotiated with Viacom and Filmways to have them distributed in the syndication circuit, where they were aired on many local television stations. The show received reasonably favorable reviews and fan response, but nevertheless did not generate high ratings. The syndication was not renewed after the first series ended in September, 1974.

The Nelsons took it in stride. Unwilling or just unable to slip into full retirement, Ozzie branched out and took on the role of producer and/or director for some popular television shows, including *Adam 12, Bridget Loves Bernie,* and *The D.A.*

Although her role as housewife, mother and grandmother, on screen and off, was still her favorite, Harriet occasionally accepted offers to appear on other shows. In 1972, she had starred in a drama on *Night Gallery,* hosted by Rod Serling. On various occasions she had made three incidental appearances on *Love, American Style.*

When faltering health began to trouble the perennially robust Ozzie, he reluctantly submitted to a medical check-up. He was diagnosed with liver cancer. With a touch of both humor and irony, he observed, "Isn't that odd for a guy who never drank or smoked?"

Treatments for various cancers had not yet seen the advances that we know today. Ozzie underwent liver surgery late in 1974, but malignant tumors recurred. He died at the Nelsons' San Fernando Valley home on June 3, 1975. Harriet, David and Rick were at his bedside. He was interred at Forest Lawn, Hollywood Hills Cemetery, following a service there at Church of the Hills.

After Ozzie's death, Harriet became somewhat reclusive. Her social life was mostly limited to activities with her family.

Possibly at the urging of her sons, though, she continued to accept various casting calls. In 1976, she had a small role in the television miniseries *Once an Eagle*. In the made-for-TV film *Smash-Up on Interstate 5,* she had a more prominent role.

The story centers on a 39-car pile-up on the California highway. In scenes before the crash, we see that all those involved are dealing with various troubles or crises. Afterward we see how their lives change. The star-studded cast included Robert Conrad, Vera Miles, Donna Mills, Terry Moore and Tommy Lee Jones. There even was a small part for David Nelson. However, the primary characters are Al and June Pearson, an elderly couple heading for a beach vacation to forget for awhile that June has a terminal illness. Those parts were played by Buddy Ebsen (the *Beverly Hillbillies* fellow) and Harriet.

In a bit of déjà vu casting, Harriet appeared in the 1979 made-for-TV movie *Death Car on the Freeway*. Other appearances during the 1970s included incidental roles on the *Fantasy Island* and *Love Boat* series and another television movie, *A Christmas for Boomer.*

During the 1970s, David devoted himself to developing his production company. Blessed with some of the business instincts of his father and a personality that felt no need to outdo the competition, he focused on building a reputation for being efficient and dependable.

The company grew and prospered without becoming so burdensome as to require all of his time and energies. In addition to other film projects, his television credits covered a wide range of comedies and dramas.

For Rick, the decade was one of multiple troubles, much of it his own doing. Like many performers of that era and since, he had taken to using drugs. In addition to regular marijuana use, he at times experimented with other stronger drugs. His sexual appetite led to many infidelities, often one-nighters. His wife, Kris, was not unaware, and she raved at him to spend more time at home with her and their children.

She, meanwhile, had taken to drinking heavily and eventually reached the point at which her dependency qualified her as an alcoholic. She also engaged in a lavish lifestyle and spent money not just freely but recklessly. Although Rick berated her, he also was prone to extravagant spending, at one time leasing a Lear jet.

Rick was still immensely popular, but although his recordings still sold well, they did not reach the top of the charts. His last Top 40 hit, was "Garden Party," ironically written in response to being booed by fans. At concerts, he was frustrated when wanting to try new material and other styles, such as rockabilly. His fans wanted only to hear all the old favorites that had taken him to his peak.

In 1977, Kris filed for divorce, asking for alimony, custody of their children and a portion of community property. They reconciled for awhile, but had recurring spats, and Kris kept her lawyer on retainer. Both Rick's and Kris' families tried to intervene and help the couple resolve their difficulties, but the handwriting was on the wall.

One of Rick's many paramours was a woman named Georgeann Crewe. In February, 1981, she gave birth to a son whom she named Eric. A blood test confirmed that Rick was the father. Whether or not that was the final straw, Kris reinstated her divorce suit and the marriage ended in December, 1982. There was much legal wrangling before and after. The split cost Rick well over a million dollars.

Ironically, one of Harriet's cameo appearances was in a 1982 episode of *Happy Days*. She also had a supporting role in the television film *The First Time*. In 1983, she played a college professor in *The Kid with the 200 I.Q.,* with the kid being played by the popular black child star Gary Coleman.

With her film work tapering off, Harriet had more time to devote to her family. She was a doting grandmother to the younger bunch, and despite Rick's troubles she remained close with both her sons. Then she was struck another blow in December, 1985.

After the family's Christmas gathering, Rick and his band left on a three-stop tour. They traveled in a rented DC-3 that had a history of mechanical problems, although no crucial ones. Their last stop was to be Dallas, Texas, but the plane crash-landed two miles short of the airport, striking some trees on the way down.

After a long investigation, the National Transportation Safety Board determined that the cause of the crash was a cabin fire resulting from a faulty cabin heater. During the inquiry, some witnesses said the plane was afire as it came down, although others said they saw no flames until after the crash. Traces of marijuana were found in the cabin, but the NTSB concluded that that had no bearing on the cause of the crash.

The pilot and copilot, although badly burned, were able to climb out the windows. All those in the plane's cabin perished. In addition to Rick, the passengers included his current girl friend, Helen Blair, guitarists Patrick Woodward and Bobby Neal, drummer Rick Intveld, keyboardist Andy Chapin, and Donald Russell, who acted as road manager and soundman.

Rick's funeral service was held a few days later at Church of the Hills, attended by 250 mourners. Over 700 of his fans gathered outside. A private burial service for family only was held a few days later, and Rick's body was interred at Forest Lawn, Hollywood Hills Cemetery, along side his father.

With Ozzie gone, the loss of her younger son was especially hard on Harriet. For David, it meant not just the loss of his brother, but a bitter court battle with Rick's ex-wife.

Rick had bequeathed his entire estate to his children and made no provision for Kris. Kris attempted to claim her ex-husband's life insurance payout, as well as control of his estate. David was administrator of Rick's estate and contested all of Kris' claims, which were eventually disallowed by the Los Angeles Superior Court.

Perhaps to assuage her grief, Harriet accepted a few more television roles when they were offered. In 1987, she appeared in *Time Out for Dad.* Dealing with a former football star's attempted adjustments to retirement, the film starred real-life football great Dick Butkus.

In 1987, David produced his film tribute *Rick Nelson: A Brother Remembers.* In what was both an uplifting and poignant task, Harriet worked with David for eight months, helping him sort through and select family photos, publicity stills and snippets from home movies. The finished film included concert footage and interviews with Rick's musical colleagues, friends and family. It aired in November on the Disney Channel, undoubtedly watched by millions of Rick's fans.

Harriet's last made-for-television role was in a 1989 episode of the *Father Dowling Mysteries.* This minor part was one she found especially appealing because one of the regular cast members was her granddaughter, Tracy Nelson. The loveable crime-solving priest was played by Tom Bosley, who had been Richie Cunningham's father on *Happy Days.*

In October, 1989, Harriet was an honorary guest at the annual Winners Circle Charity Ball, held at the Ritz-Carlton Hotel to benefit the South Coast Medical Center. She had been named the Los Angeles Times' "Woman of the Year."

Just a few week later, as she stepped off the porch of the Nelsons' South Laguna home, she slipped and fell down the front steps. She suffered a fracture to her upper thoracic spine and was hospitalized for several days at the Medical Center. She recovered from her injury, but was troubled thereafter with frequent back pain.

Unlike her husband, Harriet had been a heavy smoker for most of her life. She studiously avoided smoking in public or in any of her film or stage roles, believing it would diminish the Nelsons' image as a wholesome American family.

In her later years, she paid a painful price when she contracted emphysema. In September, 1994, she was hospitalized at the Medical Center, where she spent four weeks recovering from an attack of congestive heart failure. When she was basically stabilized, David was able to bring her home, but her condition remained frail.

She died on October 2, 1994. Ozzie's younger brother Donald was present at her bedside. A private memorial service was held at Church of the Hills, attended by about 200 friends of the family. Harriet was then buried beside Ozzie and Rick at the Hollywood Hills Cemetery.

Like his brother, David had some marital troubles. He and June avoided the angry confrontations and bitter court battles in which Rick and Kris had engaged, but their marriage ended in 1975. Their sons, Daniel and James, remained with their mother.

David later married Yvonne O'Connor Huston. She had two sons, John and Eric, and a daughter, Teri, by a previous marriage. David adopted all of them. This time the marriage was successful.

David made no effort to continue as a performer, except for a 1990 role that he may have accepted as a lark. *Cry Baby*, starring Johnny

Depp as a 1950s teen rebel, was a parody of teen musicals such as *Grease*. In that film, David and Patricia Hearst (yes, *that* Patti Hearst) played the parents of teenager Traci Lords.

Otherwise, David persevered as the head of his company, Casablanca Productions, producing mostly television commercials, industrial films and an occasional feature film. He made no effort to "grow" the company into a predominant entity. Rather, in his quiet, unassuming fashion, he built a company that met schedules, charged reasonable fees, and produced quality results. His steady but low-key management of his firm enabled him to avoid becoming engulfed in his work and able to spend off hours with his family.

No doubt he could have continued in that fashion and eventually eased into a comfortable retirement. Sadly, at the age of 74, he developed colon cancer. He died at his Century City home on January 11, 2011, with family members nearby.

Probably with a view to enabling his new family to be buried together, David chose not to be interred with Ozzie, Harriet and Rick. Instead, his body was cremated and buried in the outdoor Garden of Serenity in Westwood Memorial Park.

Noting that he was the last of the original four Nelson family members, some news reports referred to David's death as the end of an era. That term might more aptly apply to the sale of the Nelson family's Laguna Beach home in 1998. Although they had had more than one abode, the Nelson home had been an integral part of their adventures since their first sponsor slipped in a weekly plug by giving it the imaginary address of 1847 Rogers Road. Instead of moving into the single-story, three-bedroom house, the new owners had it demolished and built a large two-story Italian style country house.

In an interview not long before she died, Harriet lamented that critics often faulted the Nelsons' television adventures for presenting an idealized version of American family life in which the only problems were comic mishaps or misunderstandings easily resolved within a half hour.

David acknowledged that aspect in a 1971 *Esquire* interview when he noted that they had one family that was real and another that wasn't. "For your sanity," he explained, "you had to keep that clear. We kept up the front of this totally problemless, happy-go-lucky group. There might have been a tremendous battle in our home, but if someone from outside came in, it would be as if the director yelled, 'Roll 'em.' We'd fall right into our stage roles. It's a big load to carry, to be everybody's fantasy family"

Even so, Harriet pointed out that their show was being judged by standards of family life in the 1980s, and tremendous changes had taken place in the past couple of decades. Moreover, she noted that the show was not presented as a documentary on American family life, but rather as a family-based comedy; i.e., entertainment.

Indeed, the Nelsons' adventures may have set the standard for other comic or semi-comic family series such as *Father Knows Best* and *Leave It To Beaver*. David and Ricky, who once were dubbed "The Crown Princes of Radio" by *Radio Life* magazine, could well have been the models for the Beaver and his big brother, Wally.

Moreover, as Gerald Nachman notes in his book *Raised on Radio,* the families of most listeners dealt with disagreements that were more heated and difficulties more challenging than anything the Nelson family dramatized. For them, the Nelsons may have represented a weekly opportunity to briefly submerge themselves in the camaraderie of a surrogate family whose troubles were less stressful, more readily resolved, and even afforded a bit of fun.

The Adventures of Ozzie and Harriet aired on radio from October, 1944, until June, 1954, a total of 402 broadcasts. Recordings of a great many episodes found their way into the hands of fans and collectors and were thus preserved. Because they are in the public domain, they have become available on cassette tapes and CDs from various commercial suppliers. They also are frequently heard on programs that re-broadcast old time radio shows, such as *Those Were the Days,* heard over public radio station WDCB-FM in the Chicago metropolitan area.

Rights to original film elements of the television series are owned by the Rick Nelson Company, LLC. That company and David Nelson's trust hold copyright ownership for any new material derived from the films. In 2007, the company released a video of *The Best of the Adventures of Ozzie and Harriet.*

However, episodes of the series from before 1964 are in the public domain. As a result, collections of numerous episodes have been released by various companies on both VHS and DVD home videos. Moreover, public domain episodes of the series have been continuously shown as late-night reruns on some stations and as an on-going series on stations that air late-night reruns of many defunct series.

Between 1985 and 1994, episodes remastered from the original 35mm films were aired on The Disney Channel with new introductions by Harriet. She was delighted with the response. She told an interviewer, "I have little people come up to me when I'm in stores. It's such a thrill for me, because little five- and six-year-olds look up and say, 'I watch you on television.' Do you know how wonderful that is?"

All four of the Nelsons have been honored with stars on the Hollywood Walk of Fame. Rick Nelson was posthumously inducted into the Rock and Roll Hall of Fame in 1987.

Ozzie, Harriet, David and Rick appeared in a total of 435 television episodes. *The Adventures of Ozzie and Harriet* ran for a total of fourteen television seasons. It holds the record as the longest-running live-action sit-com on American television.

Five years before she died, Harriet was asked what was the best time of her long career. Without hesitation, she replied, "I loved radio best. It was the best of all worlds. It was big time (but) you could have a life of your own. You did it live. You had the thrill of working in front of an audience and having one crack at it. You didn't dare make a mistake, so you were absolutely on your best. It only happened once a week, so you could live like a human being the rest of the week. You could go to the movies (or) have people in for dinner. When we went to television, it was twenty-four hours a day, seven days a week. I still get such a kick out of those radio shows."

Films of Harriet Hilliard

1936 *Follow the Fleet* RKO Radio Pictures
1937 *New Faces of 1937* RKO Radio Pictures
1937 *The Life of the Party* RKO Radio Pictures
1938 *Cocoanut Grove* Paramount Pictures
1941 *Sweetheart of the Campus* Columbia Pictures
1941 *Confessions of Boston Blackie* Columbia Pictures
1942 *Canal Zone* Columbia Pictures
1942 *Juke Box Jenny* Universal Pictures
1943 *Hi, Buddy* Universal Pictures
1943 *The Falcon Strikes Back* RKO Radio Pictures
1943 *Gals, Incorporated* Universal Pictures
1943 *Honeymoon Lodge* Universal Pictures

1943 *Swingtime Johnny* Universal Pictures
1944 *Hi, Good Lookin'!* Universal Pictures
1944 *Take It Big* Paramount Pictures
1952 *Here Come the Nelsons* Universal Pictures (as Harriet Nelson)
1976 *Once an Eagle* TV Mini-Series (as Harriet Nelson)
1976 *Smash-Up on Interstate 5* TV Movie (as Harriet Nelson)
1979 *Death Car on the Freeway* TV Movie (as Harriet Nelson)
1979 *A Christmas for Boomer* TV Movie (as Harriet Nelson)
1982 *The First Time* TV Movie (as Harriet Nelson)
1983 *The Kid with the 200 I.Q.* TV Movie (as Harriet Nelson)
1984 *High School U.S.A.* TV Movie (as Harriet Nelson)
1987 *Time Out for Dad* TV Movie (as Harriet Nelson)
1989 *Father Dowling Mysteries* TV Series (as Harriet Nelson)

Short Films

1931 *Musical Justice* Paramount Pictures (uncredited)
1932 *Harem Scarem* Paramount Pictures
1932 *The Campus Mystery* Warner Bros.
1943 *Ozzie Nelson and His Orchestra* Warner Bros.

Films of Ozzie Nelson

1941 *Sweetheart of the Campus* Columbia Pictures
1942 *The Big Street* RKO Radio Pictures
1942 *Strictly in the Groove* Universal Pictures
1943 *Honeymoon Lodge* Universal Pictures
1944 *Take It Big* Paramount Pictures
1944 *Hi, Good Lookin'!* Universal Pictures
1946 *People Are Funny* Paramount Pictures
1952 *Here Come the Nelsons* Universal Pictures
1968 *The Impossible Years* Metro-Goldwyn-Mayer

Short Films

1941 *Doin' the Town* Universal Pictures
1940 *Ozzie Nelson and His Orchestra* Warner Bros.
1943 *Ozzie Nelson and His Orchestra* Warner Bros.
1944 *Wave-a-Stick Blues* RCM Productions

George and Gracie ham it up a little.
CREDIT: Nostalgia Digest collection

George Burns and Gracie Allen

George Burns was born on January 20, 1896. Gracie Allen made her first appearance on July 26, 1905. Given his almost ten-year head start, one might expect that George would have been a headliner by the time he teamed up with Gracie. Fate would have it otherwise.

George actually entered the world as Nathan Birnbaum, the ninth of twelve siblings. His parents, Louis and Dora Birnbaum, were Orthodox Jews and dirt poor. They were then living in a tenement on the Lower East Side of Manhattan. Except for newborn Nathan, all the children slept huddled on one oversize mattress.

After Nathan's birth, the family moved a few blocks to the relative luxury of a three-room cold-water flat, a third-floor walk-up with a backyard outhouse. It was here that sister Theresa and brothers Sammy and Willie would be born.

Louis Birnbaum sometimes served as a cantor at their local synagogue. He also worked as a helper at the kosher butcher shop downstairs. His income from both sources was meager, but Dora was adept at managing their money and keeping her family fed. Then, one evening in 1904, Louie dozed off in his chair and died.

At age 43, Dora was a widow, with twelve children and no source of income. Relatives helped as they could, but they, too, were poor. Thus the older children began to earn a few coins wherever they could.

By the time Nathan was six and entering first grade, he already was bringing home small sums from shining shoes and selling newspapers. On the street one day an organ grinder stopped to play. Little Nat improvised a Spanish dance and passersby applauded. Burns later remembered that as his first experience of having an audience. He liked it.

When he was eight years old, Nat and two other boys named Heshy and Mortzy worked for Mr. Rosenzweig, who ran a candy store. While mixing and stirring syrups in the basement, they harmonized on favorite songs. One day Lewis Farley, the mailman, stopped in and heard them. He was impressed. He told them what they needed was a fourth voice to form a quartet. He recommended a boy he knew named Moishe.

When the boys met Moishe, everyone was agreeable, and he became a member of the group. They dubbed themselves the Peewee Quartet. Mr. Rosenzweig let them rehearse in the cellar when they weren't working, and their four-part harmony came together nicely.

Mr. Farley became their manager. He took them to street corners around town and round trips on the ferry. As they sang, he passed a hat. Whatever was collected was later split among the boys, with a manager's cut for Farley. On one occasion Farley got them into an amateur night at a neighborhood theater, where they won the five-dollar group prize. It worked out to more than they'd take home from a typical day of singing on street corners.

When he was ten, Nat dropped out of school. He was not a particularly studious pupil, and his poor eyesight compounded his inability to keep up. It appeared he was not going to be promoted from fifth grade.

While looking for odd jobs, he left the quartet and joined up with a boy named Abie, who was a talented dancer. Abie taught him some basic steps. They became a team and spent much of their free time practicing to polish up an act.

Wanting a more stage-worthy name, Nat remembered the Burns Brothers Coal Yard, where he sometimes sneaked in to steal coal. Burns would make for a nice name, he decided, and would fit nicely on a marquee. He dropped Nat in favor of George. His brother Isadore, who hated that name, had taken to calling himself George. Nat figured if it was good enough for Isy, it was good enough for him.

Thus did Nathan Birnbaum become George Burns. Or so George told it in later years; but, as he often admitted, after telling some story in his monologues, "I lie a lot."

George and Abie became "the Burns Brothers." In the idiom of show biz, they were more often than not "at liberty." In their free time they practiced new dance routines and expanded their song repertoire. George often mingled with other out-of-work performers who lingered outside theaters where they had played or hoped to play. They cheered one another with stories of their successes and flops.

When George was sixteen, he took a full-time job with a manufacturer of women's clothing. It paid twelve dollars a week, half of which went to his mother. Most of the rest was spent on clothes. One wanted to look sharp if given the opportunity to audition; and if lucky enough to get hired, one couldn't always wear the same outfit on stage. With his hair already receding, he even treated himself to a straw hat.

He invested in some photos, a "must have" for posting in the theater, and began making the rounds of booking offices. At seventeen, he became a dancing instructor, which afforded some steady income. It also was a great place to meet girls, and George was becoming a bit of a ladies man.

Thanks to the hundreds of small-time vaudeville theaters, always in need of acts, George did frequently get hired, sometimes as a solo, sometimes with Abie. Depending on what the theater manager needed, he often was teamed up with other song and dance partners or took on a new name.

He once was "Willie Saks and His Little Derby Hat." At one point he became Willie Delight, because for two dollars he was able to buy 2,000 cards from a retiring vaudevillian that said "Willie Delight, Songs, Dances and Syncopated Chatter." He was first Brown and then Williams of "Brown and Williams." From that brief partnership came the song "The Red Rose Rag." It became one of George's favorites, from which he sang the first line or two during many guest appearances on television decades later.

These were always short-run performances and often earned him just enough to pay for his meals. Somewhere along the way here he discovered a way to eat for free by requesting a cup of hot water and then filling it with ketchup.

George was still living at home, even as most of his siblings married or simply moved out. He gave some of his modest earnings to his mother. She was in poor health, yet took in washing and sewing to make ends meet.

Well into his twenties, George continued teaming with various partners, always hoping for that better spot on the bill. When Abie decided to try a solo, George took on a girl partner named Hannah Siegel. She was Jewish, but she could pass as a Latin lass, which enabled them to utilize some Spanish dances that George had mastered.

A year-long partnership with Sid Gary was one of his longest. He stuck with Gary because he thought their matching brown suits, spats, ties and derbies made them look snazzy and might improve their status. They didn't.

The last of a long string of partners was Billy Lorraine. Billy was a good dancer and had a fine singing voice, which compensated for

Burns' rather gravelly sound. Billy sang beautifully, but when he spoke he stammered. So George did all the patter. That was fine with him, because he was always trying out new (or borrowed old) gags.

In the winter of 1923, he and Billy came to their final booking in Union City, New Jersey. By mutual consent they had decided to each seek new partners and create new acts. George could not have imagined it, but his lackluster career on stage was about to take a dramatic turn for the better.

Grace Ethel Cecile Rosalie Allen was the youngest of five children born to George and Margaret Allen. With her sisters Bessie, Pearl, and Hazel, and brother George Jr., they lived in a white stucco house in San Francisco.

Grace's father had performed as a clog dancer in saloons and honky-tonks in the pre-vaudeville days. He taught all of his offspring to dance. Grace made her debut at the age of three, performing a well-executed Irish jig on the stage at a church social.

She got her first taste of show biz in her early teens. During summer vacation from school, she landed a job singing between shows at several local movie houses.

For reasons unclear, George Sr. deserted his family two years later. Although she was a devout Catholic, Margaret obtained a divorce. She later married a policeman named Edward Pidgeon. That earned her the nickname "Pidgie," by which her children thereafter addressed her more frequently than "Mother."

Notwithstanding their feelings toward their departed father, all of the girls found that they, too, felt the draw of the stage. Bessie, the oldest, became a professional tap dancer and singer. When they were old enough, her sisters joined her to form a harmony quartet. They called themselves "The Four Colleens." When not singing Irish tunes, they lined up in Scottish kilts to do a nicely synchronized Highland fling.

The group did well until Pearl decided to drop out and open a dance school in San Francisco. Her sisters carried on by hooking up with a fellow named Larry Reilly and continuing the Irish routine as "Reilly & Co." Reilly was able to get them booked for a tour that would take them east all the way to New York. Before they'd gotten halfway there, however, Hazel and Bessie decided they'd rather stay in San Francisco, and they left the group to go teach dancing at Pearl's school.

Grace opted to continue the tour with Reilly. Then he had the nerve to rename the act simply "Larry Reilly." That did it for Grace. She could endure being "& Co.," but having no billing at all was too much. When they reached New Jersey and played their last theater, she parted company with Reilly.

That year, 1922, Grace spent six months searching unsuccessfully for someone with whom to partner. Her sisters sent her money, and she moved into a rooming house, where she became fast friends with her two roommates, Mary Kelly and Rena Arnold. To end, or at least reduce, her dependence on her sisters, she entered a stenography school, hoping to find work as a secretary.

Rena also had show biz ambitions and was modestly successful. She currently was part of a comedy act at a little theater in Union City. The team of Burns and Lorraine was playing there, and Rena had heard that they planned to split when their run ended. She urged Grace to come see them perform and try to get teamed up with one of them.

Grace took in a show and liked the act. With Rena's help, she arranged to meet both men separately. Her first meeting was with Lorraine. His stammering conversation took Grace by surprise and ended any thought of teaming up with him.

Then she met with Burns.

George had been thinking that his song and dance routines were becoming like a treadmill on the "also playing" bill. He told Grace that he was thinking of doing what was called a "talking mixed double" or "flirtation" act. That involved a man and woman engaged in a sort of gag-oriented courtship.

George, who always had an eye for pretty women, was sizing her up as they spoke. Grace was five feet tall, 102 pounds, dainty enough to add to her natural attractiveness. She had long, beautiful, blue-black hair and, if the light wasn't playing tricks on him, eyes that were two different colors.

He wasn't mistaken. The seemingly dainty Grace dealt with a number of misfortunes that plagued her most of her life.

To begin with, she was born with heterochromia, which caused her to have one blue eye and one green eye. As a youngster, she had two frightening accidents that impacted her personality the rest of her days.

She had limited vision in one eye as a result of a glass shard becoming stuck in it when she dropped and broke a glass lamp. On another occasion, she knocked over a pot of boiling tea and scalded her upper left arm. Because of the scar that it left there, she wore only dresses and tops that had full- or half-length sleeves. As an adult, she suffered from frequent severe migraine headaches.

George saw only an attractive young woman who might be a good partner for his act. He suggested that they meet for lunch the next day, which they did.

Around the corner from the Palace Theatre, just off Times Square, was a restaurant named Wiennig and Sberber's. There George skipped his ketchup in hot water routine and splurged on lunch for the two of them. He explained that what he had in mind for Grace was the "Dumb Dora" role played by many attractive young women. She would feed him the straight lines, and he would do the jokes. Grace considered herself an actress as well as a singer and dancer, and she felt certain she could play this part, provided she got equal billing.

They agreed to give it a try and George said he'd put together an act. It was a new and challenging chore. As a song and dance man, he had often inserted a bit of comic patter, but this was his first attempt at an actual comedy act. Most of his gags were taken from *College Humor*, *Captain Billy's Whiz Bang* and other such publications. Hot off the presses, but not necessarily new material.

When they got together to rehearse, George told Grace that from now on they would call her Gracie, because "George Burns and Gracie Allen" has a more syncopated sound to it. Gracie agreed. It was a minor change, but it became her permanent name except among family and friends. For her part, she always called him Nat or Natty off stage, as did all his friends.

George was nervous about a couple of things. Gracie had a high-pitched giggle, and she viewed herself as a dramatic actress. She was professional enough not to giggle during a performance, so that was a minor consideration. But he worried how a too-serious delivery of her straight lines might impact his punch lines. As he was to discover, Gracie's delivery was to became the essence of their routine, albeit not in a fashion he could have imagined.

After several weeks of compiling gags and rehearsing, George decided it was time for a try-out. He was able to get them booked for three days at the Hill Street Theatre, a small vaudeville house in Newark, where they would do four shows daily.

On their first day, Gracie wore a dark dress and high heels. The heels put her a little closer to eye level with George, who was only five feet, eight inches tall.

To empathize that he was the comic, George wore pants that were too short and a hat with a turned-up brim. Something funny happened during that first appearance, but not in the way that George had hoped or anticipated.

Something about being in front of a live audience caused Gracie to deliver her lines differently than she had in rehearsal. Her straight lines were spoken with such innocent sincerity that the audience found it hilarious. George's punch lines fell flat, because the audience did not hear them. They already were laughing at Gracie's delivery of her line. In his book *Gracie: A Love Story*, George wrote that "some magical transformation had taken place. I realized that the audience felt it too. They loved her. It was the most amazing thing, and it happened just like that."

If he was a bit crestfallen that his comedic debut was not going over, George was sharp enough to know that some script changes were in order. In between shows, he worked feverishly to switch gags around, giving most of the punch lines to Gracie. After a quick run-through, they were ready for their second turn on stage.

George offered most of the straight lines, to which Gracie would respond with her unique innocent nonsense.

Gracie: My sister just had a baby.

George: Was it a boy or a girl?

Gracie: I don't know yet, and I can't wait to find out if I'm an aunt or an uncle.

The audience loved it. And they loved Gracie. George knew immediately that they had something on which they could build. It was a marvelously uplifting feeling to know that he had the potential, with Gracie as a partner, to at last be a success in show biz.

Audience response throughout the remainder of their short run was proof that Gracie's serious silliness was the elixir that made their role reversals a hit. With their spirits and their hopes uplifted, they hired an agent. They soon had another booking for a full week at a theater in Boonton, New Jersey.

George began honing their routine to fit Gracie's personality. The audience did not respond if she was sarcastic. They did not see her as a wise guy. Rather, she was a sweet lovable gal who said things that were nonsensical to others but made perfect sense to her.

Feigning bewilderment at one such comment, George asked, "Did the maid ever drop you on your head when you were a baby?"

Gracie's reply: "Don't be silly, George. We couldn't afford a maid. My mother had to do it."

George was always a shrewd business manager. Even though they now had an agent, he personally cut a deal with the B. F. Keith Agency. For six months, he and Gracie would be a "disappointment act." They would be available on short notice to fill in for an act that, for whatever reason, dropped out unexpectedly. It meant always having bags packed and being ready to make a quick trip to whatever city where the theater was located.

The year 1924 was a turning point, starting with an appearance at the relatively large Hurtig and Seamon Theatre in Harlem. Despite one of the awful migraine headaches that Gracie frequently suffered, she gave a performance that quickly won over the audience.

As he came to better understand the appeal of their act, George continually refined and polished. He sought to give a sense of continuity to their routines. While expanding their stock of gags to cover more subjects, he retained some of the "flirtation" gags that usually went over well.

George: If I take you home after the show, will you let me kiss you?

Gracie: Alright, if you take me home, you can kiss me.

George:	Well, wait a minute. If I take you home, will your mother be there?
Gracie:	My mother will be there, but my father won't let you kiss my mother.

Doing comedy required some adjustments after years of singing and dancing. For George, one problem was what to do with his hands. When dancers, musicians, magicians or animal acts performed, their hands were always busy. As part of a comedy duo, albeit the straight man, his hands had nothing to do. To stuff them in his pockets or leave them dangling loose at his side would look awkward and detract from the act.

Some comics solved the problem by wearing a hat onstage, then taking it off and passing it from hand to hand periodically between gags. Others affected the use of a cane, which could also change hands periodically. If a gag bombed, it could even be used in a feigned loss of balance and stumbling to one side.

Jack Benny solved the problem with his patented use of one arm held across his middle so that the hand could be used to prop up the elbow of his other arm. That arm was held upright, with Jack's chin resting in his palm.

George opted for smoking cigars. He'd already become fond of cigars in his early teens and now smoked them frequently. "Back then," he once said, "for seven cents you could buy a cigar so big you'd have to wear a supporter."

These days he could afford to enjoy better brands that he'd had to bypass before. Instead, when on stage, he chose to continue the use of cheap cigars because they burned more slowly.

The cigars necessitated that he check for drafts on stage before a show to make sure that he and Gracie stood in positions that would not cause the smoke to drift into her face. Audiences didn't like that, and it affected their response to the gags.

For her part, because she thought of herself as an actress, Gracie got terribly uncomfortable if she had to look out at the audience. Instead, she stood facing George, answering his comments or questions with what he came to call her "illogical logic." Perceiving herself as an actress rather than a comedienne, Gracie delivered her lines in a light-hearted but serious fashion, which made her all the more appealing. Only at the end of the act did she turn with George and bow to the audience.

George's cigar proved to be more than just a prop. When Gracie gave out with a comic line, he turned to the audience with a shrug and took a puff. They looked back and laughed. It was a classic example of waiting for the laugh.

That year they began earning $300 a week, not small change in those times. When they played at a theater near his mother's home, George felt confident enough to invite her to a show. Afterward he introduced her to Gracie and took them out to dinner. Dora raved over Gracie's performance. Gracie was pleased, but she asked, "What about Natty? Wasn't he terrific?"

Dora shrugged and replied, "To tell you the truth, I sometimes think he acts like a relative got him the job." Jewish mothers are not easily impressed.

Nevertheless, she and Gracie hit it off well from the start and became good friends. For George, the relationship underwent a more gradual maturation.

Always with an eye for the ladies, George had found Gracie attractive from the first. At that point, however, he was thinking in terms of how she would appeal to audiences as his partner. Once they began working together, they spent much off-stage time together eating out, attending shows and fraternizing with friends in and out of the theater. He slowly began to realize that his affection for Gracie was something more than he'd ever felt for the many young women with whom he'd had carefree flings.

At last he was obliged to try expressing his feelings, hoping that Gracie might confess to having the same sort of feelings about him. When he did, the response was not encouraging. Gracie merely laughed and said, "I can't get romantic with you, George. I'm engaged."

It would have been more correct had she said she was "involved." While in steno school, she had made the rounds of theaters, hoping to find someone with whom to partner. She didn't; but in the process she met a handsome Irish dancer named Benny Ryan. He already was part of a successful team, Ryan and Lee, but he and Gracie hit it off nicely and began dating.

Before long, they were a steady pair whenever Ryan was not out of town. Their relationship progressed to the point of discussing marriage, but as yet Gracie did not have a ring, and no wedding was planned until Benny might be booked in town for some extended stay. Gracie nonetheless was certain that she would become Mrs. Benny Ryan sometime soon.

George knew this, because Gracie had shared it all with him in their off-stage times together. Nevertheless, he also knew that Gracie wrote to Ryan frequently while he was touring, and he seldom replied. This gave George hope that Ryan was not as serious about marriage as Gracie was. He was encouraged by the fact that she allowed him an occasional kiss on her cheek when they were out dancing. He also got to kiss her goodnight at the end of an evening together, although she showed no emotion. She seemed to permit it as a form of thank-you for an enjoyable evening.

George gradually came to acknowledge to himself that he was feeling for Gracie something that he had never felt for any woman before, and that feeling was love. The realization at last gave him the incentive and the courage to proclaim that he loved her and ask her to marry him. Gracie just laughed and told him, "Oh, Natty, don't be such a kidder."

Having learned to deal with discouragement professionally, George was not so easily put off. He repeated his proposal periodically as they toured and insisted that, in this matter, he was not kidding.

Still certain that she was in love with Ryan, Gracie became distressed and decided that her only course was to leave the act. She could not, however, bring herself to just tell George that she was quitting him. Smarter off stage than on, she found a tactful way out when they received an offer from the Keith-Orpheum chain.

The newly formed giant consisted of multiple Keith theaters in the East and Orpheum theaters in the Midwest. George and Gracie were offered a ten-week tour, which amounted to being on the doorstep of the big time. The booking would be worth $350 per week, the most they had ever been paid. To George's surprise and dismay, his usually agreeable partner told him she would not sign the contract unless they were paid $400 a week. Gracie felt certain that the chain would refuse, and she could then gracefully leave the act.

George suspected that might be what she had up her sleeve. He dreaded the prospect of the act breaking up and his losing Gracie, but he was obliged to make the pitch to the Orpheum management. To his surprise and great relief, they merely shrugged and agreed.

Thwarted, Gracie signed the contract. For George, a bonus of this good fortune was that they would be on the road for another ten weeks, making any Allen/Ryan nuptials unlikely. George also took some small comfort in the fact that Ryan had yet to offer Gracie a ring.

That year, 1925, they caught another break as replacements for an act that had dropped out at New York's Fifth Avenue Theatre. At the bottom of the bill, last after the star, was not exactly the big time, but they played sixteen weeks in some of Keith-Orpheum's better theaters.

With the holidays approaching, George decided to make a final stand. At the risk of losing the perfect partner, he screwed up his nerve and gave Gracie an ultimatum: "Agree to marry me within ten days or we split up." An argument followed that led to George storming out and Gracie in tears.

At a Christmas party hosted by Gracie's friend Mary Kelly, George mostly avoided Gracie by hamming it up playing Santa Claus. Gracie was miserable. In spite of herself, her feelings for George were growing stronger, and Benny Ryan had yet to produce a ring.

After the party, Ryan telephoned Gracie, and she had a revelation. She told him she didn't love him any more. As soon as she hung up, she called George. When he answered, without preamble, she told him, "You can buy the wedding ring."

Years later she told him, "You're the only man who ever made me cry. I decided that if you could make me cry, I must really love you." For his part, George later claimed that they made love for the first time the next night. Given Gracie's Catholic upbringing, this may have been one of George's boastful lies.

Nevertheless, Gracie had no qualms about being married by a justice of the peace at an informal ceremony on January 7, 1926. Nor did she let that prevent her from continuing regular attendance at mass. For his part, George was always aware of his jewishness. He often drew upon it in his gags, but he had long since ceased being a practicing Jew.

Mary Kelly was the maid of honor, and George's baby brother, Willie, was the best man. As time progressed, Willie was to become a key player in the Burns and Allen success story.

Prior to their Orpheum tour, George had decided to stop relying solely on his own collection of mostly "borrowed" gags. He hired an eccentric but very talented New York writer named John Medbury to put together some material for them. One of the first routines Medbury sent them proved very popular. It was titled "Lamb Chops" because of a typical "Dumb Dora" gag at the opening.

George: Do you like to love?
Gracie: No.
George: Do you like to kiss?
Gracie: No.
George: Well then, what do you like?
Gracie: Lamb chops.

George polished some of the material to suit Gracie, and worked with Medbury to substitute new gags for some that did not go over. Back on the road, a revamped "Lamb Chops" was a huge success in Cleveland and in Detroit, where audience response kept them on the stage for a full thirty minutes. George threw in lines from other routines. Gracie, the competent actress who knew her material, never failed to give the right goofy response with her usual deadpan seriousness.

Married six weeks, they completed their tour at the Jefferson Theatre in New York. Keith-Orpheum acknowledged their success with a new five-year contract. With just two performances a day, it would guarantee them an annual salary in excess of $25,000. In 1926, that was a handsome salary, and it was safe to say that they had entered the big time.

Like many Orpheum tours, the Burns' tour began in Chicago. They had moved up to the number four spot on the bill. By now they had begun using "The Love Nest" as their theme song, a tune George remembered from a flopped 1920 musical comedy.

George had refined "Lamb Chops," saving all the best gags and cutting any that didn't get a hearty laugh. They entered with a little soft shoe. With the closing gag, the music came up again and they exited the same way.

Upon completing the circuit, their tour ended at that New York pinnacle, the Palace Theatre. The act went over just as well there. The only down side was that George's aging mother, Dora, was too ill to take in a show.

When the couple returned from their next tour and again played The Palace, George arranged for two of his brothers to bring their mother to the theater in a limousine. They carried their mother down to her front row seat. Afterward, Dora announced that now she was ready to go.

Life was good with a guaranteed five years of bookings. When the stock market crashed in 1929, many of their friends lost their life savings. George later was thankful that his ignorance of the market prevented him from investing.

Being financially secure, the Burns decided to escape the chaos and treat themselves to an extended vacation abroad. They convinced Keith-Orpheum to allow them a six-month sabbatical.

Before they sailed, they used a little of their free time to enter the world of cinema. In one of those serendipitous moments that now and then happen, they were attending a party and talking with Jack Benny. A Paramount producer joined them and asked if Jack would like to make an easy $1,800. Fred Allen had been lined up to do a 9-minute comedy short but had had to renege. The producer was desperate not to let the project die.

Invoking his persona of a man with a great fondness for money, Jack said that he would sadly have to decline because of a busy schedule. Observing the producer's crestfallen response, George interposed that he and Gracie would be happy to substitute. The producer was relieved and happy to accept the offer. He and George worked out a schedule to film that week.

There was no time to prepare a new act, but George told Gracie they could use the "Lamb Chops" routine, which would be new to any movie-goers who hadn't seen them on the stage. If anyone at Paramount knew they were not getting fresh material, no one objected. Filming went well. George and Gracie had their act down pat, and no retakes were required.

Gracie was not happy with the way she photographed, but when the film was released it was a hit. Paramount was sufficiently pleased to extend them an offer to do ten more. George's friend Abe Lastfogel, president of the William Morris Agency, negotiated the deal for them, and got the price bumped up from the initial offer of $1,800 to $3,500 per picture.

In addition to a pleasant six months in Europe, the Burns had their initial exposure to that new medium, radio. The BBC, having gotten wind of their visit, asked them to do five short spots at various stations as they toured England. They proved popular with the British, even though some of their material did not come across to listeners. As Gracie observed, "They took us too seriously."

Even so, the experience gave George pause for thought. Radio was coming into its own, and it had some distinct advantages. Comics could skip the song and dance routines, and no extensive wardrobe was needed. Best of all, as he later noted, "Radio was easy. If you could read your lines without rattling the paper, you were a star."

The Burns returned with a year left on their contract and were pleased to put in almost all of their time in New York, including seventeen weeks at various Broadway theaters. In the final weeks, they were thrilled to play with such established stars as Eddie Cantor, W. C. Fields, the Ritz Brothers and George Jessel.

Perhaps with a premonition of vaudeville's coming demise, George decided that they would not renew their contract with Keith-Orpheum, which all but insured that their theater days were over. They could subsist for awhile on the income from their short subject films, but they were now a hot property, and Paramount wanted them. George cut a deal for them to appear in some full-length films.

Meanwhile, he began pursuing the possibilities of working in radio. Eddie Cantor had already made the transition. He had contacted them, wanting Gracie, alone, to be a guest on his program. George agreed, as long as he could write her material. Gracie and Eddie did a routine together, with Eddie reading what would have been George's lines. She was a hit. George stood by silently as Gracie stole the show from its star.

Many early programs on radio featured mostly music by big name bands, but they often included little comic interludes. Crooner/bandleader Rudy Vallee brought the Burns in to fill this role. They were guests several times on Guy Lombardo's show, which led to a year-long commitment.

In 1931, Paramount called upon them for their first full-length film appearance. *The Big Broadcast* drew upon the growing popularity of radio. It was set in a radio station, and was essentially a series of short skits by various vaudeville people, with Bing Crosby acting as host. George and Gracie simply did one of their old routines.

During the filming, the director worried that Gracie's black hair would not photograph well on black and white film. Gracie accommodated him by becoming a blond.

Another film followed in 1932. *International House* had George and Gracie joining the popular W. C. Fields. George had the rare opportunity to do a sketch without Gracie, as a foil for Fields.

Meanwhile, their radio guest appearances led to a first program of their own.

With General Cigar Company as the sponsor, George enjoyed a fringe benefit in the form of a steady supply of quality cigars. To his amusement, however, he appeared as a sort of tag-along. Because the sponsor was enamored of Gracie, the show was called *The Adventures of Gracie*. Their wedded state was not mentioned on the show. Rather, they were paired as a comedy duo, using material from, or similar to, their old stage act, the "flirtation" routine.

In early 1932, the first broadcast began on CBS with their "Love Nest" theme. It ended with what became classic lines throughout their radio and television years.

George: Say good night, Gracie.

Gracie: Good night.

Unlike their stage experience, the show was not a smash. The network made some adjustments, moving it back a half hour and changing the name to *The George Burns and Gracie Allen Show*. Typical of George, he had a more creative idea.   Gracie had a real life brother named George. In their stage act, Burns would often ask Gracie, "How's your brother, George?" That would lead to ten or fifteen minutes worth of gags. Burns invented a story that brother George had disappeared and Gracie was looking for him.

It began with Gracie making a surprise visit on the Eddie Cantor program to interrupt him in the middle of a joke and say, "I'm Gracie Allen. I'm looking for my brother." A couple of gags followed, and she departed. Half an hour later, she interrupted Jack Benny to ask, "Have you seen my brother?"

With similar comic interruptions, Gracie visited every Sunday evening program on CBS. Then she spent the following week making innocently goofy appearances on musical and dramatic programs and some of the daytime soap operas. She even popped up in a movie newsreel, still searching.

Listeners who had never seen Burns and Allen on stage or screen came to know Gracie, and they liked her. She was a bit of a tonic in the misery of the Great Depression. CBS received over 250,000 letters from listeners, mostly amused, but some truly concerned for this poor lady whose brother was missing.

Gracie's real-life brother, George, didn't find it amusing, however. A quiet, unassuming accountant in California, he was eventually tracked down by enterprising reporters. When they hounded him to come forward, he instead took time off and went into hiding. He sent his sister a telegram asking, "Can't you make a living any other way?"

The Burns abandoned the hunt, but it took awhile to cool down. Even the New York police got into the act, bringing Fred Allen in for questioning. By the time the gag had run its course, *The George Burns and Gracie Allen Show* was one of the most popular on radio.

The downside to radio—and it was a significant one—was the vastness of its audience. In vaudeville, you could put together a good routine and tour the United States for a year. Playing hundreds of theaters, you repeated the same routine for audiences to whom it was new material. In radio, you told a joke once, and everyone listening heard it. You could not use it again next week.

There was a limit to how much material George could draw from *Captain Billy's Whiz Bang* and other gag magazines. He had his own creative talent, but he was obliged to begin utilizing paid writers who were tuned in to Gracie's character and could come up with gags that worked for her and George.

With their help and his oversight, he and Gracie continued as comedy favorites for the next eight years. The show was popular enough to attract several big name sponsors, including Hinds Cream, Swan Soap and Chesterfield (in an era before the Surgeon General's report ended on-air cigarette advertising).

Comedy shows reversed the practice of the big band shows, including one or two musical interludes between the skits. George and Gracie utilized Paul Whiteman and his orchestra, later replaced by Meredith Willson, who went on to fame as writer/composer of *The Music Man*. Tony Martin was one of several singers who provided vocals.

In 1934, eight years into their marriage, the Burns were still childless, and not for lack to love-making. Although neither of them ever visited a physician for testing, Gracie assumed that she simply was unable to become pregnant. George was not so sure.

He never confessed it to Gracie, but he had contracted a case of gonorrhea in his early womanizing years. The cure had had some unpleasant side effects, and he was convinced that he had become sterile. Prior to his infatuation with Gracie, his mishap didn't deter him from numerous escapades with various women, but he henceforth never engaged in unprotected sex.

From a practical point of view, George was in no rush to start a family. For show biz couples, becoming parents posed a problem. The wife would need to drop out of the act for an extended period. That meant the husband would need to switch to a single act or find a fill-in partner. George was well aware that Gracie was key to their success.

Either option was likely to mean a reduced income, just when there was about to be another mouth to fill.

Nevertheless, keeping his beloved Gracie happy outweighed such economic considerations. So when she suggested an adoption, he readily agreed. They applied to a Catholic agency in Illinois, the Evanston Cradle, because of its excellent reputation. One stipulation, of course, was that the adopted child must be raised in the Catholic faith. George readily concurred.

A few months later, they were told that a baby girl was available. Without having seen her, they agreed to accept the infant. They even had a name selected: Sandra Jean.

While making arrangements to go to Evanston, Gracie contacted her dear friend Mary Kelly and asked her to meet them and help bring the baby back to New York. The Burns had heard through friends that Mary had fallen on hard times and was trying to drown her troubles in alcohol. When she met them she was looking quite unkempt, overweight, her hair uncombed, clothes messy.

Gracie gave her a warm, non-judgmental greeting, then helped her to clean up and get to looking a bit like her old self. She then let Mary "help" her by playing cards on the long train ride back to New York. George had already hired a private nurse to accompany them and provide most of the child care for Sandra Jean. Gracie and Mary simply took turns holding the infant and cooing to her when she was awake, clean and fed.

Once back in New York, George hired Mary to be a reader while he and the writers worked up radio scripts. She would read Gracie's lines as they tried out various routines to see how they came across. It was, of course, a make-work job, meant to help Mary get sober and put herself back together. The Burns also invited her to move in with them.

They continued to commute to Los Angeles and take part in a number of Paramount films, none of them memorable. *We're Not Dressing* was a typical mediocre example, even though their co-stars included Bing Crosby, Carole Lombard and Ethel Merman. Nevertheless, Depression era audiences welcomed light-hearted distractions. The work was plentiful and profitable for the Burns.

The networks had begun switching many of their operations to Los Angeles. So when George and Gracie were filming *The Big Broadcast of 1936,* for which they were paid $75,000, they decided it was time to leave New York. They rented a large and beautiful house on Sunset Boulevard and simply let the lease run out on their apartment in New York.

They also decided that it was time for Sandy (as their lovely daughter came to be called) to have a sibling. They contacted the Evanston Cradle again, asking this time for a boy. The agency soon informed them that a handsome lad had been born July 9, 1935. They again made the trip to Chicago to bring home the little fellow, whom they named Ronald Jon.

Like his sister, Ron was brought up in the Catholic faith. Again it was no deal breaker for George. He was always aware of his Jewish background, and often drew upon it for material. In practice, though, he seldom visited the synagogue except to attend weddings and funerals. When asked if it ever bothered him that his children attended the Catholic church, he smiled and replied, "I'm the only Jew in this family."

Gracie was a loving and attentive mother, but she was not maternal, nor was she cut out to be a homemaker. There was always a nurse when the children were small. Later there were various hired help, such as the live-in couple who served as housekeeper/cook and general maintenance man.

Nevertheless, her children later remembered her as "a regular mother" and their home life as quite normal. The family had regular home-cooked meals (albeit by the housekeeper). They had regular bed times and assigned chores to earn a weekly allowance. Their parents took them visiting relatives and show biz friends.

The latter included Jack Benny and his wife Sadie, who on the Benny radio program became a regular as Mary Livingston. George had met Jack early in his vaudeville days, when he was struggling and Jack had already started his climb to stardom. They hit it off from the start and became lifelong best friends.

In 1937, the Burns starred with the inimitable dancer Fred Astaire in *A Damsel in Distress*. Fred played a dancer (what else?) on tour, with George as his press agent and Gracie as his secretary. It was a rare departure from their appearing as a couple, although Gracie still played Gracie.

George pulled off a unique coup by convincing Astaire to include a novelty dance that he and Gracie had learned from two vaudeville friends. Called "the whisk-broom dance," it involved some intricate dancing around one another while producing a rhythmic whooshing sound by brushing whisk-brooms on their shoulders and thighs.

They auditioned the dance for Fred and asked if he thought it could be worked into the film. Fred loved it. He improvised some changes to insert himself into the number, and they did it as a threesome. The twenty-minute dance was a highlight, if not the best scene, in the picture.

George was a take-charge type. With their growing success, he leased three adjoining rooms at the Hollywood Plaza Hotel and turned them into an office complex. He and his writers met there to put the radio shows together.

Many years later, in books that he wrote and as a television talk show guest, George always emphasized Gracie's role as the key to their success. Without her, he said, he'd have continued stumbling along as an "also appearing" act, if he could get hired.

In reality, it was his instinct for what Gracie would say or do in various situations that kept her in character. A scripting session might be a babble of writers tossing out ideas. When George heard a gag that sounded right for Gracie, he hushed everyone and dictated Gracie's line to his secretary. He knew exactly how his Gracie would say it.

Mary Kelly remained part of the staff, reading Gracie's lines when they did run-throughs before the final scripts were drafted. This was partly to give Gracie more time at home with their children and to socialize with her girl friends. More important, it was a way to provide Gracie's dear friend with a steady income and an opportunity to get her life back together. Unfortunately, Mary had begun drinking again. Because of the children, Gracie soon asked her to leave their house.

Having left school after the fourth grade, George struggled with reading any but the simplest text. His poor eyesight added to the problem. Those thick, heavy glasses were not a prop.

Unlike vaudeville, where you repeated the same well-rehearsed routine day after day, radio required reading a script that was new for each broadcast. So when not working with the writers, George began bringing in a tutor. It was a long tedious undertaking, broken at intervals by work schedules and George's frustration, but over time he became a little more proficient, even if still a bit slow with larger words.

To help run the new office, George hired his brother Willie and gave him the title of Producer. In reality, Willie was a do-it-all go-fer. He already arranged George and Gracie's travel and hotel stays. Now he ran errands, supervised the secretary and did assorted flunky tasks.

Willie also shared some of George's natural comic wit. Though not officially on the writing staff, he often sat in on the gatherings. While not as quick and sharp as his brother, he had a keen sense of humor and understood the Burns and Allen act well enough to contribute some good lines. He even occasionally suggested story lines that got the nod from George.

One negative aspect of Willie's role was that he also served as a target for George's sometimes short fuse. When the writing or rehearsals were not going well, George did not want to let off steam at the writers or actors. Instead, he found some reason to find fault with Willie and took him to task to get it out of his system.

Willie knew what was happening and generally took it stoically. On one occasion, though, he stood his ground and said, "I don't have to take this from you, Nat. I could go back to doing what I was doing before I came here."

Taken off guard, George raised his eyebrows and asked, "What was that?"

Willie replied, "I was sitting at home in Brooklyn and you were sending me fifty dollars a week." That broke George up and curtailed his temper.

About three times a week, George would leave the writers to themselves and go to lunch at the Hillcrest Country Club. There he joined a motley group of stage, screen and radio stars that included George Jessel, Edward G. Robinson, Al Jolson, Eddie Cantor, the three Ritz brothers, Groucho and Harpo Marx and George's buddy, Jack Benny.

It was a leisurely lunch, followed by a couple of hours during which they would have a few drinks, smoke cigars and tell jokes. The comics were best at this, of course, and they most enjoyed aiming wisecracks at fellow funnymen. It was mostly good natured, although occasionally a bit raunchy. George remembered that Groucho's humor tended at times to be a bit mean-spirited.

During the 1930s, with the Depression weighing heavily upon most of the population, George and Gracie entertained enough listeners to attract a series of sponsors, including White Owl Cigars (1933 to 1935) and Campbell's Soups (1935 to 1937). Grape Nuts picked up the program and moved them to NBC in 1937.

In 1940, radio was still providing the Burns with a comfortable lifestyle. For most of the past eight years, their show had been rated among the top five comedy programs. But they had now begun to experience a ratings decline. It was a sharp enough decline that the possibility of being cancelled was a reality. They needed a boost.

Gracie provided George with one of those light bulb ideas. Busy knitting a sweater for one of their children, she put her needles down with a sigh and said, "I'm tired of knitting. I think I'll run for president."

Of course! Why not?

George had recently replaced Johnny Medbury (who never left his apartment) with Sam Perrin as head writer. Perrin was a man of multiple talents and highly regarded. He later spent many years cranking out scripts for Jack Benny.

Perrin and George kicked off Gracie's campaign with a few political jokes on their own show. Then, as in the search for her missing brother, Gracie began popping up on other programs to announce her candidacy, making political statements and promises in her illogical logic fashion.

She had been a surprise to her parents, so she would run as the Surprise Party candidate. Her campaign slogan would be: "Down with Common Sense. Vote for Gracie!" Charles Henderson, a songwriter and close friend of the Burns, even composed the Surprise Party's campaign song, a modest ditty entitled "Vote for Gracie." One line proclaimed, "If the country's going Gracie, so can you!"

Noting that she had no running mate, Gracie explained that there was no vice-presidential candidate because she would tolerate no vice in her administration.

Listeners were delighted with her unexpected appearance on *The Texaco Star Theatre*, the *Doctor I.Q.* quiz program, the *Jack Benny* and *Fibber McGee and Molly* shows and others. They laughed, and sometimes nodded in agreement with her unconventional political positions.

Asked about the Neutrality Bill being debated in Congress, she said, "If we owe it, we should pay it."

Would she replicate President Roosevelt's fireside chats? "Yes, but not between April 15 and October 15. Washington is too hot in the summer."

Asked if she would recognize Russia, she hesitated a bit. "I don't know. I meet so many people...."

On *The Texaco Star Theatre,* Ken Murray asked Gracie which party she was affiliated with. As if affronted, she retorted, "I may take a drink now and then, but I never get affiliated." In a twist of that gag, someone asked her what party she was with. Gracie's reply: "Same old party George Burns."

Did she favor a living wage? "Of course. Wages aren't any good when you're dead."

One of her proposals would no doubt appeal to today's voters as much as it did then: Put the Congress on a commission basis. If the country prospers, they get a percentage. If not, too bad.

Since it was a leap year, Gracie chose a kangaroo as the Surprise Party mascot and adopted the slogan "It's in the bag." She also advocated sew-on campaign buttons so that supporters would not have a midstream change of heart.

With some help from the writing crew, Gracie even authored a book: *How to Become President*. The table of contents listed a dozen pointers for achieving that lofty office.

Chapter 1: *Government Jobs Pay Big Money*

Chapter 2: *Others Make Good, Why Not You?*

Chapter 3: *Why A Woman President? Well, Why?*

Chapter 4: *How To Attract Attention And Be Drafted*

Chapter 5: *Issues And How To Pick Them*

Chapter 6: *How Not To Offend Anybody*

Chapter 7: *Buying A Good Used Platform*

Chapter 8: *Secrets Of Unsuccessful Speechmaking*

Chapter 9: *How To Shake Hands And Make It Stick*

Chapter 10: *Five Good Games To Play At A Convention*

Chapter 11: *Where To Spend Election Night*

Chapter 12: *To The Victor Belongs The Spoiled*
(*Hints On Remodeling The White House*)

The campaign proved so popular that the city of Omaha, Nebraska, offered the use of a convention hall in May. W. Averell Harriman, the Union Pacific Railroad's chairman of the board, offered the use of his private car. Sam Perrin and George hopped on board with the idea of a whistle-stop tour en route. They prepared a series of short speeches for the Surprise Party candidate.

Given her fear of facing an audience, Gracie was not thrilled with that idea, but George was persuasive. To ease the tension for her, he arranged for her sister Hazel and Mary Kelly to accompany them. Between stops, the ladies relaxed by chatting and playing gin rummy.

The train made thirty-four stops and drew crowds as large as 3,000. Gracie was lovingly received and cheered by all of them. In Omaha's

Creighton University Stadium, on May 17, 1940, thousands of laughing and cheering "delegates" nominated Gracie Allen as the Surprise Party candidate for president. The event and her acceptance speech were broadcast nationwide on NBC.

George tries to show Gracie who's boss; but we all know better.
CREDIT: Nostalgia Digest collection

That was the peak of the campaign, and the Burns returned home exhausted. Despite her popularity, Gracie was not able to garner more votes than F.D.R. She was a gracious loser, noting philosophically, "This year's president is next year's postage stamp."

She did enjoy a small victory along the way. Midway in her campaign, write-in voters in Menominee, Michigan, had elected her mayor. She was, however, disqualified as a non-resident.

The only down side to the adventure was that Mary Kelly's drinking problem was still evident during the whistle stop tour. Gracie and George continued to give her what support and encouragement they could, but Gracie soon was mourning the loss of her dear friend.

Ironically, despite the enthusiasm over Gracie's run for the White House, the Burns and Allen program was still struggling in the ratings. George knew that they had to do something, and he thought he saw the problem.

For eight years, their on-air personalities had been a vaudeville couple doing the kind of Dumb Dora material they had done on the stage. It was becoming dated, and the comical pretense of the "flirtation" act no longer suited them. As George explained it, "Our jokes (were) too young for us."

George conferred with Sam Perrin and they made a major change in the show's format that henceforth set it apart from all other sit-coms. At the beginning of the first show of the 1940-41 season, George addressed the audience as himself. He informed them that he and Gracie were actually married in real life and had two young children. With a little additional background about their home life, he announced that henceforth they would be playing themselves.

Which they did. The situations were exaggerated and the audience understood, if they hadn't before, that Gracie wasn't *really* that dumb. But the formula worked, and it was to continue through both their radio and television years. In subsequent weeks the program's popularity surged.

As the program entered a new phase, George hired a talented your writer named Paul Henning. In a letter to his mother, Paul proudly told her that he would now be writing for George Burns. His mother wrote back saying, "Congratulations, that's wonderful, but who writes for Gracie? She's the one who says all the funny things."

Now that they were portraying a real life show biz couple, albeit in a situation comedy format, George and the writers began working Hollywood stars into sketches that usually involved one of Gracie's mischievous schemes or nonsensical mix-ups. Guests on the show included Cary Grant, Ronald Reagan, Shirley Temple, Jack Benny and others. One episode involved Gracie having a crush on Clark Gable.

Scripts were expanded to include a number of new characters who appeared in most episodes. Bea Benaderet (she of television's *Petticoat Junction*) and Hal March played the Burns' neighbors, Blanche and Harry Morton.

In radio adventure series, the hero having a "sidekick" helped move the stories along as they discussed where they were going, what they were seeing, what their plan was, etc. Harry was a sounding board for George when he suspected Gracie was up to something, and would offer advice on how to deal with the matter.

For Gracie, Blanche was a confidant for comic schemes she cooked up or some mess she wanted to keep secret from George. Blanche was a sympathetic ear, but when she tried to give Gracie advice it usually went unheeded.

When not doing commercials, the Burns' announcers appeared

as friends who would stop by to visit and have a comic exchange with Gracie. Harry Von Zell, who also spent many years with Eddie Cantor, attempted to maintain a dignified persona as he was confronted by Gracie's illogical logic.

The handsome Bill Goodwin later replaced Von Zell. When not hawking the sponsor's product, Bill would usually have a comic story to tell Gracie about his latest romance. On one program Gracie was awed by reports of how Bill's kisses made ladies swoon. To find out if it was true, she badgered him into agreeing to give her a sample kiss. At that point, George interrupted.

George: Wait a minute. Gracie, are you going to kiss Bill right before me?

Gracie: Well, all right, George. If you want, you can kiss him first.

Mel Blanc was the voice of Bugs Bunny and numerous other Looney Tunes characters, as well as Jack Benny's long-suffering violin teacher. He played the Burns' "happy postman," whose visits usually included some tale of misfortune in a mournful tone of voice. After a few comic exchanges as he handed Gracie her mail, he would depart saying, "Remember, Mrs. Burns, keep smiling."

Gale Gordon, who later became a foil for Lucille Ball, played the Burns' wealthy Texas oilman neighbor. He always addressed Gracie as "Ma'am." His visits often included an account of how he had just become a tad richer. He was helping his wife plant some petunias, or digging for worms to go fishing, "'n' up popped another durned oil well!"

The show's popularity continued into the 1940s, with several changes of time schedules and sponsors. As was often the practice in the 30s and 40s, the program's title would usually incorporate the sponsor's name or a particular product they were going to be advertising. Programs would begin with the announcer proclaiming that name and then adding, "...with George Burns and Gracie Allen."

Thus, when Maxwell House took over the show, it became Maxwell House Coffee Time. On those programs, after the initial introduction, the stars themselves would plug the product.

Gracie: Another cup of Maxwell House coffee, George?

George: Thank you, Gracie. You know, Maxwell House is always good to the last drop.

Gracie: And that drop's good, too

When Lever Brothers took over the show in 1941, they acknowledged their stars' popularity by changing the program's title to *The George Burns and Gracie Allen Show*.

Lever Brothers continued as their sponsor through 1945, with George and Gracie helping to promote sales of Swan Soap. During that period, the Sportsmen quartet joined the show, using the alias of The Swanset.

It was the Sportsmen who for many years on Jack Benny's show sang songs that would evolve into a Lucky Strike commercial. A couple of verses into a popular tune, they would inject lyrics that extolled the virtues of Lucky's smooth taste and managed to work in the slogan "L-S-M-F-T" ("Lucky Strike Means Fine Tobacco.") When Jack realized what was happening, he would say, "Fellas, wait a minute." The boys would continue as if they did not hear him. That prompted Jack to say, "Wait a minute!" a couple more times, his voice growing louder and more agitated each time.

Finally, as the Sportsmen neared the end of the tune, Jack would shout: "WAIT...A...MIN...NIT!" The orchestra would be cut off, the quartet would halt in mid-syllable, and the audience would erupt in hysterical laughter. They knew all along what was going to happen, and waited in gleeful anticipation. Lucky Strike got in a unique singing commercial and the audience didn't mind at all. In fact, they loved it.

On the home front, with their children now school age, life was comfortable, secure and pleasant. Except for one discordant incident.

A happy marriage and home life and his unswerving love for Gracie had not cured George of his wandering eye. On one occasion, he gave in to his hormonal instincts and strayed from the nest for a brief encounter with a willing and winsome young woman. Afterward, he phoned Jack Benny and expressed his guilt at having given in to his masculine urge.

Gracie overheard the conversation, but never said anything about it. As George explained it years later, Gracie knew. He knew that she knew. And she knew that he knew that she knew. In the end, making up cost him a mink coat. Sometime later, Gracie related the incident to a close friend and said, "I wish Natty would find another girlfriend. I could use a silver fox jacket."

In 1939, Gracie made one of several film appearances without George. She previously had been in a couple of Paramount's short films doing a solo. This time she starred in a full-length feature, albeit a "B" picture, *The Gracie Allen Murder Mystery*. It was adapted from the novel of the same name, one of a series by S. S. Van Dine, about his detective hero, Philo Vance. Gracie, playing herself, "assists" Vance in solving the crime in order to save a friend. The film version was more a comedy than a drama, so it did not disturb audiences when Gracie interrupted the action at about midpoint to sing a comic song

Gracie also appeared without George in 1941's *Mr. and Mrs. North,* a film version of a Broadway play. Created by the husband and wife writing team of Frances and Richard Lockridge, Pam and Jerry North were a crime-solving New York couple featured in twenty-six novels. Pam was the sharper of the two and usually solved the case after Jerry unwittingly unearthed a clue. The pair found their way onto radio in 1941, and the program was popular enough to continue until April, 1955.

Gracie appeared once again without *George* in 1944's *Two Girls and a Sailor*. If George felt slighted or jealous, he never let it show. He was ever mindful that, in their partnership, he was the straight man and Gracie was the star.

He recalled a reviewer who had caught their early vaudeville act and wrote a rave review of Gracie, praising her singing, dancing and comedy timing, with only passing mention of George. The reviewer concluded: "There is no telling how far Miss Allen could go if she worked alone."

As they approached the end of the 1940s with their program still doing well, George was invited to pay a visit to William S. Paley, the brilliant and tough chairman of CBS. He had an inkling beforehand of the reason.

Throughout the 1940s, Paley had been striving to build CBS into a major network that would no longer stand in the shadow of the mighty NBC. He had brought Bing Crosby, Red Skelton and others into the fold, and persuading Jack Benny to join them had been a major coup. Now he wanted Burns and Allen.

More specifically, Paley wanted to add George and Gracie to his television lineup. For better or worse, the medium that Newton Minow later called "a vast wasteland" was coming into its own.

In 1946, there were an estimated 44,000 families, about one percent of the U.S. population, with television sets in their homes. With only eighteen stations broadcasting, the choice of programs was limited. But postwar prosperity and mass production were making television sets more affordable. By 1952, 225 stations were broadcasting to over 24 million viewers. Even with small screens and flickering pictures, television's novelty appeal was having an impact on radio.

As he had for the other stars, Paley offered George an interesting incentive. He would buy the rights to the Burns' programs so that the stars could report what they were paid as capital gains rather than personal income. For George, who never forgot his struggling early years, it was a tempting offer.

He consulted his pal Jack Benny. Although not really the pinchpenny he portrayed, Benny was a smart businessman. He urged George to go for it. George was persuaded. Now all he had to do was persuade Gracie.

Gracie was not interested in moving to television. If it were up to her, they would simply retire. Either her migraines were getting worse, or getting older was making them harder to endure. She and George could certainly retire comfortably. George had avoided the stock market, but over the years he had made other good investments, thanks to businessmen friends who had pointed out good places to put his money. The Burns were already millionaires several times over.

For George, though, retirement had little appeal. Performing was what he did and what he wanted to do. He was quite persuasive, and Gracie never could say no to him. Reluctantly, she agreed.

The show would be aired from a New York theater, so the Burns temporarily relocated. CBS put them up in a suite at the Algonquin Hotel. They brought along Willie Burns, Paul Henning and their wives. George hired more writers.

They were still committed to another year on radio at CBS. George knew that doing two shows on two media would be a strain on Gracie.

He insisted that the television program be aired every other week. This would gave George and the writers more time to prepare scripts that were up to what their radio audience would expect from them. CBS agreed. George and Gracie began alternating with the anthology series *Starlight Theatre* and later with *Star of the Family*.

As on radio, the Burns would be playing themselves, albeit not "the real Gracie." She would continue to be the slightly out-of-kilter wife, possessed with what George described as an "illogical logic" that made her comic comments seem sensible...almost.

George: Gracie, those are beautiful flowers. Where did they come from?

Gracie: Don't you remember, George? You said that if I went to visit Clara Bagley in the hospital, I should be sure to take her flowers. So, when she wasn't looking, I did.

To help ease Gracie's discomfort going before the television cameras, George arranged to have a set built that replicated the living room in their California home. The first television episode of *The George Burns and Gracie Allen Show* aired on October 12, 1950.

George is credited with setting a sit-com precedent by using the live theater technique of "breaking the fourth wall." The program opened with the music fading and George walking off the set to stand beside a curtain at the front of the stage. There he set the scene with a brief monologue consisting of wry jokes about what was going to happen.

He spoke straight into the camera. After each gag, he took a puff on his cigar to wait for the laugh. When he was done, he nodded to the audience as if to say, "Well, you've been warned." Then he stepped back into the set and the action began. As the episode progressed, there would be one or two more intervals when everything paused for a bit as George returned out front to crack wise about whatever scheme Gracie had going. Then he stepped back and the story continued.

George was uncertain about the stunt at first. It was unique for a comedy show, and he wasn't sure the audience would buy it. But they did, and it became a hallmark of the show.

The show was a hit, and a second year was in the bag, but Gracie continued to yearn for retirement. George had more persuading to do. It helped that they were able to move the show back to California at the end of the first season.

Lucille Ball and husband Desi Arnaz had already set the stage for much of what was to come in television entertainment. All their *I Love Lucy* shows were on film. They created a production company, Desilu Productions. They pioneered the technique of filming from three different directions and selecting the best "take" for the final edited program. They had complete control over their show, owned the rights to rebroadcasts, and were among the first to take advantage of what came to be called syndication. In the process, they made a fortune.

From the outset, George saw the advantages of filming. In radio, actors had only to stand at a microphone and read from a script in a voice suitable for whatever emotion they were experiencing. On television, they had to perform as on the stage, with all the possibilities for a physical mishap or forgotten line. He decreed that their show would be filmed.

Once back in California, he contracted for the use of General Service Studios, where Desilu was already filming. He set about creating his own production company. He purchased equipment and hired operators. He was unable to think of a name for the company until he overheard brother Willie tell someone that he lived on McCadden

Avenue. That had a nice sound to it. In 1951, McCadden Productions went into business.

When the new season began, George set up a schedule with his staff for writing, rehearsing and filming. Ever mindful of not overworking the writers, he made sure that they had a weekend day off. Once a show was filmed, it was shown to a sample audience of about two hundred people. Chuckles and laughter were recorded and would be inserted onto the film track at the point they occurred.

George wasn't a fan of "canned" laughter being added to augment a gag that got little response, but he reluctantly went along with what quickly became a standard technique on filmed television shows. The theory was that viewers at home were more likely to laugh aloud if they heard the studio audience laughing.

Because she wasn't really the ditz that she portrayed, Gracie had difficulty memorizing her nonsensical lines. For her, cue cards were a blessing. George had a different problem. With his poor eyesight and limited reading skills, cue cards were of little help. Though it took an effort, he read through each script repeatedly until he knew all his lines and was confident to go on stage as in the vaudeville days.

The show followed the same story line as their radio show. Some characters were dropped and others introduced. Blanche and Harry Morton were still their next door neighbors, still played by Bea Benaderet and Hal March. Hal later left the show and was replaced, first by Fred Clark, then Larry Keating, and later John Brown, who played Irma's boy friend Al on the *My Friend Irma* radio show.

Blossom Seeley and Benny Fields were dear friends of the Burns from their vaudeville days. They lost most of their savings in the stock market crash, and then vaudeville died. Their type of song and dance act was no longer in great demand. From time to time, George would see an opportunity to work one or both of them into a script and provide them with a little income.

Another long-time friend, Rolfe Sedan, took over the role of Mr. Beasley, the "happy mailman," who always stopped to chat with Gracie.

What became a running gag on the program was a closet filled with hats left by various visitors who had departed hastily when confounded by Gracie's illogical logic.

When Paul Henning left to pursue other interests, George made Fred De Cordova director. De Cordova was a respected director of many films. He later became Johnny Carson's long-time director on *The Tonight Show*. Apart from that, he probably is most fondly remembered as the director of the film *Bedtime for Bonzo,* in which future president Ronald Reagan co-starred with a chimpanzee.

Although George was clearly in charge, the production company was sort of a family affair. Sandy worked there for awhile as a production assistant. She could have been worked into the cast, but show biz did not really hold a great appeal for her. She eventually left to continue her education at UCLA.

Ronnie joined the staff as an assistant film editor. On October 18, 1954, he appeared on the show in a brief supporting role. On October 10, 1955, he began appearing as himself. It was a bit disorienting for a time. At home, Gracie was just a regular mother, but on the show he had to react to her as the slightly off-center character that she portrayed.

On the real-life home front, Sandy was at the center of another distressing family incident during her seventeenth summer. She had graduated from high school and was anticipating going off to college.

She had been dating a fellow named Jim Wilhoite and it had become serious. One evening her parents were out for some event. As Sandy and Jim fantasized about a future wedding, they simultaneously came to the decision to elope.

Sandy called her dear friend, Joan Benny, who shortly arrived in her sporty Pontiac convertible. Sandy told her that she and Jim were going to elope, and she had to come along as a witness. Surprised but game, Joan said, "Great, let's go!" Jim rounded up a friend named Marvin and they took off for Las Vegas.

Finding an all-night chapel was easy. But a problem arose after the ceremony when they discussed finding a motel and realized that none of them had more than a few dollars with them. Credit cards were not yet in vogue.

As they drove aimlessly about town, they saw a marquee at the Flamingo Hotel flashing the name "Tony Martin." Tony was a close friend of the Burns from the days when he had sung on their program. Sandy was sure he would help them.

They got to Tony's room as he was getting ready for bed after the late show. He let them in, heard their story and, to Sandy's dismay, he was furious.

"You didn't tell your folks?" Tony declared incredulously. "How could you be so thoughtless?" He ordered up some late night snacks, and then demanded that they call home.

The Burns had returned home to find Sandy out past her curfew. They waited up for awhile, only mildly irritated, but by midnight the irritation turned to worry. George went to wake Ronnie and demand, "Where's your sister?" Unaware of what was going on, Ronnie could only say groggily, "I don't know." Then his head dropped back onto the pillow and he went back to sleep.

George and Gracie began calling the police, hospitals and any friends they thought Sandy might have gone to visit and stayed too late. When George called Jack Benny, he learned that Jack had been about to call them. Soon the Bennys came over to join the Burns.

They were still taking turns making calls when Sandy's long distance call came through. It was a distraught Gracie who answered. With her eyes cast down from Tony Martin's stern gaze, Sandy blurted out what she had done. When Gracie heard it, she had just three angry words: "Get home. NOW!"

Having received money from Tony Martin for gas and breakfast, the wayward foursome arrived at the Burns house about ten o'clock. As a sort of tag-along participant, Marvin got off easy by being sent on his way. Then George launched into a tirade at the remaining three offenders. He adored Sandy and normally would keep his temper in check when angry with her. This time, however, anger was coupled with the anxious concern that her absence had caused.

When George's outburst was over, Gracie lit into Sandy, while Sadie lit into Joan for being a part of this thoughtless escapade. Only Jack, who was always a mild mannered sort, stood back quietly. Though he looked down or nodded at much of what the two mothers said, he voiced no anger at any of the parties involved.

When at last Gracie and Sadie had exhausted their wrath and paused for breath, Sandy sheepish looked over at her "Uncle J." She recalls that he simply nodded and gave her a look that said, "Everything's okay."

Finally, all parties sat down to have lunch and discuss where did they go from here. A few weeks later, Jack and Sadie threw a big party for the newlyweds. Jim was accepted into the family, and within a couple of years George and Gracie were thrilled to be spoiling two adorable granddaughters, Laura and Melissa.

Though the Burns were already comfortably well off, it was McCadden Productions that eventually made them multi-millionaires. They were already enjoying the benefits of producing their own show when Paul Henning came to George with an idea for a show he wanted to write. George liked it and they cut a deal to film it at McCadden with George as executive producer. The amiable, handsome movie actor Robert Cummings starred as a womanizing photographer in *Love That Bob*. It became a popular series running from 1955 to 1958.

George recruited the amiable and talented Rod Amateau to produce the show. When Fred De Cordova departed the Burns and Allen show in 1954 to direct *December Bride*, Amateau replaced him as director.

Not long after Paul Henning's visit, a writer named Irving Brecher came to George with his idea for a show to be titled *The People's Choice*. He summarized the story line, and when he mentioned that it involved a talking dog, George raised his eyebrows and told him to pull up a chair so they could cut a deal. When they were done, McCadden owned half the show, and it was filmed at General Service Studios. It ran from 1955 to 1958 and starred Jackie Cooper. A versatile veteran of many films, he nevertheless was perhaps best remembered for his childhood appearances in the *Our Gang* series.

From a talking dog, George later moved on to a talking horse when he took over production of *Mr. Ed*. When the concept was presented to him and he agreed to take it on, George said to brother Willie, "Get Alan Young. He looks like the kind of guy a horse would talk to."

Alan Young was a popular stage and screen actor. He was on radio with *The Alan Young Show* during the 1940s, and had made the transition to television. He would now become famous by co-starring with a horse that talked, but only to him, and each week helped get him out of comic troubles that usually began when he listened to earlier advice from the nag.

George maintained a hands-off approach on all the shows, but wandered in and out during rehearsals and productions to offer assistance or advice if problems arose. When something in the script didn't seem to click, he often would suggest doing this or changing that, but in a manner that said "only if you think it will work." Most times it did, and changes were made.

The production company was flourishing and George was involved and overseeing everything that went on there. One might think that doing his and Gracie's show plus the activity at McCadden would wear him down. Instead, it seemed to energize him. Show biz was his life.

That was not the case for Gracie, who continued to yearn for retirement. Their current sponsor had the Burns appearing in newspaper and magazine ads as "Carnation's Contented Couple." But each year it took more persuading for George to get Gracie to agree to one more season.

Her migraine headaches continued, and she became progressively more tired. Then, early in 1958, she suffered a series of prolonged and severe chest pains. The doctors' diagnosis was that she had had a mild heart attack. She was prescribed nitroglycerine pills and told to get as much bed rest as possible. For the remainder of her life, Gracie would occasionally suffer what she called "heart episodes." Slipping a nitro pill under her tongue usually brought relief.

With a sense of guilt, George quickly changed gears. He became more solicitous and hired a live-in nurse. Then he had the McCadden office issue a formal announcement that this would be the last season of their television show. Gracie's retirement was such big news that she made the September 22 cover of *Life* magazine.

Trouper that she was, Gracie paced herself and made it through the end of that program season. She and George filmed their final episode together on June 4, 1958. It was one shy of number 300.

Before the last episode aired, George began working with the writers and director Rod Amateau to produce a replacement, aptly titled *The George Burns Show*. In it, he and Ronnie still lived in the house modeled to look like their real home. A spare room was rented out to two college girls.

Without Gracie, however, it was just another situation comedy. It struggled through one season, and then NBC dropped it.

What next? Why not simply retire? The Burns financial status would be more than adequate to sustain him to age 100 if he should live that long. Friends made solicitous suggestions that he do so. To which George responded: "And do what?" He was a performer, and being "on" was the fuel that kept him energized.

After so many years of being a straight man for Gracie, he determined, with some trepidation, that he would return to live performances as a solo. Brother Willie and his chief writer, Harvey Helm, worked with him on a stand-up act. By the summer of 1959, he had himself booked at Harrah's in Lake Tahoe, Nevada, and the Sahara Hotel in Las Vegas.

Harrah's was a sort of trial run to see how the act went over. George interspersed gags with some singing and stories (really jokes) that involved Gracie and himself. Despite her frail condition, Gracie was there for the opening, along with Sandy and Ronnie, Sadie and Jack. Later, when they were alone, she diplomatically critiqued the act, suggesting a few changes. In particular, she noted that George seemed nervous. She advised him, first of all, to relax. Then she encouraged him to just be himself and present his material in the same one-on-one fashion in which he often kept their show biz friends entertained with one anecdote and gag after another.

George knew she was right. Gracie knew him as well as he knew

Gracie. Working alone and trying to be the funnyman after so many years of depending on his partner for the laughs made him nervous, and it showed. He made a conscious effort to be more relaxed, and hoped that in the process he would be funnier.

The Sahara was more a casino than a hotel, but they had a show room that presented popular performers and drew good crowds. A star has to have opening acts. George used his connections to have a popular trio, the De Castro Sisters, on the bill, along with a dance team. He also had a young singer named Bobby Darin, who went on to stardom before his untimely death. The show went well, even if George didn't get rave reviews.

In the Fall of 1959, he produced a television special for NBC called *George Burns in the Big Time*. It was a nostalgic look back to the days of vaudeville and a salute to the entertainers thereof. His guests included George Jessel, Eddie Cantor and, of course, Jack Benny. It was a fun get-together of old friends, with singing, much reminiscing about the good and tough times, poking fun at one another, and old routines reprised.

During the next few years, George was gratified to enjoy numerous engagements. Most were within an easy drive from home, and Gracie would be in the audience on the first night, along with their son and daughter and various friends.

Even though his appearances went well, George had determined that he simply wasn't cut out for a solo act. He began recruiting a series of female partners that included Connie Stevens, Madeline Kahn, Jane Russell, Connie Haines, Dorothy Provine, Bernadette Peters and Ann-Margret. Borrowing liberally from the old Burns and Allen vaudeville days, he put together routines in which the ladies got most of the laughs.

The act would begin with George walking out to the tune of "Love Nest," the radio and television theme. He would tell gags between a couple of songs and some soft shoe. Then his partner would be introduced. Those who were singers would do a couple of songs. Then the audience would be treated to some of the best of the old George and Gracie routines.

His partners all enjoyed the comedy and got into the spirit of the thing, but they weren't Gracie. No one could replace Gracie. Carol Channing came the closest. Already a Broadway star, she relished the opportunity to play the dumb blond role and show her comedic side. She and George were invited to bring the act to the 1962 World's Fair in Seattle, Washington, for a 14-week run.

In between engagements, George kept up a busy-work routine, spending mornings at the production company. He took on another series, *No Time for Sergeants*. It starred Andy Griffith, who later moved on to long-running popularity as the sheriff of Mayberry in his own series. Around noon, he went to the club for lunch and an afternoon with the regulars and occasional guests.

From the club, he went home for a martini and dinner with Gracie. They now spent most evenings quietly watching television. Even in her frail state, Gracie was intent on enjoying their time alone together. Then on a Thursday evening in August, 1964, she suffered another severe attack. George called for an ambulance, held her hand, and spoke reassuringly to her as they rushed to the hospital. The doctors did what they could, but around dawn on August 27, Gracie died. She was fifty-eight years old.

After breaking the news to Sandy and Ronnie, George called Jack Benny. Jack, Sadie and Joan came immediately to the house at 720 North Maple and, as Joan remembered, "We just camped there." Jack and Sadie took turns making calls and the news spread quickly. What followed was a sort of unorthodox version of the Jewish shiva, or mourning period, that was more like an Irish wake.

George was secluded in an upstairs bedroom, accompanied most of the time by Sandy, Ronnie and George's sister Goldie. All of Gracie's sisters were deceased except for Bessie, who was in a nursing home.

Downstairs there was a continuous flow of friends from every stage of George and Gracie's past and present, most of them with some connection to the world of show biz. Indoors, on the front lawn, out back around the pool, they mingled and shared loving memories of Gracie as food and drinks were continuously delivered. The performers took turns putting on their acts to entertain one another. Thus the mourning was softened by the remembrance of happier times.

On Sunday evening, George emerged, his eyes red from crying. Grateful for the presence of so many friends, he joined the celebration of Gracie's life by telling some stories about her and recalling some of their favorite times together.

On Monday morning, Gracie's body was laid to rest in a vault at Forest Lawn Memorial Park. Outside the Church of the Recessional, speakers were placed on the grounds so that the huge overflow crowd could hear the service. Then, comforted by Sandy and Ronnie, George returned to the home that he and Gracie had shared for so many years.

The next day, he resumed his usual routine, spending the morning at the office and the afternoon at the club. He needed to maintain a routine. The production company had fewer programs on its agenda and operated smoothly with or without him. It was, more than ever, busy-work to occupy his time. The club still afforded good lunches and good company, but many of the older members had died off. George got along well with the new, younger group of comics, which included Danny Thomas and Sammy Davis Jr. Still. it wasn't the same as the old Round Table circle.

Though he may not have realized it, George had entered what became a long period of depression. His main outlet was a practice that he began and continued almost to the end of his days.

Once a month he visited the mausoleum. He sat on a bench near Gracie's vault and lit a cigar. For the time that it took to smoke the cigar, he talked to Gracie. He told her about things that were going on in the family and among their friends. He confided to her, as he would not to anyone else, how lost he was without her and any pains or problems he was currently experiencing. When the cigar was at its end, he said goodbye to Gracie and told her he'd be back next month.

Years later, he told interviewers about this and said, "I don't know if Gracie hears me. But I always feel better after we've talked."

A bright spot occurred in 1966 when long-time bachelor Ronnie was married. A reception at the Bel-Air Hotel was replete with entertainment, much good food and a well-stocked and well-staffed open bar.

But the celebrating was short-lived. George's brother Willie overindulged and became quite intoxicated. He somehow managed to drive himself home without having an accident or being pulled over. Once there, however, he evidently felt a need for sleeping pills and overdosed. He was found dead the next day.

After seeing to a proper funeral for his baby brother, George resumed seeking engagements where he could arrange them. In May, 1967, he opened at the Riviera Hotel in Las Vegas. With Gracie gone, he felt he could no longer use "Love Nest" as a theme. He chose the familiar old tune "Ain't Misbehavin'" for his intro tune. He could quip that at his age he was no longer capable of misbehaving'.

That booking was most memorable for his meeting with an attractive young blond member of a dance team that was also on the bill. Between shows, he discovered her practicing tap dance steps backstage. Pleased to see a youngster interested in the old soft shoe, he made her acquaintance and asked her out to dinner. It resulted in a series of dinners almost every night for three weeks.

Their age difference—she was nineteen and George was seventy-one—seemed no deterrent to their mutual attraction. They continued dating off and on when their paths crossed.

Lisa became the first of several younger women with whom George had brief or extended affairs. None of them seemed to be looking for a sugar daddy. Neither did any seem to be thinking of marriage, which was the last thing on George's mind. His appetite for romance did not override the fact that Gracie would always be his true love.

The fact that he still could appeal to the ladies, including some much younger than him, gave a boost to his morale during a long period when he frequently struggled with depression. It helped, also, that he was in good physical shape for a man his age, maintained a reasonably healthy diet (largely thanks to his at-home cook) and was physically active.

He had given up his frequent golf outings when his legs began to complain halfway through eighteen holes. But he had long used the backyard pool to do laps every morning. Afterward, he would walk around the perimeter for fifteen minutes. Now he had begun a regimen of sit-ups, deep knee bends and other exercises that had become popular after being implemented by the Canadian Air Force.

Bookings now were scattered and hard to come by. There was a lot of bright younger talent out there. So George was less reluctant than he might otherwise have been when Buddha Records invited him to record an album.

George thought the idea was to have him do a comedic singing routine. He arrived at the studio with his proposed script, and was met by Larry Fallon, who would lead the orchestra. To his surprise, Larry told him no, this was not going to be a comedy album with a little piano music. Buddha wanted him to sing.

Apart from his boyhood quartet days and some lighthearted duets with various partners in vaudeville, George did not take his singing seriously. Nevertheless, with a bit of coaxing from Fallon, he succumbed. The album was titled "Ain't Misbehaving." It included a mix of oldies ("You Made Me Love You" and "The Red Rose Rag") and contemporary tunes that George had never before sung ("Mr. Bojangles" and "Feeling Groovy").

When it was released, Buddha gave it the same kind of promotion they would for one of their top-rated pop stars. They even booked George into Avery Fisher Hall in Lincoln Center, where he was accompanied by a full-size orchestra, with Larry Fallon conducting. Jack Benny introduced George by saying, "Tonight, for the first time, a man is going to play this hall who can't spell it."

The album was not a smashing success, but George was reinvigorated by his efforts to promote it. He appeared as a guest on various television programs, including two visits to *The Dean Martin Show*. He even went to England and visited on Tom Jones' program.

Johnny Carson invited him to appear on *The Tonight Show*. During the taping in July, 1974, George had some difficulty getting his words out and seemed to be losing his train of thought during the conversation. He shrugged it off, and a bit of editing erased it from the later broadcast. But on August 8, at a concert with Ronnie, he began to suffer chest pains. The next day he was admitted to the hospital and underwent triple bypass surgery. Ronnie recalled, "At that time, he was the oldest person ever to have that operation."

George recovered nicely from the surgery, but 1974 proved to be a very bad year in other respects. His sister Goldie died. She was the last of his siblings, the only one who lived nearby, and had been very close with Gracie. At her funeral, George could not bring himself to toss the traditional shovelful of dirt into her grave.

Meanwhile, Jack Benny was in declining health, though he was unaware of the severity of his problem. He had experienced dizzy spells and been diagnosed as having suffered a mild stroke. During tests, it had also been determined that he had pancreatic cancer. Sadie and Joan were informed, but Jack's personal physician, wanting to spare him, told him he had a case of "pancreatitis."

Jack left the hospital feeling fine, but the doctors' advice was that he needed time to recover and should slow down. That presented a problem. He recently had done a screen test and been chosen for a role opposite Walter Matthau in a film version of Neil Simon's Broadway play *The Sunshine Boys*. Meanwhile, he had a month-long booking at the Fontainebleau Hotel in Miami Beach. The demands of the latter would not qualify as slowing down.

Jack instructed his long-time agent, Irving Fein, to see if George could substitute for him at the Fontainebleau. George's recent bypass surgery and the fact that he was seventy-eight years old did not deter him from accepting. He also felt that by filling in he might be aiding in his friend's recovery.

Three days before Christmas, Joan Benny received a call from her mother to come quickly. Jack had fallen into a coma.

Word spread quickly, and during the next few days, a stream of friends from the entertainment world flocked to the Benny home. After offering comfort and support to Sadie and Joan, they milled about inside and outside the house, sharing memories of the good times in general and stories about Jack in particular. Sadie and Joan left Jack's side periodically to welcome newcomers and arrange for a steady flow of food and drink.

George was one of the first to arrive. He, too, shared some Jack stores, albeit with less hilarity. When allowed to visit briefly at Jack's bedside, he spoke to his dear friend of the good times they had shared, hoping that he was being heard, but knowing it probably was not so. Other than returning home to sleep, he spent most of the next few days at the Benny home.

On December 26, just a short while after George had paid him another brief visit, Jack died. He was eighty years old.

Jack's funeral was at Hillside Memorial Cemetery in Culver City. On December 27, over 2,000 people assembled, most of them outside, where speakers were set up as at Gracie's funeral. Inside, Sadie and Joan sat in the front, surrounded by members of the Round Table. Behind them were dozens of top show biz stars, including James Stewart, Henry Fonda, Dinah Shore, Johnny Carson and Danny Kaye. Governor Ronald Reagan and his wife were near the front.

With great trepidation, George had agreed to be the first eulogist. It had been many years since he had worn a yarmulke, but today he donned one and a talles (prayer shawl) around his shoulders. His throat went dry as he stepped to the lectern and he made a valiant effort to mouth the words he had rehearsed. He began, "What can I tell you about Jack? I've known him fifty-five years. I can't imagine my life without him."

He got no further. First came tears, then uncontrollable sobbing. He fled from the podium, and returned to his seat. For all that, it was perhaps the most moving of all the eulogies Jack received that day.

Allowing for what he felt was a respectful period of mourning, Irving Fein waited until after the new year had begun before visiting George at his General Service Studios office. With little preamble, he asked if George would be willing to play the part of Al Lewis in *The Sunshine Boys*. George replied that he didn't think he could do it, knowing that it was the role Jack was going to play.

Irving then played his ace. He told George about a phone conversation Jack had had with director Herbert Ross just weeks before he died. Having realized that he was not getting better, Jack had told Ross that he might not be up to taking on the role. If he wasn't, he urged Ross to consider George, saying, "He would be wonderful in the part." Ross promised to keep George in mind, and after Jack's death he contacted Irving.

Now Irving reminded George that he had been Jack's manager for twenty-six years and knew him as well as Jack knew himself. "Take my word for it," he said, "nothing would make Jack happier than for you to take that part."

With a flourish, he reached into his briefcase, withdrew a copy of the script and dropped it on George's desk. "Read it," he said, heading for the door before George could respond, "and call me in the morning."

Given his limited reading ability, it took George a bit longer to read through the script, but he liked it, and he told Irving that he'd be willing to give it a try. A few days later, he met with Ross, Neil Simon and producer Ray Stark at Ross' home. He did not bring his script. When he asked what scene they'd like him to play, they handed him a script, but he said he did not need it. He had memorized his part.

That left the threesome speechless for a moment. They were even more impressed with George's performance when they picked a scene for him to run through. George took it in stride and did fine on the first try. "I'm perfect for the part," he said. "You're looking for an old Jewish vaudevillian, and I'm an old Jewish vaudevillian."

The Sunshine Boys was about two aging comics named Al Lewis and Willy Clark, a.k.a. "Lewis and Clark," who had been a team for fifty years, but split up after some spat, and had not spoken to each other since. A television network putting together a history of comedy wants to use them. Clark's nephew, played by Richard Benjamin, has been recruited to try to get them back together.

In addition to Jack Benny, Groucho Marx, Phil Silvers and Red Skelton had been considered for the role of Al Lewis. Other than Jack, none of them seemed quite right. Now Matthau and the others knew that they had found the perfect Al Lewis. Walter and George clicked immediately, and they became fast friends in the course of the filming.

In an early scene, before the two comics' reunion, George was persuaded to remove his toupee so that he looked his age. It was the only time he appeared on stage or on the screen without it. When viewing the finished film, he quipped, "I never knew that I was bald."

Appearing on Johnny Carson's *Tonight Show* to promote the film, Richard Benjamin told of George's scriptless audition. Someone, he said, asked a bit incredulously, "You memorized the entire script?" To which George innocently replied, "Isn't that what I'm supposed to do?"

In reality, George had been in the practice of memorizing since his early vaudeville years. His poor eyesight and limited reading skills made cue cards and teleprompters of little use to him.

Walter Matthau was paid a million dollars for the picture. George got about a third of that. That didn't sit well with Irving Fein (who, of course, got a percentage) but, unsure if George could pull it off, he bit his lip and held his peace.

It didn't bother George. He was working, it wasn't hard work, and he was enjoying himself. He didn't really need the money. From his perspective, it was far more gratifying to realize that he was, at long last, a star in his own right. He knew Gracie would be proud of him.

The film was not a smash, but it did well at the box office. Reviewers, some too young to remember Burns and Allen, singled George out for high praise. At the age of eighty, he was nominated for 1975's Best Supporting Actor and was proclaimed the winner at the Academy Awards ceremony in February, 1976.

Accepting the Oscar, his head just barely visible above the lectern, he told the audience that he had not made a film since 1939. "I've decided," he said, "to keep making one picture every thirty-six years."

Fame is fleeting. Winning an Oscar did not result in a string of movie offers, and personal appearances were still few and scattered. He was, after all, an octogenarian who was relatively unknown to younger film and show patrons. Still, he was paid well for what engagements Irving was able to arrange, and the work was not demanding. Mindful of the age and health history of his new meal ticket, Irving signed him to only two- or three-day weekend appearances. That may have contributed to mostly full houses, since those who wanted to see him perform had limited options.

He found time to author his second book, *Living It Up (Or, They Still Love Me in Altoona)*. His first book had been published back in 1955. *I Love Her, That's Why!* was dubbed an autobiography. It actually was an "as told to" type book, written by Cynthia Hobart Lindsay, an actress turned writer, whose several biographies included a later one about Boris Karloff. Lindsay took notes as George rambled about his early life and his life with Gracie, interjecting old and new gags as they occurred to him. When she had enough notes, Lindsay reassembled it all and produced a book that became a best seller.

George, of course, could not have written a book alone, since he was still semi-literate. But now he had writers and secretaries working for him at the production company. He utilized their talents to put together the new book. Over time he produced ten books, all of them with a similar format: vaudeville memories, stories about Gracie, reminiscences of show biz friends, with a plentiful supply of Burns-style jokes scattered throughout.

Another break-through came late in 1976, when Warner Brothers called on Carl Reiner to direct a film called *Oh, God!* In it, God comes down to earth because He is concerned that the world is in such a mess that even believers are losing faith. He selects Jerry Landers, a young, unassuming assistant supermarket manager, to spread the word that He is still around and still cares about His creation and the people in it.

Folk singer John Denver was to play the store manager, his first and only film. His natural soft-spoken, laid-back personality made him a good fit for the role. As Jerry, he has to deal with the disbelief of everyone that he encounters in an effort to convey God's message that He is still there and He still cares about them.

Mel Brooks had already agreed to play God. He and Reiner had long ago achieved fame with their 2,000-year-old man routine. But Carl felt that Mel was just not right to play the Almighty. He shared his concern with the play's writer, Larry Gelbart. Larry agreed. Having seen and loved *The Sunshine Boys*, he suggested that Reiner consider George Burns.

Reiner leaped at the idea. He contacted Irving Fein, who quickly got a script into George's hands. When he finished reading it, George had no doubt that he wanted the part. He gave Irving a thumbs-up to work out the contract.

George Burns as God is a quiet-spoken but persuasive little old man in a baseball cap, who prompts Jerry through various semi-comic situations as he confronts the disbelief of people that he could be God's messenger. Religion is easy, God says; faith takes an effort.

In a wise, fatherly voice, God/George offers such uplifting thoughts as: "I know it's hard to have faith in these times, but maybe if you start with faith, you could change things," and "If you find it hard to believe in me, maybe it would help to know that I believe in you."

John Denver's popularity drew many younger people to the theatres, while older folk who remembered Burns and Allen were drawn to seeing the aging Oscar winner playing the Almighty so believably. Reiner, George, et al were gratified that the film played in some theatres for almost a year.

The film cost a little over two million dollars to make. It grossed almost one hundred million. Carl Reiner, who may have been a tad biased, enthused that "For many people, young and old, it was like a religious experience."

A second successful film demonstrated both George's staying power and that he could still be a "draw." Between 1977 and 1979, Irving was able to book him at top venues in Atlantic City, Las Vegas and elsewhere at fees ranging from $25,000 to $50,000. He also appeared in four—count 'em!—four more films.

Hollywood loves sequels, especially if the original was a big success. Writers are adept at picking up where the plot left off, and audiences are easily enticed to see what happens next. *Oh, God!* Resulted in two sequels.

In *Oh, God! Book II,* God comes to Earth again and uses a precocious schoolgirl to continue Jerry Landers' work spreading His word. In *Oh, God! You Devil,* George had the delightful opportunity to play both God and the Devil, competing for the soul of a young would-be songwriter. In George's portrayal, the Devil is a charming, good humored fellow who could endear himself to his prey.

When an interviewer spoke of his role in the three *God* pictures, George recalled, "I got nervous when I was asked to play God. We're both around the same age, but we grew up in different neighborhoods."

At a celebrity roast in George's honor, Dean Martin told the attendees, "When George was growing up, the Top Ten were the Ten Commandments." For his part, when it was his turn to speak, George observed, "You know, people often ask me about the young girls I go out with." A puff on his cigar as his audience waited, then he continued, "I would go out with women my age, but there are no women my age."

In his nightclub performances, he often entered behind a puff of smoke from his ever-present cigar, then opened by telling the audience, "I usually get a standing ovation just for standing." With his newfound popularity, he could no longer use the line because audiences, especially the older crowd, often did give him a standing ovation when he walked out onto the stage.

Instead he did a new twist on the gag. He took a few puffs on the cigar and smiled at the audience until the applause subsided. Then he'd say, "That's good. If I can stand, so can you."

Joking aside, standing up for a typically one-hour performance was becoming so tiring that he needed a nap when he returned to his dressing room. He confessed this to a friend, who suggested that he sit down.

"If Perry Como can sit on a stool," he said, "why can't you? You're older."

That wasn't the way it was done in the old days, and George resisted the idea at first. After awhile, however, he tried the stool on a few appearances and found that he could still relax and do his shtick while seated. Eventually, he decided to go the whole way and had an easy chair set on the stage. After the applause died upon his entry, he told the audience, "Now I'm going to do something I enjoy more than anything else." Then he sat down.

In 1978, at the age of eighty-two, George made a cameo appearance with the Beatles in their film *Sgt. Pepper's Lonely Hearts Club Band*. He appeared as a guest on television's *The Muppet Show*, and made a movie for television called *The Comedy Company*.

He also found time and energy to make two more films. In the forgettable *Just You and Me, Kid* he played an aging vaudevillian. Typecasting? His daughter was played by Brooke Shields. Like John Denver, she probably attracted a lot of young people who would otherwise have passed on the film.

Going In Style was (pun intended) another story. George teamed up with veteran actors Lee Strasberg and Art Carney (who played Jackie Gleason's pal Ed Norton on the popular television series *The Honeymooners*). The three play retired New York buddies, getting by on Social Security and spending most of their time sitting together on a park bench. One day they decide, just to be doing something, to rob a bank.

George and Gracie chat with Bea Benaderet and Larry Keating, who played Blanche and Harry Morton. CREDIT: Nostalgia Digest collection

Borrowing pistols from Lee's son's collection and donning Groucho Marx nose masks, they actually pull it off, although their loot is a modest $36,000. Since none of them has a car, they make their getaway in a cab. The hold-up and what happens after have the makings of a Damon Runyon story.

To keep himself in the public eye, and in demand, George made frequent guest appearances on many late-night television talk shows. Johnny

Carson had him on the *Tonight Show* frequently. Johnny knew that George was good for an endless supply of jokes and anecdotal memories.

When the question about retiring came up, George said, "Six years ago, Sinatra announced his retirement. He's still working. The happiest people I know are the ones that are still working. The saddest are the ones who are retired." When asked about Gracie, he said, "For forty years, I had one joke. Then she died." Or: "For forty years, I fed Gracie straight lines, and she fed me."

He also continued to crank out books, with the help of his co-writers. When he published *How to Live to Be 100* in 1983, it may have seemed like tempting the Grim Reaper. Son Ronnie recalled him saying, "I want to celebrate my hundredth birthday by playing the Palladium in London." Irving Fein actually got him booked, but it was not to be.

Nevertheless, even if he was slowing down a bit, he kept active. If his age was brought up on his television guest appearances, he quipped, "I can't die. I'm booked." Indeed, in 1984 Irving negotiated a five-year contract with Caesar's Palace for George to perform in Atlantic City, Lake Tahoe and Las Vegas.

In 1985, George hosted a comedy anthology series for CBS called *George Burns Comedy Week*. Numerous well-known comedians appeared in various episodes, including Don Rickles, Martin Mull, Robert Klein and Don Knotts. Valerie Perrine and Harvey Korman starred in what came to be a pilot for their short-lived sit-com series *Leo & Liz in Beverly Hills*. Even with Gracie appearing via old film and television clips, *George Burns Comedy Week* lasted only from September through December.

On January 17, 1986, CBS celebrated George's ninetieth birthday with a television program called *A Very Special Special*. It was hosted by John Forsythe, a Hollywood actor who currently was enjoying prolonged popularity on the television series *Dynasty*. Among other guests, fittingly enough, were John Denver and Walter Matthau.

George told a few jokes and sang one of his favorite oldies: "Boom, boom, boom, boom. Down in the garden where the red rose grows...." Much of the program was taken up with clips of George and Gracie from their many early films, including their wonderful dance with Fred Astaire in *A Damsel in Distress*. In his closing comments, acknowledging how blessed he had been to have Gracie as a partner, George said, "By the time I found out I had no talent, I was too big a star to do anything else."

The 1988 film *18 Again!* was a variation on a plot used in more than one movie previously. A shy, awkward college lad and his grandfather are almost killed in a car accident. Their souls trade places. Now the young man becomes popular with fraternity brothers, coeds, etc. George is mostly an off-screen voice making wry comments about his grandson's marvelous transformation.

In November of 1989, George was a guest of Larry King to promote his book *All My Best Friends*. King made sure they covered that subject, and then moved on. He was good at drawing out his guests. Knowing how many famous comics George had associated with, he asked about several.

George had words of praise for such as Al Jolson and Jimmy Durante. King caught him off guard when he asked bluntly if he had liked Groucho Marx. George paused and then hedged. "I liked Harpo," he said. When King pressed him, he reflected for a moment, then shrugged and said, "I liked Groucho. I just never danced with him."

Knowing of their friendship, King observed that Jack Benny's death must have been very hard on him. George seemed unable to reply for a moment. Then he said simply, "He was my best friend."

"Was his death sudden?" King asked.

Again a pause. Then George said, "It was sudden for me."

As if he did not have enough going on, George made a 45-minute videotape that year called *The Wit and Wisdom of George Burns*. It would be, like so many others, sold on television with a loud-voiced promo and little teaser clips. In it he talks about his daily routine and actually demonstrates his exercise program. The video ends with him performing before a college audience, As he takes his bows, he says, "You didn't think I would be around this long."

His last television special, *George Burns Celebrates Eighty Years in Show Business*, was in 1993. The format was similar to a Friar's Club roast. Seated at long tables was a Who's Who of show biz stars, including Milton Berle, Buddy Hackett, Bob Hope, Phyllis Diller, Carol Channing, Red Buttons and Johnny Carson. The comedians took turns directing old guy jokes at George, who endured it all with a patient smile.

A high point of the program was Bernadette Peters singing the lyric of the Burns and Allen theme "Love Nest," mostly unfamiliar to those present, or long forgotten. For George, the evening was at least restful. He got to sit through most of it. When he finally got to speak, perhaps thinking there'd been enough jokes, he rendered one of the patter songs that had been his trademark in the pre-Gracie days.

George's last film role was a cameo in the 1994 comedy mystery *Radioland Murders*. He no doubt savored the role of Milt Lackey, a 100-year-old stand-up comedian.

It's said that most accidents happen in the home. In September, 1994, George slipped in the shower and fell, striking his head on a tub fixture. In addition to a mild concussion, he suffered a nasty gash on his head. At the hospital, Sandy and Ronnie were told that there was pressure on his brain from an accumulation of spinal fluid. It would need to be drained.

That required drilling into his skull. It was a simple procedure that the doctors considered fairly routine. But this patient was approaching one hundred years old. On September 14, 1994, George suffered a heart attack and a mild stroke while on the operating table.

Despite that, the operation itself went well, and George was soon in a recovery ward. A speech therapist was encouraged when George not only answered correctly, though weakly, but interjected a few jokes.

Still, reality had to be faced. Irving Fein cancelled the London Palladium gig. A long-planned engagement for January, 1996, at the Las Vegas Caesar's Palace was in doubt. As was a two-hour special that CBS had planned to tape and broadcast on or near George's hundredth birthday.

When released from the hospital, George made a determined effort to return to a normal routine. He had his driver/valet Daniel D'Hoore help him from his new wheelchair into the car and drive him to the office. At noon, Daniel drove him to the club for lunch. Most days he spent an hour or two playing bridge with some of his old buddies. He could not shuffle or deal, and he made mistakes he would never have made before, but his friends pretended they didn't notice.

Around three o'clock he went home and napped for a couple of hours. When he awoke, the housekeeper fixed his afternoon martini, using just enough gin to be tasted. Around six, he had his dinner in the upstairs bedroom.

Because he didn't read and seldom watched television, his evenings were mostly uneventful unless members of his family stopped by, which they did as often as possible. Otherwise, he took to his bed early.

By August of 1995, Irving Fein was required to confirm that

George would be up to doing the CBS television special. Reluctantly, he acknowledged that it was doubtful. The special was cancelled.

That left only George's birthday engagement at Caesar's Palace. The nervous management told Irving that they needed to be assured by October that he would be there. Irving wanted this big finish for George almost as much as George wanted it, but he couldn't bring himself to be that hopeful. The engagement was cancelled.

Staying active, i.e., being "booked," had kept George energized well into his nineties. He had always been a small man. Now he had shrunk to an even smaller size, and looked like the old man that he had refused to be even as he joked about his age. His declining health, coupled with the realization that he would do no more performing, robbed him of the zest for living that he had long embodied.

By the beginning of 1996, he was spending more time in bed than out of it. He achieved his goal of reaching his one-hundredth birthday, but the celebration was a quiet one, with only family and household staff present. His children read him newspaper accounts that heralded the event and recalled his long career with and without Gracie. In a somewhat gravelly voice, he was able to interject a few jokes and elaborate on incidents cited.

George died in his bed at home on March 9, 1996, with Ronnie, a nurse and a housekeeper nearby.

His body would be entombed next to Gracie's at the Forest Lawn Memorial Park mausoleum. The funeral was a much smaller, quieter one than hers, held at the nearby Wee Kirk o' the Heather Chapel, attended by family members and show biz people who had been closest to him.

His longtime pianist, Morty Jacobs, played a medley of tunes that George loved, old tunes that he had sung in his vaudeville days, including "Sidewalks of New York," "By the Light of the Silvery Moon" and "Love Nest."

One eulogizer noted that George was probably most fondly remembered for his razor wit. "People would say, 'Oh, Mr. Burns, it's so nice to see you,' and George would reply, 'At my age, it's good to see anybody.'"

Irvine Fein gave the final eulogy. The agent who had spent most of his career representing Jack Benny, and then George Burns, said, "George, we'll miss you. I know you took your music with you. So wherever you are, I hope they're playing it in your key."

* * * * * * * * *

Sandra Jean Burns married James Wilhoite on August 6, 1953. They had two daughters, Laura and Melissa. That marriage ended in 1957. George Burns' producer, Rod Amateau, had long had a secret crush on Sandy. After her divorce, he was emboldened to express his interest. They began dating and were married on September 1, 1959. Sandy had two more daughters, Grace and Brooke, before that marriage also ended in divorce in 1962. Sandra died in 2010

* * * * * * * * *

Ronald Jon "Ronnie" Burns, despite his appearance in numerous Burns and Allen television episodes and several minor film roles, was never enamored of show business. After producing his father's short-lived television series *Wendy and Me* (1964-65), he ventured into the real estate business and prospered. He raised horses on a ranch that he purchased in Santa Ynez. Ronnie and his wife Janice had three sons, Brent, Brad and Bryan. In 2007, Ronnie died of cancer at the age of seventy-two at his Pacific Palisades home. He was survived by Janice, their three sons and six grandchildren.

* * * * * * * * *

For her contributions to the television industry, Gracie Allen was honored with a star on the Hollywood Walk of Fame on the 6600 block of Hollywood Boulevard. In 1988, she and George Burns earned a joint injunction into membership of the Television Hall of Fame.

* * * * * * * * *

George Burns has three stars on the Hollywood Walk of Fame: for television, on the 6500 block of Hollywood Boulevard; for live performance, on the 6600 block of Hollywood Boulevard; and for film, on the 1600 block of Vine Street.

George Burns and Gracie Allen Short Films

1929 *Lambchops,* a Warner Brothers "Vitaphone Varieties" short
1930 *Fit to Be Tied,* Paramount Pictures
1931 *Pulling a Bone,* Paramount Pictures
1931 *The Antique Shop,* Paramount Pictures
1931 *Once Over, Light,* Paramount Pictures
1931 *100% Service,* Paramount Pictures
1931 *Oh, My Operation,* Paramount Pictures
1932 *The Babbling Brook,* Paramount Pictures
1932 *Your Hat,* Paramount Pictures
1933 *Let's Dance,* Paramount Pictures
1933 *Walking the Baby,* Paramount Pictures

George Burns and Gracie Allen Radio Programs

1933-1934 *The White Owl Program,* CBS
1934-1935 *The Adventures of Gracie,* CBS
1935-1937 *The Campbell's Tomato Juice Program,* CBS
1937-1938 *The Grape Nuts Program,* NBC
1938-1939 *The Chesterfield Program,* CBS
1939-1940 *The Hinds Honey and Almond Cream Program,* CBS
1940-1941 *The Hormel Program,* NBC
1941-1945 *The Swan Soap Show,* NBC, then CBS
1945-1949 *Maxwell House Coffee Time,* NBC
1949-1950 *The Amm-I-dent Toothpaste Show,* CBS

Books by George Burns

I Love Her, That's Why, recollections shared with bio author Cynthia Hobart Lindsay, Simon and Schuster (1955)
Living it up: Or, They Still Love Me in Altoona!, Putnam (1967)
The Third Time Around, Putnam (1980)
How To Live To Be 100 – Or More – The Ultimate Diet, Sex and Exercise Book, Robson Books (1983) (Over the years, various doctors advised George to change his diet and give up martinis and cigars. He dedicated this book to the widows of his last six doctors.)
Dr. Burns' Prescription for Happiness: Buy Two Books and Call Me in the Morning, Putnam (1984)
Dear George: Advice and Answers, Putnam (1985)
Gracie: A Love Story, Putnam (1988)
All My Best Friends, Putnam (1989)

Wisdom of the 90's, Putnam (1991)
100 Years, 100 Stories, Putnam (1996)

Gracie Allen's Recipe for Roast Beef

Buy 1 large roast of beef.
Buy 1 small roast of beef.
Take the two roasts and put them in the oven.
When the little one burns, the big one is done!

Classic Burns and Allen Gag

George: Gracie, why should I give your mother a bushel of nuts? What did she ever give me?
Gracie: Why, George, she gave you me. And I'm as good as nuts.

Jim and Marian Jordan as themselves in a studio photo pose.
CREDIT: Nostalgia Digest collection

Jim and Marian Jordan
Fibber McGee and Molly

He would later be known by a much different name, but on November 16, 1896, he entered the world as James Edward Jordan. With his three brothers and three sisters, he spent his early years on a farm just outside of Peoria, Illinois, and attended a rural school.

Up the road a piece (as the country folk were wont to say), the Driscoll family welcomed their daughter, Marian Irene, on April 5, 1898. Growing up with three sisters and nine brothers, it was easy for her to get lost in the crowd. Fortunately, her father had steady work in the area coal mines, and the family never wanted for food or other needs.

When James, who by now was called Jim, was twelve years old, the rest of his family moved into the city. Jim stayed behind to live and work on his cousin's farm until he was almost fifteen., When he joined his family in town, he was enrolled in St. Marks School to complete eighth grade.

After graduating, he entered Peoria's Spaulding Institute. One of the pals with whom he played basketball there was nicknamed "Spike" Sheen. Spike later became Archbishop Fulton J. Sheen, revered as a spiritual guide by millions of Catholics and non-Catholics alike for his uplifting messages on his 1950s television program *Life Is Worth Living*.

Despite its rural location, Peoria in the 1890s was a lively town, with many bustling businesses that catered to farmers from the surrounding countryside. Its population of 50,000 made it the second largest city in Illinois. Although they were about the same age and lived not far apart, Marian and Jim had not yet connected. Their shared musical talents would eventually make that happen.

In addition to being blessed with a lovely contralto voice, Marian took both piano and violin lessons. Jim took vocal lessons to master the use of his pure tenor voice. In December, 1915, Fate used their mutual musical interests to bring them together.

Jim had joined a choral group at St John's Church that planned to give a Christmas recital. After rehearsal one evening, there was a social gathering. The group sang various popular tunes together and as soloists, duets, etc. The pretty and perky Marian caught Jim's attention doing a lively jig.

He bravely introduced himself, complemented her on her impromptu dance, and struck up a conversation. Marian kept up her end long enough to convince him that she liked him, but he lost his nerve at the point when he should have asked her for a date.

The next day, however, he recovered sufficiently to do so by telephone. She accepted, and they made it a New Years Eve date. That gave them the excuse to stay out a bit later than would otherwise have been deemed proper by their parents.

More dates followed. They soon eliminated any other dating partners and agreed that their relationship had progressed beyond casual dating. Marriage became a serious subject.

Marian was by now an accomplished pianist and gave lessons in her parents' home. Jim had tried his hand at several jobs, including door-to-door sales and clerking in a drugstore. His real ambition, however, was a theatrical career as a singer. He was the tenor in a trio that sang for various local events. They were paid for these, but he agreed with his own and Marian's parents that it was not enough to support a wife. Marriage plans were indefinitely postponed.

In September, 1917, with a recommendation from his vocal teacher, Jim went to Chicago and auditioned for a singing group in need of a tenor. He got the job. The quartet joined a larger drama/comedy group that was to make a 39-week tour of Canada and the United States on the Western Vaudeville Circuit.

It was not the glamorous life that Jim had envisioned. There were long train rides, nights in dingy hotels, and meals, often consumed in haste, that were a far cry from Mom's home cooking. All of which were paid for out of pocket, leaving only a modest net income. After the last of 260 performances, he decided it was time to head home.

Once there, he was able to obtain a job carrying mail for the U.S. Post Office. It was steady work, paid well, and he could sing to himself as he made his deliveries. Meanwhile, Marian had a steady clientele of young would-be pianists. Both she and Jim tucked away as much of their incomes as possible. They eventually had a nest egg that they considered adequate for launching a life together. With the blessings of both families, they were married on August 31, 1918.

They honeymooned in St. Louis, where they visited one of Jim's sisters. The honeymoon was a short one. America was at war, and a week after their wedding Jim received notification that Uncle Sam required his service.

Jim reported for duty and spent six weeks in basic training for the infantry. He then was dispatched to France as part of the 122nd Engineers. Soon after his arrival, and before he could be assigned to any unit, he contracted a severe case of dysentery. It resulted in a prolonged hospital stay that lasted until the Armistice had been signed. The discomfort notwithstanding, it proved to be a mishap with an up side.

As he was recovering, he spoke to some officers and succeeded in getting himself assigned to the Entertainment Division. He then organized a camp show that he called The Premiere Review. It was a group of thirty-five men with a variety of talents who began touring U.S. hospital units for the next six months. Jim sang tenor in one of the group's two quartets.

During one of their performances, Jim ran into his brother Mickey. Mickey played piano and Jim knew the group could use him. At Jim's suggestion, Mickey requested and was granted a transfer, and he became part of the entertainment team.

In July, 1919, Jim returned home with discharge papers in his pocket. After a joyful reunion, he and Marian put a down payment on a modest little four-room house and moved in. Jim somehow got a job in a machine shop, but his mechanical skills were not up to the requirements. To spare his kindly boss the unpleasantness of firing him, he left voluntarily. He tried his hand at selling washing machines, vacuum cleaners and life insurance. In spite of his outgoing nature, his efforts convinced him that he was not cut out to be a salesman.

One day he sat down to have a serious talk with Marian. She had encouraged him in his short-lived stage performing. She, too, had taken to singing and playing piano, unpaid, at numerous events in and near Peoria. Would she consider teaming up to give show business a serious try? Marian's response was close to "I thought you'd never ask!" Indeed, she would.

Buoyed by her enthusiasm, Jim went to work. He had some scenery made up. Then he began making a list of organizations that were convenient to rail lines and held various events featuring professional entertainment. Together, he and Marian shopped for a wardrobe. Finally, he hired three musicians to be part of a group that their posters and handbills would call The Metropolitan Musical Entertainers.

They would be traveling by train, so to finance their start-up the Jordans sold their old car for $125. Then the group got on the road.

They offered a mixed menu of music. There were instrumental pieces by the entire group, with Jim playing a passable guitar. In between, Marian played piano pieces and accompanied herself and/or Jim on solos and duets. Audience response ranged from lukewarm to enthusiastic. At least they never were booed.

Jim was able to arrange enough appearances so that the ensemble was in a different town each day. There were matinee and evening shows performed in high school auditoriums, meeting halls and theaters, large and small. Favorable comments from a performance in one place sometimes opened a door for them down the road.

Playing to audiences of varying sizes meant working for varied payment, but they did well for the most part. In their best year, the group took in $25,000, a respectable total, even though it had to be divided five ways.

Determined to be successful, Jim and Marian continued the tour when Marian learned that she was pregnant. She took just a brief time out when their daughter, Kathryn, was born on June 18, 1920. She soon resumed her place at the piano, with Jim's parents watching over their new grandchild back home.

When Jim Jr. was born on August 3, 1923, she and Jim agreed it was time for her to take some time off to be a mother at home. The group was disbanded, but Jim continued touring as a tenor soloist. He used house pianists to accompany him in theaters, and local talent in other venues.

Marian joined him periodically, bringing Kathryn and Jim Jr. with her. On these occasions they billed themselves as Marian and Jim Jordan, Harmony Team. While they were on stage, fellow performers watched over the children.

It was during this period that Jim had his first inauspicious encounter with that new medium called radio. While he was appearing at a Minneapolis theater, he was invited to come sing on a local station. After an evening performance, he went to the studio and sang several songs over the air. He neither spoke nor was paid, but his introduction by the announcer included a plug for his theater appearance.

Jim's solo performances were not as much fun or as financially rewarding as working with Marian. As the holidays neared in 1924, he decided to take a breather and return home.

He found work as a clerk in a dry goods store. Without requiring him to be a salesman, it afforded him the opportunity to be as helpful as he was able and to engage customers with his naturally outgoing, chatty personality.

Marian found time to continue giving a few piano lessons. Her modest income was salted away in their savings.

When an opportunity presented itself, the duo continued performing together at nearby events. In between their regular and irregular jobs, they enjoyed being at home with their youngsters.

An evening spent with Jim's brother and his wife at their Chicago home planted a seed that led to their ultimate career. After dinner and some socializing, the couples sat around a table radio in the living room. They spent the evening tuning in to see what was being presented on various stations.

Across the country, small radio stations were starting up as families began placing receivers in their homes. Much of their air time was filled with music, so they had a constant need for musicians and vocalists. Those with sufficient finances offered modest payment. Others drew performers who wanted to be heard by the potential large audience that could result in personal stage appearances.

The Jordans saw the possibilities of selling themselves to one of the stations that paid its performers. While continuing to do whatever stage work they could find close to home, they kept their eyes and ears open. Opportunity presented itself in 1925 at a little station, WICO, just outside of Chicago. They were hired to do a 15-minute program three nights a week for the sum of $10 a week. They were introduced each night as "Marian and Jim in Songs" and experimented a bit with some humorous patter. The salary was mere pocket change, but their names were mentioned several times during each broadcast, and they had a six-month contract.

Several similar jobs followed, with and without pay, and they continued doing personal appearances that they could work into their schedule. In 1927, they took on their first program with a sponsor. The Williamson Candy Company, makers of the O'Henry candy bar, paid them $35 a week to perform on a Friday night show with other vocalists. They became The O'Henry Twins.

A break-through occurred in October, 1927. They were having dinner in Chicago when they met an old friend named Howard Newmiller. He was a pianist with whom they had worked on the road. Howard was now working at Chicago radio station WENR. He told the Jordans that if they came by the station he felt certain he could help them find a paying job there.

WENR went on the air in late 1924, operating on a mere 10 watts. Its founder, E. N. Rauland, owned a manufacturing company. One of his products was a brand of radios called the All-American, so he had a vested interest in fostering the growth of the new medium. By late 1925, the station was using a 1,000-watt transmitter designed by Rauland himself.

In 1927, industrial magnate Samuel Insull purchased the station for $1 million. Insull was a co-founder of General Electric and Commonwealth Edison. His financial enterprises included ownership or part-ownership of Peoples Gas, Federal Signal Corporation, and other large companies. Recognizing the potential of rail transit, he obtained controlling interests in numerous companies, including the Chicago South Shore, the Milwaukee Road, and Chicago, Aurora and Elgin railways.

A patron of Chicago's Civic Opera, he sought to bring its performances into people's homes through the new medium of radio. After forming a company called Great Lakes Broadcasting, he bought several stations. He moved all of them, including WENR, into the Civic Opera House. WENR later became an affiliate of NBC's Blue Network.

Insull was one of many super-rich investors who lost their fortunes during the Great Depression. In the 1920s, however, he was a man of great wealth and influence. Thanks to his deep pockets, WENR was able to pay generously to hire talented performers, while many small stations paid only a token or simply offered hopeful performers the opportunity to be heard.

Jim and Marian were aware of the stature of WENR, and they were happy to accept Howard's invitation. He did not let them down. When the Jordans left the radio station, they had a contract to do a quarter-hour children's program called *The Air Scouts*. It was sponsored by People's Gas, Light and Coke Company. They would be paid, as a team, just $40 a week. That meant they would still need to find other work, but this job was a turning point. They would never again be without steady work.

At 5:00 p.m. on Monday, October 3, 1927, the Jordans were heard for the first time on *The Air Scouts*. It also marked the first time that they spoke on the air. All of their previous radio performances had involved singing and/or piano pieces only. The only spoken segments were done by staff announcers.

The Air Scouts was a sort of adventure and fun program for the youngsters. It involved story telling and bits of make believe. In both of these areas, the Jordans began for the first time using a variety of voices. They were pleased to discover that they shared a talent they had not previously tapped. Marian began using the little girl's voice that would one day be the neighbor kid, Teeny, who visited the McGees and drove Fibber nuts. Jim took on the role of an old man who told such tall tales that even their young listeners weren't taken in.

Once they had their feet in the station door, they began finding opportunities to play incidental or continuing characters on other programs. One was called *Grab Bag*. It featured dramatizations of current comic strips. Their newfound talent for doing voices served them well here. Marian once did a dozen different voices on a single broadcast.

In 1928, they began to portray Luke Gray and his long-suffering wife Mirandy on a show created for them by staff writer Harry Lawrence. It was called, simply, *Luke and Mirandy*. Once again Jim played a character who was prone to lengthy stretches of the truth. Mirandy spent much of her time separating fiction from fact.

Marian had the distinction of playing the mother in a serialized drama that may have been the first of what came to be called "soap operas." *The Smith Family* mixed drama with some humor as it portrayed the lives of Nora and Ed and their two daughters. Jim played the boyfriend of one daughter. The program, also written by Harry Lawrence, followed the couple's courtship and later marriage. One extended series of episodes had Nora running for a local office and winning against a formidable opponent—her husband.

The program was sponsored by National Tea Company. It premiered on June 9, 1929, and was heard twice weekly. It was sufficiently popular to continue the family's stories of mostly everyday American life until April 3, 1932. During the last year of the show, WENR was pleased enough with the Jordans' performances to increase their salary to $60 a week.

The Jordans also were charter members of a comedy classroom that aired as *Kaltenmeyer's Kindergarten*. Subtitled "The Nonsense School of the Air," it starred Bruce Kamman as Professor Kaltenmeyer. A trumpet player and former vaudevillian, Kamman created the program as a one-time special. It received such a favorable response from listeners that the station encouraged him to develop it into a regular series.

In a half-hour format, the show was performed on Saturdays before a live studio audience. It began on a sustaining basis (unsponsored) in October, 1932. It was popular enough to continue that way until January, 1935, when the Quaker Oats Company picked it up. Along with Kamman and a fellow named Johnny Wolf, Jim and Marian were the first four cast members.

Other actors joined the cast as more "students" were enrolled in the school and parents or other school staff visited the classroom. Marian sometimes played a Mrs. Van Schuyler and a giggly lady named Gertie Glump. Jim was heard as a fellow named Cy Wintergreen and the rather dense Mickey Donovan.

It's doubtful that any of the school's students every became scholars. The lack of learning was personified by the theme song sung by the cast at the beginning of the show:

"Kaltenmeyer's startin',
Let's all go to school.
In his kindergarten,
Where everyone's a fool.
Boy, do we pull boners!
Mischief we all raise.
Lots of it, and you'll admit,
Were in those good old days."

The Jordan's also found time to be occasional guests on Don McNeill's popular program, *The Breakfast Club*. They were known as the bucolic twosome Toots (Marian) and Chickie (Jim) in a routine that was heavy on country bumpkin humor. In its early years, *The Breakfast Club* had no studio audience at its 7:00 a.m. airing. Laughter was provided by the orchestra, Don and other cast members.

The Jordans' skits always opened with them enthusiastically greeting one another.

Marian: Good morning, Chickie.

Jim: Hi ya, Toots.

Then they launched into the cornball gags. On one occasion, Jim muffed his opening line.

Marian: Good morning, Chickie.

Jim: Hi ya, Tits.

Neither Jim nor Marian caught the flub. They went into their gags and read through a page or more before it dawned on them that there was an unusual degree of laughter. A glance toward the orchestra found them almost rolling on the floor in hysterics. Jim remembered thinking, "Gee, are we *that* funny?"

Don McNeill happened to have gone down the hall to get a cup of coffee, so he missed the uproar of unintended comedy. Only after the show was over was the incident shared with him. Don reflected that it was lucky he had been absent. Had he heard Jim's flub, he might have been unable to fulfill his Master of Ceremonies duties through the remainder of the program.

Despite, the Great Depression, Jim and Marian were doing well in 1931. In addition to starring in or being part of the cast of several radio programs, they managed to work in two or three live stage performances most weeks at theaters in and near Chicago. Their combined income from both venues ranged from about $600 to $800 dollars a week.

Somewhere along here they began thinking about having their own comedy show. Various vaudeville friends had often suggested that they add some comedy to their routine. Singing groups typically inserted gags or light patter between songs. The Jordans had long felt that comedy was not their forte, that their theater audiences did not come to hear them tell jokes.

Still, most of their work on radio had involved a mixture of singing and comedy, in some cases heavier on the latter. Radio appeared to have great potential, and in these hard times listeners were especially responsive to comedy. With their talent for doing multiple voices, they should be able to carry a good comedy program, and perhaps insert a little music here and there.

One day Jim found himself with some idle time on his hands. Wandering about the WENR lobby, he pondered half a dozen hazy ideas for a program that would make good use of his and Marian's combined talents. He was not coming up with any brainstorm.

As he paced, a fellow named Don Quinn happened by and greeted him. The Jordans knew Don only casually. They had met him at a party. Don told them he had been working at an advertising company when the firm went under. Now he spent much of his time roaming from station to station, taking on writing assignments wherever he could find them. It was, he told Jim, an iffy way to make a living, but he was getting along. Jim allowed as how that was a coincidence, because he was wrestling with the notion of putting together a humorous program, but his mind was a blank.

Noting that he had a lot of free time on his hands, Don offered to do some writing for Jim and Marian on a commission basis. If he could produce a program that the Jordans were able to sell to the station, he would get a percentage of whatever they were paid. Jim liked the idea and agreed.

This proved to be a milestone in the careers of Jim and Marian Jordan, and Don Quinn as well.

Don had heard the Jordans on the *Luke and Mirandy* program. He thought Luke Gray could be at the center of a program on which he was visited by other colorful characters whose personalities afforded a basis for the gags. Jim agreed and encouraged Don to give it a try.

At their next meeting, joined by Marian, Don presented the scenario for a program he tentatively called *Marian and Jim in Smackout, The Crossroads of the Air*. The setting would be a little general merchandise store, complete with a tinkling bell over the front door, located at a rural crossroads. It would be run by a fellow who was long on story telling and short on merchandise. Whenever a customer asked for some item, he would regretfully tell them that he was "smack out," but should have it in the next day or two.

The storekeeper may have reminded the Jordans of Luke Gray, or perhaps they just liked the name. Whatever the reason, they chose to use the name again, although this time there was no Mirandy. Luke would be unmarried and living in a rear room of the store.

Don had mapped out some characters to be store customers, with gags to suit their personalities. Jim and Marian suggested other characters, based on their ability to do various voices and dialects. With their approval of the basic format, and their added ideas, Don quickly put together a program that the Jordans could audition for the station.

At that stage, Jim chose to make a bit of a detour. WENR had by then become part of NBC. Unlike the station's previous management, the network did not allow performers to have their stage appearances announced on their programs. This was a decided deterrent to the Jordans' efforts to promote themselves to theaters in the listening area. Theater owners knew that many in their audiences were drawn in by the promotional announcements that were made on most stations. For many struggling newcomers, this was their only "payment" for performing on the air.

Rather than offer WENR a program that he felt had real potential, Jim decided to shop it around elsewhere. He found a receptive audience at Chicago's WMAQ. The station management liked the sample script and the concept. They were familiar with Jim and Marian's versatility from having heard them on various programs.

Jim left the station with a contract for a fifteen-minute program to be aired six days a week, Monday through Saturday. The station had no qualms about occasional plugs for the Jordans' personal appearances. Although the program would initially be sustaining, Jim was able to negotiate a 26-week contract, double the usual thirteen weeks for an untested start-up program. The Jordans would be paid $200 a week. Out of that, Don would get $40, a 20% commission the Jordans and Don had agreed upon.

After some initial self-congratulations, the trio's next meeting was spent fine-tuning the format of the program and the characters who would populate it. Jim and Marian suggested some types they knew they could portray. Don tried out others on them, and they selected the ones that worked.

Had his advertising career not been short-circuited, Don Quinn doubtless would have risen to the top there. His fertile imagination and wit soon produced an ample supply of scripts to get the program up and running.

Recognizing that his original proposed title might leave the announcer a bit breathless, he shortened it. It became, simply, *Smackout*. The audience would pick up the meaning quickly.

Jim's character got fleshed out in early programs. In addition to spouting unbelievable stories, he wrote poems and limericks, which he recited for customers in lieu of finding whatever they were shopping for. When alone, he often sang a few lines of "Go Tell Aunt Rhodie the Old Grey Goose is Dead." His conversation included many country cracker expressions: "By Timothy… How in the tunket?… Wouldn't that just cut ye in two and plow ye under?"

In the radio section of newspapers and elsewhere, WMAQ sometimes promoted the program with a picture of Jim as Luke Gray. He sported a gray goatee, wore spectacles, and his wide-brimmed hat had a G.A.R. badge attached.

Luke had a lady friend named Marian who came by the store daily. After being told that he was smack out of whatever she wanted, she would sit down at the piano. (Yes, in the middle of the country store, for reasons never explained, there just happened to be a piano.) With a little introductory riff, she would play and sing some favorite old song. Jim often would join her for a duet, and occasionally she accompanied him on a solo.

One of the frequent visitors to the store was a little girl who lived across the street with her aunt. Voiced by Marian, she came seeking lollypops and had a knack for charming Luke into a free hand-out. She also played piano and sang. In her case, it was such tunes as "Rockin' Horse Parade," "I Got the Mumps" and, near the holidays, "Santa Claus is Coming to Town."

The program premiered on March 2, 1931, and was a hit from the start. The station soon began hearing from listeners with favorable comments. In addition to the store's big Franklin stove and aisles cluttered with unsorted merchandise, there was a Post Office window. Luke began receiving cards and letters from listeners requesting to hear Marian sing favorite tunes.

Don Quinn began creating a host of characters for both Jim and Marian to bring to life. Marian was the well-fixed widow Bedelia Thomas, who aspired to a singing career but had no talent, which she freely demonstrated. Geraldine (no last name) was an oversize lady, giddy and gabby. When she needed something badly enough, Mrs. J. Highhat Upson, who owned a mansion on a nearby hill, lowered herself to visiting the store. Whatever she was looking for, Luke was "smack out," but during their conversation, he managed to slip in some cracks about her uppity attitude, usually without her catching on. During the show's lifespan, Marian played sixty-nine characters, including a flapper, a Kentucky matron, a Scandinavian and a middle-aged country gal.

In addition to producing and directing the show, Jim also got to play a range of characters concocted by Don Quinn. He was August Carl Pigmeyer, "Augie," a farmer with a heavy German accent. He was a delivery boy, an Irish policeman, an Italian professor, and the dim-witted Perky McSnark, who delivered a sack of mail from the train station each day. In all, Jim portrayed seventy-one characters with such names as Sam Tappit, Lump Murphy, Jorp Cankle and Snipe McFee.

Every voice heard on the show was Jim's or Marian's. In addition, Quinn created about 120 characters never actually heard, but whose personality quirks and misadventures were the subject of conversations between Luke and various customers. Quinn had Luke expounding about woodpeckers trained to tap out Morse code messages and a farmer who developed a hybrid square tomato that fit perfectly on bacon/tomato sandwiches.

Things were going along nicely when, on November 1, 1931, the station was bought by NBC. Once again the rule prohibiting performers' on-air plugs was in effect. It was a bit ironic, but Jim decided they would shrug it off and carry on. They were still able to line up occasional live theater performances, and they drew extra income by performing on a number of other radio programs.

They stuck with the program at WMAQ, and the station was happy to have them. The show never did pick up a sponsor, but because it was so popular the station continued to carry them on a sustaining basis until May, 1933. Network executives then decided the show didn't warrant continuing on an unsponsored basis.

Their decision proved premature. They soon were swamped with letters from listeners insisting that they bring the program back. They did. It resumed on September 25, and continued until August 3, 1935, about four months after the *Fibber McGee* program first aired. The Jordans had by then chalked up 948 broadcasts.

A Little Sidebar: On April 26, 1931, long-time friends Chester Lauck and Norris Goff premiered their creation *Lum and Abner* on station KTHS in Hot Springs, Arkansas. The story revolved around the two owners' operation of the Jot-Em-Down store in the fictional town of Pine Ridge, Arkansas, modeled on their actual home town of Waters.

The two were more countrified than Luke Gray, to the point of qualifying as what was then called hillbillies. Many episodes involved them getting drawn into some get-rich-quick scheme by the fast-talking Squire Skimp. Things never went as planned, and they would then come close to losing the store before being saved by some serendipitous stroke of luck.

In the midst of these and other misadventures, numerous colorful locals stopped in to shop at the store. Their visits were the occasion for exchanges of down home humor. Like the Jordans, Lauck and Goff between them portrayed all of the characters who appeared on the show, though not nearly as many.

The program proved so popular that it soon had Quaker Oats as a sponsor and was picked up by NBC. It began as a daily fifteen-minute serialized comedy/soap, and later was heard weekly with stories that fit into a half-hour format. It spawned no less than seven feature films, with Lauck and Goff playing the lead characters.

Coming on the air just eight weeks after the first *Smackout* program, one might suspect that Lauck and Goff were inspired by the latter. In fact, however, they had for some time been doing a comedy dialect routine together at local events. When they expanded the idea and found their way onto the airwaves, their homespun humor was an instant hit.

With a few blips in their scheduling, *Lum and Abner* remained on the air until 1954, long after television had dealt a death knell to most radio drama. The town of Waters had its name officially changed to Pine Ridge.

In 1935, something wonderful happened. S. C. Johnson & Sons, better known as the Johnson Wax Company, brought out a new auto wax product dubbed Car-Nu. That's not the wonderful thing that happened, but it was the seed.

The company wanted to introduce its product in a big way to promote sales to car owners nationwide. In addition to print advertising, they sought a radio program on which to vocalize the benefits of Car-Nu in keeping those cars looking bright and new.

Johnson had sponsored a musical program on NBC for awhile, so they asked the network what they had available. A dozen or more programs were auditioned for them, but none of them was deemed suitable by the Johnson folk. *Smackout* was never suggested.

Jack Lewis, a partner in the Needham, Louis and Brorby Advertising Agency, handled advertising for Johnson. He also happened to be married to the former Henrietta Johnson, daughter of H. F. Johnson, who was the head of the family company.

Jack had been listening to numerous radio programs, hoping to find one that would work for the Johnsons. Nothing he'd heard thus far had seemed right. His wife, meanwhile, was a devoted listener to *Smackout*. She encouraged Jack to tune in to the clever couple who did that show. He did.

The *Smackout* format wasn't what the Johnson Wax Company was looking for. It would be difficult to promote their product at a store where the owner was always "smack out" of everything. Yet Jack quickly recognized the appeal of the couple doing the show, and he agreed with his wife that they had potential.

A meeting was arranged at the Johnson headquarters in Racine, Wisconsin.

Based upon what Jack Lewis told them when he called, the Jordans and Don Quinn put together a comedy sketch that incorporated a dozen or more characters, all voiced by Jim and Marian.

In a conference room at the headquarters, they stood before Jack and several S. C. Johnson reps and performed. There was plentiful laughter among their small audience. When they were done, there was some back-and-forth among Jack and the others. Then, speaking for the group, Jack said that they felt this was what they were looking for.

Everyone then moved to a large conference table and got seated. Jack began by explaining that the Johnson people wanted Jim and Marian to play a married couple. That certainly wasn't a problem for them.

Next came the question of a format that would facilitate the maximum potential to promote Car-Nu. That was an easy one for Don Quinn. He proposed that Jim and Marian would be a couple touring the country by car. Along the way, they would meet a number of interesting people with whom to interact, just as Luke did on *Smackout*. He got a "yes" vote all around. Details would need to be worked out, but the basis for the program was already in place. There were hand shakes all around, and another meeting was set for two days later.

Jack began that meeting by noting that the Johnson company would want to have the last say over the story content, as well as the commercials. Jim and Marian agreed, while noting that it was never their practice to use any risqué material. Don simply observed that he and the Jordans had a pretty good fix on what would get a laugh and what wouldn't, and being second guessed would be a deterrent. Jack assured him that Johnson didn't intent to exercise that kind of control.

They moved on to further discussion of the show's format. Jack said that the Johnson people liked the idea of Luke Gray's far-fetched story telling. To make the most of that, they felt that the husband's name should reflect this trait. In the discussion that followed, Jim, Marian, Jack and the Johnson reps took turns tossing out names that might work. Some were too silly. Others had possibilities, but none seemed to be quite what they were looking for.

Meanwhile, Don Quinn sat quietly doodling on a piece of paper.

When there was a pause in the back-and-forth, he pushed the paper across the table to Jack Lewis. Jack looked at it, grinned and passed it along to the Johnson people. They took turns smiling and nodding their agreement.

Then they passed the paper to the Jordans. Jim and Marian looked and saw that Don had drawn a curlicue flower design all around the edges of the paper. In the center, using an advertiser's fancy printing, he had written "Fibber McGee."

No further discussion was needed on that issue. As they moved on to a name for Marian, the Jordans glanced at one another and said that they already had that covered.

When they were working together on *The Smith Family*, they had always thought that Nora was not the right name for the chief character. In discussing other possibilities, they agreed that a better name would have been Molly. They tucked that name away, agreeing that if Marian ever took on the role of an Irish woman in some future program, they would want her to be named Molly.

No lengthy discussion was required on this issue. Everyone agreed that the name worked perfectly with the surname McGee.

Next came a name for the program. The custom at the time was that the sponsor's name was coupled with the name of the star(s) in the show's introduction. Thus, a popular program sponsored by Maxwell House, for instance, had the announcer declaring: "It's *Maxwell House Coffee Time*, with George Burns and Gracie Allen!"

Jack suggested that the program probably would open with something like "*The Johnson Car-Nu Show*, with Fibber and Molly McGee." The Jordans demurred. Based on their vaudeville experience, they said their characters should be introduced as Fibber McGee and Molly. It was an accepted style on the stage, and the phrasing had a smoother flow when spoken aloud. All agreed.

A few more details would have to be worked out, but Jack said they were close enough to talk contract. S. C. Johnson was prepared to offer Jim and Marian a thirteen-week contract at $250 a week. Recognizing that Don's writing would be a key ingredient of the program, they would offer him a separate contract.

The figure mentioned was only $50 more than the Jordans were being paid for *Smackout*, but they would not have to deduct a percentage for Don. It was a reasonable offer for a show yet to be developed. Jim said they would accept, but with one provision. The contract should be for twenty-six weeks.

He and Marian had covered this territory previously when they were putting together the *Smackout* program. A practice had developed of scheduling radio programs in thirteen-week segments. Four segments would thus fill a year, and the pattern made it easier to block in replacement programs when a show was cancelled. New shows usually were plugged in for thirteen weeks to test audience response and sometimes pulled even sooner if they proved to be duds.

Jim explained that he and Marian felt their program should have the longer time frame in order to develop and prove itself and to gather up a regular listener base. Jack looked to the Johnson reps, who all nodded their agreement. The group adjourned for lunch. When they returned, the contracts were ready and were signed by all parties.

No one knew it at the time, but for the Jordans, Don Quinn, the Johnson Wax Company and millions of radio listeners, something wonderful happened that day.

An initial broadcast for the new program was tentatively scheduled for April of the next year. In the weeks that followed, Don began working on scripts so that there would be several ready when the program went on the air. The show would air only once a week for a half hour, which meant it would require less scripting than *Smackout*. Yet it presented several challenges.

Each week's program would encapsulate an episode with a beginning and an ending. There would be musical interludes. Time had to be allowed for openings, closings and commercials. Don managed to work out these details while still producing *Smackout* scripts for the Jordans.

When they had free time, Jim and Marian met with Don to go over what he had scripted. Reading scripts aloud, they worked out voices for various characters he created for the McGees to meet along the road. In the process, the trio shucked some gags, revised others and modified some characters.

The holidays were especially joyful for Jim and Marian in 1934, as they celebrated with family and contemplated a trip to New York. Perhaps because S. C. Johnson & Co. was working with NBC to be sure that there was abundant ballyhoo for the new program, it was decided that they would broadcast from the New York City station with a live audience.

In April, 1935, the Jordans boarded a train in Chicago's Union Station and sat up the entire night, too excited to sleep. Despite having spent much time in Chicago, they were awed to find themselves in "the big apple." True to their frugal small town roots, they rented a light housekeeping apartment with kitchenette near the station. Don Quinn followed them to town and rented an apartment a few blocks away.

The premiere of *Fibber McGee and Molly* took place in Studio 8-H of the NBC building on April 16, 1935. Before the show, Chester Lauck and Norris Goff, a.k.a. Lum and Abner, stopped by to wish the Jordans well. As the studio audience was being seated, they spotted the familiar faces of George Burns and Gracie Allen. They were thrilled that radio's popular couple had come to see their show.

It was the custom at that time for performers with a studio audience to dress for their parts. Marian and Jim drew from their vaudeville wardrobe for their attire. She wore a sack-like dress with a flowered print. On her head was a kettle-shaped black hat with a feather poking up at an odd angle. Jim wore spectacles, a battered straw hat and a one-button striped suit. Lest there be any doubt that he was a bit of a rube, his feet were encased in a pair of orange shoes.

As the studio clock's second hand reached the straight-up position, the "On Air" signs lit up and announcer Harlow Wilcox enthusiastically proclaimed: "*The Johnson Wax Program*, with Fibber McGee and Molly!" The studio orchestra, conducted by Rico Marcelli, began to play the theme music, "Save Your Sorrow for Tomorrow." A perky tune, it dated back to 1925, but those in the audience who remembered it would recognize its appropriateness in these hard times.

After a few bars, the men in the control room reduced the volume for the radio audience while Wilcox gave the first Johnson's Car-Nu commercial. When he was done, they brought the volume up again and signaled Conductor Marcelli, who then found an appropriate place for the orchestra to end the theme with a little riff. Harlow then set the scene for the arrival of the show's stars.

Don Quinn provided Harlow with a mellifluously mischievous flow of words that became a pleasant pattern for introductions on subsequent programs. On that premiere broadcast, Fibber was introduced as "that ambulating Ananias, that humbug of the highways." Molly was more affectionately identified as "his constant companion and severest critic." She lived up to the latter nomenclature by at times calling him up short with a harsh, "McGee!"

In subsequent shows, as audiences got to know them, Harlow would happily describe them as: "…your fugitives from formality, your flivving, four-cylinder philosophers..." and "...those gay and garrulous gadders, those gasoline gondoliers..." or "...that dippy, dizzy, duo, those distinctive destroyers of dullness...FIBBER MCGEE AND MOLLY!"

As planned, the introductory broadcast found Fibber and Molly on the road in their beat-up old flivver. They began their journey on U.S. Highway 79. Don Quinn may have selected that route because it ran on a diagonal from Russellville, Kentucky, down to Round Rock, Texas, at an intersection with Interstate 35 just north of Austin, Texas. That would take the McGees through a lot of rural areas and small towns where they could meet up with some "plain folk" like themselves.

Along the way, they occasionally stopped to ask for directions. That afforded an opportunity to mention the names of towns along their route, thus drawing in portions of their listening audience who lived in or near those towns. It also enabled them to encounter the many characters that Don Quinn would create for them.

About midway in each program, there would be a stop at a filling station. The attendant filling their tank would be Harlow Wilcox, who invariably would find a way to turn their conversation into an enthusiastic endorsement of using Johnson's Car-Nu to keep cars—even theirs—shining like new.

A musical interlude featured a comedy vocal duo known as Ronnie and Van. As the McGees continued on the road, Quinn worked in a duet by the McGees, with the jalopy motor puttering in the background. The song, "Flossie Farmer, the Snake Charmer," was aptly suited to their slightly rustic personalities. Don also had Fibber spouting a monolog about "When the red light is a dead light."

Early programs included about as much music as comedy. Don allowed spots in the script for either Jim or Marian to do a solo number, often a comic one. From time to time they did a duet. In September, they allowed young Jimmy and Kay to make a rare appearance and perform a duet together.

Sound effects played a key role in radio dramas and comedies. Don Quinn put them to good use with the McGees. When Fibber started up their jalopy, it gave out a reluctant sputtering serenade not unlike the sound of Jack Benny's beloved and much joked-about Maxwell.

The vehicle's rickety condition, illustrated by a variety of sound effects, gave Fibber opportunities to comment in his imaginative style. "Them brakes," he once told Molly, "are tighter than a forty-dollar girdle after a spaghetti dinner." When he applied the brakes, they complained with a prolonged screech. This would prompt McGee to mutter, "Gotta get those brakes fixed one of these days." It would not happen during the course of their journey, but it was a precursor to the utterance he later would frequently repeat about the infamous hall closet.

The laughs came at the right places. The reviews were mostly favorable. One referred to Fibber as a sort of Irish version of the popular Baron Munchausen. Those that found fault here and there were nonetheless mostly positive about the two stars.

Comments about Fibber's rube characterization prompted Quinn to ease up a bit on subsequent programs. He gradually had McGee become a more average small town fellow who was prone to spouting obviously preposterous claims about his talents and accomplishments, interspersed with tall tales on other subjects. Molly was, from the start, the loving and a bit smarter wife who knew her spouse's limitations all too well. She would allow him to stray just so far from the truth before cutting him short with a gentle recollection of reality; or sometimes not so gentle.

In mid-May, the Jordans returned home and the program began

airing from Chicago station WMAQ on May 14. Rico Marcelli and his orchestra came along initially. About a year later, the Ted Weems orchestra took over. Weems brought along a soft-spoken but personable young singer named Perry Como, who got some of his best early exposure on the McGee show. A female vocalist named Marvel Maxwell sometimes sang in place of, or in addition to, Perry. She went on to a successful singing and acting career after she changed her first name to Marilyn.

The show was not an instant hit, but NBC soon began receiving favorable mail. Initially, much of it was from rural areas. Listeners there no doubt appreciated Jim's overdone personification of the country bumpkin. As Don Quinn molded him into a more average fellow, albeit a boastful one, more letters began coming in from small town folk as well as those from the more sophisticated big cities.

Before the Jordans' six-month trial period was up, the S. C. Johnson Company offered to extend their contract. They also proposed a change in the show's format.

Initial sales of Car-Nu had been gratifying, and grew more so in tandem with increased listener response to *Fibber McGee and Molly*. The company now wished to focus commercials on their line of furniture, woodwork and floor wax products. Though it was never specifically stated, it was assumed from the beginning that the McGees had no permanent residence. Two comical nomads roaming the country in a well-polished but beat-up car were not especially conducive to the Johnson company's objective.

A change of venue was in order. Don Quinn to the rescue.

On August 26, 1935, the McGees found themselves in the picturesque little town of Wistful Vista. As part of a sales promotion, The Hagglemeyer Realty Development Company was conducting a raffle for one of its homes. For two dollars, Fibber bought a raffle ticket, mainly because purchasers were treated to a free lunch. He was not enthused about his ticket number: 131,313.

The McGees loitered around town, prepared to depart as soon as the drawing was over. This provided an opportunity for them to mingle and engage in comic conversations with a couple of the locals. As the winning number was drawn, they prepared to head for their car. Then the number was read aloud, and they were stopped in their tracks, as Fibber frantically searched his pockets for the ticket. It appeared that they would be lingering a bit longer, because Fibber's seemingly unlucky number was the winner.

Voila! The McGees were homeowners!

The McGees' new two-dollar home apparently was located on the main street of Wistful Vista, for the street also bore that name. It was never identified as a street, road, boulevard or whatever. Whenever mentioned in subsequent programs, it was simply identified as the house at 79 Wistful Vista. In his opening introductions, Harlow Wilcox would typically describe the scene and conclude by saying. "…as we look in at 79 Wistful Vista, home of…FIBBER MCGEE AND MOLLY!"

The pattern for the program, established in the early on-the-road shows, underwent a little modification. Henceforth, episodes almost invariably consisted of three acts. Harlow's initial declaration of the show that was about to start was followed by a few bars of the theme song, which faded for his first commercial. After that a few bars preceded his introductory description of the scene in the McGees' living room and Act 1 began.

Some gag line ended the act. The resident vocalist would then do the first musical interlude. As the orchestra struck up the opening bars, Harlow would speak over it and say, "Perry Como (or whoever) sings…." As the applause faded after the vocal piece, we would be back with the McGees for Act 2.

That, too, ended with a gag that preceded the orchestra starting up again and Harlow saying, "Rico Marcelli and his orchestra play…" When the instrumental interlude ended, Harlow did another commercial. At it's conclusion, a short musical bridge took us back to the McGees for Act 3.

Another musical bridge at the end of Act 3, usually accompanied by audience applause, preceded Harlow's third plug for the sponsor. Then Fibber and Molly returned for a very short curtain call. In a sort of philosophical manner, they would exchange one or two more comic remarks that summarized whatever nonsense had transpired. This usually involved Fibber confessing to some foolishness and being forgiven by Molly. He then would simply say, "Good night." Molly always had the last word: "Good night, all." It became a trademark closing for the show.

Theme music up, and Harlow would give an abridged plug for another wax product not previously mentioned, or perhaps an invitation to stay tuned to listen to whatever program was to follow.

Don Quinn smoothly transposed the show's format to fit the McGees' new at-home lives. A string of visitors produced the back-and-forth that provided a broad palette of comical palaver. In their traveling days, Jim and Marian provided many of the voices for the characters that Fibber and Molly encountered. Occasionally, some would be played by actors who were regulars on other programs at the station.

In their providentially provided new dwelling, the McGees now began to be visited by an amusing assortment of local residents. Two of their first regular supporting players were Isabel Randolph and Bill Thompson.

Isabel Randolph popped in on January 13 as the first of several snooty society matrons, all of whom lived "up on the hill." Presumably that was the rich folks' part of town. Perhaps just for the fun of renaming her, Don Quinn had her revisit periodically as Mrs. Dillingham-Skunkls (usually addressed by McGee as "Dilly"), Mrs. J. Mitchell-Twitchell, Mrs. J. Waldemar Loganberry, Mrs. J. Uppingham Upson and others.

She came into her own in October, 1938, when Quinn renamed her Mrs. Abigail Uppington. That name stuck for the duration of her visits, perhaps because Don and Jim enjoyed having McGee address her as "Uppy." Her imperious use of a lorgnette led Fibber to remark that her nose was so out of joint that she had to carry her glasses on a stick. When she proudly described herself as a member of the upper crust, McGee observed that said group was defined as "a bunch of crumbs, held together by dough."

The mild mannered Molly occasionally surprised the audience and Fibber by tossing in an observant one-liner. Of Uppy, she once remarked, "Abigail just rang up another no-sale on her social register."

Over time, it developed that Uppy's background might be less highbrow than she claimed. During one visit, she let slip that she had once worked in a laundry. It was later revealed that she had been a bareback rider in a traveling circus. The wealthy Mr. Uppington proposed after she was one day thrown from her horse into his lap.

In addition to his comedic skills, Bill Thompson had a marvelous talent for doing dialects. In 1934, when he was just twenty-one, he won a talent contest at Chicago's "Century of Progress" World's

Fair by performing a comic sketch in which he portrayed ten different characters with assorted dialects.

On January 27, 1936, he paid his first visit to the McGees as a cheery fellow named Nick Porkenhoppolis. In a very heavy Greek accent, his first words were, "Allo keeds!" In their conversation, he immediately took to calling Fibber "Fizzer" and addressing Mollie as "Kewpie" (presumably a mangled version of "Cutie"). In later programs, when neighbor Gildersleeve appeared, Nick called him "Mr. Gilderpuss."

In intermittent appearances, Nick's name changed, without explanation, to Nick DeMopolis and later to Nick DePopolous, who became a long-running favorite.

In exchanges between Fibber and Nick, it often was Fibber who played the straight man.

Nick: I am lending myself some friction from the Public Strawberry.

Fibber: Library...

Nick: Sure.... This story I am reading to me now is entitled to be calling itself Little Red Robin Hood.

Fibber: Whatcha mean? Little Red Riding Hood or Robin Hood? That's two different books.

Nick: No, Fizzer, it is being only one book. But I am making an allowance for you being an ignoramipuss about literacy. I am being an awful book snake myself.

With the McGees settled in their new dwelling, Don Quinn and Jim conspired on developing the flaws in Fibber's character that continually got him into trouble. On the other side of the coin, Molly would earn the audience's love for putting up with him and even sticking up for him when necessary.

For starters, Fibber was convinced that he could handle anything around the home that needed fixing. Molly, who knew her spouse perhaps better than he knew himself, would try to dissuade him, always to no avail. Thus he would attempt to repair a leaky faucet and flood their basement, fall off a ladder and pull the sagging blinds down with him, or patch up their front sidewalk, only to get his feet stuck in the quick-drying cement. He once attempted to drill for oil in their back yard.

The long-suffering but patient Molly never called Fibber by name. She would address him as "Dearie," or, when taking him to task, "McGee!" When visitors dropped in as Fibber was attempting his repairs, she would explain, "Himself here thinks he's a plumber." Or an electrician, or a piano tuner, or whatever.

A Fibber McGee cast photo, circa 1940; from left, The King's Men quartet, orchestra leader Billy Mills, Jim and Marian Jordan, Harold Peary, Bill Thompson, Isabel Randolph, announcer Harlow Wilcox.
CREDIT: Nostalgia Digest collection

For his part, Fibber inevitably would become frustrated with the task at hand, but never acknowledge that his fumbling efforts were the problem. Instead, putting the blame on the object being repaired, he would begin what became his patented line of pseudo cussing: "Dat rat the dat-ratted— "

That would prompt Molly to cut him off with a harsh, "McGee!" Then in a shame-faced voice, he would say, "Sorry, Molly."

Regardless of the subject, he had a penchant for taking the opposite view of whatever various visitors espoused. This occasioned the many laughable arguments between "Himself," and several verbal sparring partners. Molly acted as referee, hushing and chastising them if they got too rowdy.

As his name implied, Fibber also was prone to stretching the truth or sundering it completely, especially when expounding upon his own abilities and past exploits. In his imagined illustrious past, he claimed to have been the West's greater bronco buster, a wrestler known as the Mad Mauler of Muncie, the pilot of a stratosphere balloon, and the renowned deep sea diver Mudbank McGee. A comment about some enterprise or activity was apt to prompt an alliterative oration prepared for him by Don Quinn.

Recalling his youthful pugilistic career: "Punch-Bowl McGee, I was known as in those days. Pronounced by press and public as the Pugilistic Pixie of the pedigreed paper-weight pugs, pummeling pudgy palookas, pulverizing proboscises and paralyzing plug-uglies. Pounding poor preliminary pork and beaners to the pulp with a peppy pip of a pop. Positively a peach of a punch that plunked the punks on their piazzas. Ping-Pong Poppa of the pineapple punch, a peculiar poke that petrified the pit of the paunch of the pillow pushers who plopped to the platform, too pop-eyed to protest!"

Or: "I was the top tin can designer for the Town Talk Tuna Company, and I turned out tuna tins by the ton. I had a type of tin in two tones of tan that was the talk of the tuna trade, but one tan turned two tones too tawny, so I had to tone down the tawny tan and tone up the other tan so the tuna tin I turned out was the finest two-tone tuna tin in town. I used tons of tan, and tens of tons of tin, in turning out the toniest two-tone tan tuna tin they ever tinned tuna in. Kept me pretty busy turning out tons of tuna in the tan and tawny tins."

In a sort of sing-song voice, Jim spouted these nonsensical fantasies at a measured pace that avoided verbal stumbles. Midway through, he often took in a quick breath for effect. When he reached the end, he would, with a note of triumph, take a deep gulp of air, as if he hadn't been sure he was going to make it.

The audience usually breathed a sigh of relief along with him as they added applause to their laughter.

Molly often could be heard chuckling during Fibber's fantasy discourse. She never interrupted him, but from time to time would remind him that she knew full well it was all baloney.

Molly: The trouble with you, dearie, is that your memory is too good.

Fibber: How is that, Molly?

Molly: You remember things that never happened.

Nevertheless, Fibber's dissertations were popular enough that Don Quinn wrote many of them into the scripts. To insure that he got them right, Jim would practice them at home while balancing a loaded laundry basket on his head. It apparently was an effective trick. Only once did his tongue go astray in a tale about his days in a bakery.

Two thirds of the way through the routine, McGee was saying "… my batter baked better because I beat my batter on a platter, which made a better batter, scattered the batter, sputtered the butter, buttered the platter, splattered the platter…" At this point, his tongue slipped, and what came out was "splattered the bladder…"

Jim hesitated but a moment, then quickly got his tongue untied and carried on to the conclusion. But not before the audience, cast and crew were convulsed with laughter that almost drowned him out as he bravely continued to the end.

Thereafter, Don Quinn was careful to avoid using word combinations that might cause embarrassment if Fibber flubbed.

In the beginning, the McGees did not have a doorbell on their home. While they engaged in a humorous husband/wife exchange, a visitor would knock at the front door. Neither Fibber nor Molly would go to open it. One of them would simply call out: "Come in." The sound effects man would produce the sound of the door opening and closing as the visitor entered and greeted them.

The McGees apparently had been settled in their new home for awhile when we first found them there. Visitors never came to the door and said, "Hi, I'm So-and-So from down the street. Welcome to the block." They all apparently had done that by the time we first met them. When one of them walked into the living room, either Molly or Fibber would say, for the benefit of the audience, "Oh, it's Mister (or Missus) Whoever."

Improving on Harlow Wilcox's previous role as a service station attendant, Don Quinn soon had him popping in as one of the McGees' regular visitors. His visit, of course, provided an opportunity for the mid-point commercial.

No matter what the current goings-on at the McGee house, something in the conversation would remind Wilcox of the shine on a floor polished with Johnson's Glo-Coat. If need be, Molly would feed him a line. Fibber would groan at what he knew was coming.

Molly: Mr. Wilcox, why do you have such a bright shine on your face?

Fibber: Oh, Kiddo, now you've gone and done it.

Wilcox: That bright shine on my face, Molly, is a reflection of the perfect job I get every time I apply Johnson's Self-Polishing Glo-Coat to my hardwood floors!

In his mellow, ebullient voice, Harlow would enthuse about "the ease and satisfaction that housewives enjoy when they use Johnson's Self-Polishing Glo-Coat. There's no rubbing, no buffing. Just apply, and let dry."

As Wilcox continued, Fibber would interject little moaning asides to express his misery: "Oh, my goodness!" or "Good grief!"

Wilcox enjoyed the routine so much that he seldom could hold back a chuckle as he launched into his spiel. Thanks to Don Quinn's writing, his pitch was always soft-sell and good humored. The device itself became a source of aside jokes by Fibber: "What do you want, Wilcox? Though as the fellow said when he sat on a bee, I have a deep-seated suspicion."

Harlow once stopped by to pick up Fibber for an Elks Club meeting. Unbeknownst to Molly, the "meeting" was to be a card game.

When he got his opening, Harlow said, "Next time your have a *full house* over for a party, give your kitchen linoleum a *new deal* with Johnson's Self Polishing Glo-Coat. Enjoy that *royal flush* of pride you'll get from a clean, sparkling kitchen floor. See how easily spots and footprints wipe right off a Glo-Coated linoleum with a surface wax-sealed against dust and dirt. If you spill something from a *trey*, it can't raise the *deuce* with your linoleum because Glo-Coat is *aces* in protection. Get a container of Johnson's Self Polishing Glo-Coat today! It's your *dealer's choice!*"

Wilcox clearly was enjoying himself, and Molly *raised the ante* as she *bluffed* her way through half-muffled laughter.

On one program, after Harlow departed, Fibber told Molly, "Ol' Wilcox thinks the Seven Wonders of the World are the pyramids, the Hanging Gardens and five cans of Glo-Coat."

Harlow's devotion to the source of his salary led Fibber to dub him "Waxy."

For his part, Wilcox always addressed Molly as "Molly," but, like almost all of the McGees' visitors, he did not call her hubby "Fibber." Most often he addressed him as "Pal." In the show's opening introductions, he did refer to the stars as Fibber and Molly, although Don Quinn often had him use such references as "the squire of 79 Wistful Vista."

After its somewhat lukewarm initial reviews, the show began to take on a Glo-Coat shine. Its growing popularity and its low-key commercials were having the effect S. C. Johnson & Co. hoped for. A nationwide survey in December, 1936, had dealers reporting sales increases ranging from 30 to 50 percent on various Johnson polishes. A separate survey of homeowners in a selected city of 150,000 population indicated a 20 percent increase of various household polishes on their shelves. The same survey found Johnson's auto wax products in twice as many homes as in 1935.

The Johnson folk were quite pleased. When the Jordans reviewed the survey results with them, they succeeded in negotiating an increase in their salary to $2,650 per program.

That made for a substantial income in Depression-era dollars. They might not actually qualify as wealthy, but they were now comfortably well off. They took a giant step forward and purchased a lot in the Peterson Woods area of Chicago's Northwest Side. There they built a modest-sized but comfortable home. They were now bono fide Chicagoans.

It was an easy trip downtown to the station for rehearsals and the broadcasts. They had established a routine that worked well and was maintained with little change for the duration of the program.

On Thursday, they met with Don Quinn, and he outlined his idea for the next week's program. There would be an animated discussion, during which Jim and Marian would make suggestions for additions or changes. Afterward, Don did a rewrite and brought the completed script to the Jordans' home on Sunday afternoon.

Together, they read through the script aloud. Don filled in for the other actors, doing a serviceable job of imitating their vocal characteristics. After more discussing and exchanging of ideas, Don took the script home to make whatever changes were deemed needed.

On Monday morning, the full cast met at the WMAQ studio for a rehearsal. Everyone was free to put out suggestions. Some gags were modified slightly, others added or cut to fill the allotted time. Tuesday morning was a full run-through for timing and any last-minute tweaking, however slight. Then everyone returned to their respective homes to relax and be ready for the evening presentation.

That involved two full performances of the same program. In the early years, NBC and the other networks typically aired evening programs twice so that they could be heard by listeners in each time zone. The first broadcast would be heard in the Eastern, Central and Midwest area. The repeat was usually aired two hours later to reach people in the Pacific Time Zone who might have been still at work or dining during the first broadcast.

As a family man, Jim Jordan placed a great deal of importance on giving everyone some time off between programs. He adhered faithfully to a schedule that allowed for several days of family time each week. Other cast members, apart from performing on other shows, were free for most of the week.

From one coast to the other, *Fibber McGee and Molly* slowly gained more and more regular listeners. In January, 1936, the program had a modest 6.6 rating; by January, 1937, it was up to 13.0. Survey ratings always had a margin of error, but the show had about doubled its audience.

During its eighteen years in a half-hour format, the program enjoyed sixteen years of ratings in the double digits. It exceeded a rating of 20.0 ten times, and was over 30.0 seven times.

With an assist from Don Quinn's writing, Bill Thompson added the razzle dazzle man Horatio K. Boomer to the show's population. Introduced on March 9, 1936, as Mr. Blotto, he was given what Quinn thought was a more apt moniker in September. A con man by nature, Boomer behaved much like the popular film star W. C. Fields, whose on-screen character usually was a flim-flam man.

The characterization and impersonation were so obvious that Fields was well aware of it. When an interviewer asked what he thought about it, Fields replied, "It's damn good!"

After the exchange of a few gags, Boomer's visit usually concluded with him reaching into his seemingly bottomless pockets for something that he wanted to show the McGees. He seldom found what he was digging for, instead pulling out and naming a series of nonsensical items. The search always ended with him saying, "… and … a check for a short beer."

Almost as soon as the McGees moved in, Teeny became a regular visitor. The cute tyke who had charmed Luke Gray at the *Smackout* store had evidently moved to Wistful Vista. Her personality had undergone a change en route. She now was a bit mischievous, with a penchant for getting on McGee's nerves.

She usually was accompanied by her pal Willy Toops. Willy was not heard, however, because he always waited for her out on the sidewalk. Most of her visits included some tale of a recent activity of her own or Willy's or the two of them. She was given to accenting her comments with the phrase "I betcha."

Listeners came to know when Teeny was about to appear, because Molly would say that she had to go check on a pie she was baking or some other errand in another room. As she left, McGee would observe something on the order of: "Ah, there goes a good kid. She knows I ain't never gonna get this lamp fixed, but she'd rather I mess with something that's already broke than— "

At that point would come the knock on the door. When Fibber said, "Come in," the door would open and Teeny would greet him: "Hi, Mister."

Fibber was likely to respond with an unenthusiastic, "Oh, it's you, huh?"

Unoffended, Teeny would reply, "Yep, it's me, I betcha. What cha doin', Mister, huh, what cha?"

Whatever household problem or chore McGee was working on, he would briefly explain to her, which prompted a few gags back and forth. This Teeny was aware that Fibber's name was evocative of his tendency to elaborate upon his own abilities and accomplishments. Her comments would sometimes attest to her being on to him.

Teeny: My mamma, she says to take everything you hand out with a grain of salt.

Fibber: Oh, she did, eh?

Teeny: Sure. She says you can pull more wild yarns than a puppy with a sweater.

After a brief exchange, Teeny would usually start in on one of the excited tales that were her specialty. McGee would make little comments along the way. This invariably was a mistake, because at some point it would cause Teeny to lose her train of thought. He would then be caught up in a losing effort to get her back on track.

Teeny: Yesterday we had a history test 'n' Willy 'n' me did good, I betcha.

Fibber: That's good.

Teeny: Yep, we did all our home work, 'n' so we did good.

Fibber: Doing your home work helped.

Teeny: Yep. Willy and me, we both got a hundred, I betcha.

Fibber: You did, hey?

Teeny: And our teacher... Huh?

Fibber: I said, you did, hey?

Teeny: Who did?

Fibber: You and Willie Toops.

Teeny: Did what?

Fibber: Got a hundred

Teeny: Where?

Fibber: (growing frustrated): In history.

Teeny: When?

Fibber: (voice rising): Yesterday!

Teeny: Why?

Fibber: (now yelling): For doing your home work right.

Teeny: I know it!

The "I' was pronounced in a high, whiny voice, so that Teeny's response came across as a snappy rebuke: "Why're you telling me all this when I already know it?"

The upshot of these encounters usually was that Fibber, desperate to get this kid out of his hair, would say, "Alright. Look, Sis, here's a dime. Why don't you and Willy run down to the soda shop and get yourselves a couple of ice cream cones."

Teeny: Gee, thanks. So long, mister.

Sound: Door opens.

Teeny (moving away, calling out): Hey, Willie! I got it, I betcha.

Audiences loved Teeny, especially once they realized that it was Marian playing the part. They looked forward to her visits and always knew it was about to happen when Molly found a reason to leave Fibber alone in the living room.

Teeny was a staple of the program for its duration. When she had been around for quite some time, Don Quinn had Fibber ask one day how old she was.

Teeny: I'm five, I betcha.

Fibber: How many years have you been visiting us here?

Teeny: Nine. (Pause) Ain't it a wonderful world, mister?

Another early arrival on the show was a fellow who had no name. In March, 1936, the McGees made one of their occasional trips into town. En route they met an old fellow who was hard of hearing. A brief conversation resulted in a few jokes before they continued on their way.

The part was played by Cliff Arquette, who later took on the persona full time and named him Charlie Weaver. In his battered hat and rimless spectacles, he became quite well known as one of the favorite panelists on television's popular comedy/quiz show, *Hollywood Squares*.

After Arquette left the show, Don Quinn brought the character back but took him off the street and made him a visitor at the McGee house. Bill Thompson took on another role as the Old Timer. He dropped in for the first time on November 16 and took to calling Molly "daughter" and Fibber "Johnny."

Not much of his background was ever discussed, although he did once confide that his given name was Rupert Blasingame. Which might account for his not objecting to the McGees always addressing him as "Old Timer." Fibber later shortened that at times to just "O. T."

In his rambling comic discourses, Old Timer often referred to his mama and papa. He also made tender but comical references to his sweetheart, Bessie, whom he met at a wrestling match. Bessie had once been billed as "Meathook Mabel, the Milwaukee Monster."

As time passed, it seemed that half the population of Wistful Vista knew the McGees and would take turns calling on them. Late that year, they even had an off-air visit from a representative of Paramount Pictures.

Hollywood was calling!

In April, 1937, Jim Jr. and Kathryn (Kay) were out of school, or perhaps the Jordans had them excused early. In either case, the family boarded a train at the Chicago station and set off for a scenic ride to sunny California. Don Quinn joined them to help the studio writers in preparing material for the McGees' film debut.

In the so-called "Golden Age of Radio," Hollywood recruited many of the medium's stars, especially the comedians, to appear on the silver screen. The big studios produced hundreds of "B" pictures every year. They recognized that a popular radio star's name on a theater's outside and lobby posters could draw in many patrons who might otherwise pass up the advertised picture.

Fred Allen, Joan Davis, Phil Harris, Ralph Edwards, Henry

Morgan and many other radio personalities on occasion stepped away from the microphone and in front of the camera. In straightforward dramas, the radio personalities usually had supporting roles that diverted briefly from the main story line to infuse a few laughs.

Some of radio's biggest stars were given starring roles, often in films written just for them and transposing their radio personas to the screen. Lum and Abner brought their down home humor to the screen, and audiences got to see what the town of Pine Ridge looked like, including the Jot-Em-Down store. Jack Benny's films *Buck Benny Rides Again* and *The Horn Blows at Midnight* provided endless material for kidding the star on his own and other radio programs.

Singer/comic Eddie Cantor, a vaudeville veteran, had already appeared in several silent feature films and shorts before he first appeared on radio in 1931. He turned down an offer to star in *The Jazz Singer*, which proved to be a star-maker for Al Jolson. Nonetheless, he went on to star or appear in more than two dozen full-length and short films. That he was both a comic and a singer, usually of amusing novelty tunes, made him the more appealing to the film makers and their audiences.

The zany Red Skelton, who created half a dozen loveably goofy characters, was first heard on radio in 1937. In 1938, he appeared in *Having Wonderful Time*, starring Ginger Rogers and Douglas Fairbanks Jr. In a supporting role along with Lucille Ball, billed as Richard "Red" Skelton, he performed his comic demonstration of how different types of persons dunk their donuts. Like Lucille Ball, Red was one of the radio and film comics who later successfully made the transition to television.

In their first film endeavor, Jim and Marian Jordan would not star, but their supporting roles surely helped carry the film. In *This Way*

Please, a movie theater usherette has a crush on a visiting matinee idol played by Charles "Buddy" Rogers. A former vaudeville singer and actor, Rogers became a popular leading man in films. He starred in *Wings*, a silent film that won the Academy Award for Best Picture at the first awards ceremony in 1929.

Not long after the filming, Rogers married one of Hollywood's darlings, actress Mary Pickford. A co-founder of United Artists, Pickford starred in dozens of silent and sound pictures. She was known as "America's sweetheart," and Rogers was often referred to as "America's boyfriend." When they wed, their friend Clark Gable predicted that it wouldn't last a year, because Rogers was eleven years younger than Pickford. Gable was wrong. The couple stayed happily married until she died in 1979.

The usherette in *This Way Please* was played by Betty Grable, the lovely singer and dancer with the legs that became as famous as her face. Grable was then what the Hollywood studios often referred to as a "budding starlet." At RKO and Paramount Pictures, she had had numerous supporting roles, often playing a co-ed. Her billing in *This Way Please* marked the beginning of her star status. In 1940, then under contract with 20th Century-Fox, she starred in *Down Argentine Way* with Don Ameche and Carmen Miranda. For the next decade she was the studio's biggest star, appearing in many Technicolor musicals. During World War II, her popularity with GIs as a pin-up girl gave an added boost to her career. She was the world's top box office draw in 1943, and in 1947 she was America's highest-paid entertainer.

In this illustrious company, Jim and Marian provided comic relief. Dressed in rustic costumes, they reverted back to their *Smackout* personas, or the early on-the-road McGees. They arrived in Hollywood in a beat-up automobile, towing a trailer with a hand-printed sign:

"Hollywood or Bust!" Though not done in costume, Marian got to demonstrate her vocal versatility, using the voices of Teeny and the Widow Wheedledeck, from her *Smackout* days.

Willing to play up his bumpkin role to the limit, Jim agreed to a couple of scenes in which he took prat falls. In one, he tumbled off a stage and fell into the orchestra pit. In a scene reminiscent of the old Harold Lloyd films, he fell out of a window high up in a tall building and was saved by bouncing off of a providentially placed awning.

The filming of *This Way Please* afforded the Jordans the opportunity to make the acquaintance of Mary Livingston, the radio antagonist and off-air wife of Jack Benny. Her experience on the Benny program had prepared her well for her wisecracking supporting role.

While the Jordans were engaged in the filming, *Fibber McGee and Molly* was broadcast from NBC's Hollywood studios over station KFI. Many film celebrities and West Coast radio people attended the broadcasts.

In between the radio programs and filming, the Jordan family spent much of their free time touring the area and sightseeing. They liked what they saw. A seed was planted for a decision that would later bring them back to the area.

Filming was complete in July. The Jordans returned to Chicago and resumed broadcasting from WMAQ on July 12. While on the West Coast, they had spent some time with NBC executives. They came home with a new 52-week contract that boosted their salary to $3,500 per week.

The California adventure had been exciting and fun, but it also had been a busy one. Although buoyed by the movie-making experience and the new contract, the senior Jordans returned home weary. Marian, especially, was extremely tired and experiencing some health problems. The year 1937 had begun well, but a dark cloud was gathering on the horizon.

Early in the Jordans' marriage, Marian had been a social drinker; a cocktail with dinner, a couple of drinks with friends at social events. Somewhere along the way, her drinking increased. It may initially have served to bolster her energy level as she rehearsed and performed on the program while also fulfilling the role of homemaker and mother.

Gradually, however, that changed. Instead of giving her a boost, the alcohol began to drain her of energy. As her physical health diminished, so also did her mental and emotional state. In a progression familiar to all AA members, she had become a problem drinker; i.e., an alcoholic.

This Way Please had its Chicago opening at the luxurious downtown Garrick Theatre on November 18. The Jordans had looked forward to seeing themselves in their first film at a local theater, but Marian was too ill to attend.

At Jim's urging, she visited her family doctor for a check-up. He was alarmed at her condition of near physical exhaustion, as well as her mental and emotional state. He advised the Jordans that she was going to require a prolonged period of complete rest in a facility that specialized in treating her problem. If she continued to appear on the program, which he advised against, she should be there only for the broadcast, and preferably seated.

Many years later, daughter Kay told an interviewer that her mother had been inches away from a complete nervous breakdown. Prior to her diagnosis, as her condition worsened, she had even contemplated suicide.

The Jordans were staggered by the doctor's diagnosis, but they took his recommendation seriously. They immediately began making arrangements to have Marian check herself into a clinic with a reputation for confidentiality and results in helping people with mental, emotional and stress-related problems, including those stemming from alcoholism.

They were warned up front that it could be a long process. Marian could check herself out at any time, but the clinic would not officially release her until they were confident that she was rehabilitated and capable of returning to a normal home life and the rigors of a performing career. For the first time, Marian missed a broadcast.

A brief announcement on the program simply stated that Molly was being treated for extreme fatigue. The vast majority of Fibber and Molly's audience did not even know their real names, and would not have made the connection if some whisper of Marian's illness slipped out.

The cast and crew of *Fibber McGee and Molly* undoubtedly knew what the problem was. Some close friends and radio associates probably did also, but all were discreet.

Marian and announcer Harlow Wilcox had developed a brother/sister closeness. Harlow corresponded with Marian frequently while she was away, which was a great comfort during her confinement.

Fortunately for the Jordans, they did not live in an era of in-your-face media reporting such as we know today. Other than public incidents that would be seen and gossiped about by others, the press generally adhered to a policy that people's private lives were just that, private. Even the very obvious partial paralysis of President Franklyn D. Roosevelt was never discussed in the press. Indeed, the press and newsreel photographers took care to photograph him from the waist up.

Marian's absence nevertheless necessitated some hasty program changes by Don Quinn and Jim. McGee could not be left alone in the house at 79 Wistful Vista. He needed someone with whom to exchange gags and idle talk between visitors.

Enter Silvus Leviticus Deuteronomy Watson, nicknamed "Silly." He became a houseboy for McGee. Molly was away visiting a sister, and the master of the house was no master of housekeeping. Silly took care of that, as well as the cooking and other incidental chores.

Silly Watson was played by a versatile actor named Hugh Studebaker (no relation to the automobile manufacturer). Like Goodman and Jane Ace, Studebaker was a product of station KMBC. After a brief break-in period at a small station in Omaha, he migrated to Kansas City. There he found work playing the organ on one program and acting on several daytime serials. Most were heard only locally, but one was carried on the CBS network.

In 1934, he felt that he had outgrown KMBC, and he decided to try his luck in the Windy City. There he soon was participating in numerous daytime series. He was heard on such popular soap operas as *The Romance of Helen Trent*, *The Road of Life*, *Bachelor's Children*, *The Right to Happiness*, *Backstage Wife* and *The Guiding Light*.

Perhaps just for a change of pace, he joined the cast of the kid's adventure series, *Captain Midnight*. There he became Ichabod "Ikky" Mudd, the chief mechanic and provider of occasional comic relief in the captain's Secret Squadron. Many years later, he was a co-founder of the American Federation of Television and Radio Artists, AFTRA.

During Molly's prolonged absence, the program was renamed *Fibber McGee and Company*. Silly Watson, who was a Southern boy with a pronounced slow drawl, had a few comic exchanges with McGee between visitors. Don had McGee venture outside a bit more often, and some new characters were introduced.

On October 4, another versatile actor joined the cast. Harold Peary was an old friend of the Jordans. They had first met him when he worked with them on *Kaltenmeyer's Kindergarten*, playing a pupil's Italian father. In Peary's first visit with McGee, he was heard as a blustery mayor named Appleby. McGee quickly dubbed him "Applepuss."

Though Appleby clearly was a precursor of the future Mayor LaTrivia, he was quickly sidelined by a series of other characters Peary would play. In personas that often appeared only once, he was a piano salesman, a bombastic retired Army general, a doctor, a lawyer, a veddy British Lord Bingham and the Wistful Vista druggist, Mr. Kremer.

Don Quinn evidently liked the name Gildersleeve. Peary appeared as several men with that surname but a different given name each time. He once was manager of a girdle factory and on another occasion was president of the Gildersleeve Baby Carriage Company. It was some time before he evolved into the long-running character of Throckmorton P. Gildersleeve.

The first night of Marian's absence was a test of Jim's stage presence. Fearful that he might break up at some point, he took a deep breath before his first line and charged ahead. By reminding himself that everyone else was depending upon him, he made it through the half hour. As the program was ending, he leaned in close to the microphone and said softly, "Good night, Molly."

On subsequent shows, he repeated the message or varied it with "Hurry back, Molly." The holidays came and went, with Marian still undergoing treatment. In January, 1938, as Jim continued with his show-ending message, the Federal Communications Commission took note and objected. They advised NBC that there was a rule prohibiting "point to point communication" on regulated stations. With apologies, NBC told Jim that he must desist. He did.

The FCC took some flack from several columnists who chastised their hard-nosed insistence on "the rules." No doubt there were members of the Commission who were fans of Fibber and Molly. After a time they reconsidered. Molly was a fictional character on a radio program; thus Jim was not addressing a real person. Rather, the fictional Fibber was speaking to another off-stage character on the program. A notice was sent to the network rescinding the earlier judgment that the messages were not allowable. On March 15, McGee again ended the program with a soft-spoken, "Good night, Molly."

Years later, Jimmy Durante would end his television programs by stepping back out of a spotlight and saying, "Good night, Mrs. Callabash, wherever you are." Perhaps to avoid a run-in with the FCC, Jimmy never explained whether Mrs. Callabash was a real person or imaginary.

In January, regular listeners may have noted a difference in the music heard on the program. Ted Weems and his band left the show and were replaced by Billy Mills and his orchestra on January 17.

Billy Mills was a talented composer and arranger who got his early start playing the organ in church and the piano in a hometown theater. He served as an Army bandmaster during World War I. After working for a short time as arranger for a band, he formed his own orchestra. By 1932, he was an arranger on the Chicago staff of CBS, where his talent eventually moved him up to the position of General Music Supervisor.

The Billy Mills orchestra was comprised of a nicely balanced mix of wind and string instruments. The former included trumpets, trombones, saxophones, clarinets and flutes. Strings included guitar, viola, cello, three violins and usually two pianos. The composition produced a rich, full sound that made the Mills orchestra stand out among the many that enhanced various radio programs.

Over the years, Billy Mills composed a number of tunes for the program, and he was fond of presenting special arrangements of older or currently popular tunes. With a sense of humor that made him fit well on the program, he led his orchestra in many novelty pieces. Mills later composed a piece called "Wing to Wing," which became the long-time familiar theme music for the *McGee* program

On the May 10 program he featured a young multi-talented drummer named Lindley Armstrong Jones. In addition to his drums, young

Jones played cowbells, slide-whistle and an assortment of other unusual "musical" instruments in a wacky rendition of "Kiss Me Again." The audience loved it. They later came to love Jones as he went on to form his own group known as Spike Jones and His City Slickers.

Perhaps just to keep himself busy during Marian's absence, Jim took on his first solo performance on another show since their *Smackout* days. On January 21, he appeared with Barbara Luddy and Les Tremayne on the popular *First Nighter* program. He was a hard-boiled theatrical agent in a story called "Four-Door Blinky."

In March, there was a landmark change at the National Broadcasting Company. As a result of anti-trust litigation, the network was mandated to divest itself of either the so-called Red Network or its counterpart, the Blue Network. Both were owned and operated by NBC as independent entities with some overlapping programming. When required to choose, NBC retained the Red Network. What had been the Blue Network eventually became the American Broadcasting Company, ABC. The *Fibber McGee* program remained on NBC.

Until the later introduction of "transcribed" (recorded) programs, the majority of programs continued to broadcast two complete shows. The first would be heard by the Eastern and Central time zone listeners; the later show would be heard by those in the Mountain and Pacific time zones.

On March 15, *Fibber McGee and Company,* was broadcast only once, at 8:30 p.m. Central Standard Time. It was a welcome change that lightened the work load for the cast and crew. It meant, however, that Pacific area listeners would have to be tuned in at 6:30 p.m. That decision by the sponsor and NBC indicated their high regard for the program's appeal and its ability to attract faithful listeners.

May was a good month. *Radio Guide* magazine announced the results of its annual "Star of Stars" guide. *Fibber McGee and Molly*, even in its temporary reformat as *Fibber McGee and Company*, ranked third. It still trailed the Jack Benny and Edgar Bergen programs, but was ahead of such other popular stars as Eddie Cantor, Fred Allen and Burns and Allen.

Even more cause for rejoicing, Marian Jordan came home. The clinic doctors deemed that they had done all that they could for her. It was now up to her to return to her normal surroundings and try to move forward. They told Jim that they felt she was ready, but cautioned that her physical health was still fragile. She should exert herself as little as possible and focus on resting and regaining her strength.

As much as she longed to be back on the program, she and Jim agreed that it was best to wait a bit. On June 28, the last program of the season, she made a one-time return. To minimize the physical strain of her appearance, Jim and Don Quinn arranged for her to sit at a folding table and use a small gooseneck microphone. In addition to being Molly again, Marian prevailed upon Don to include a little encounter between Fibber and Teeny. The broadcast tired her some physically, but it also gave a significant boost to her morale.

By mutual consent, the Jordan family focused their summer free time on giving Marian the opportunity to rest and relax. Kay and Jim Jr. were now teenagers and capable of pitching in with many chores while making sure that their mother was as comfortable as possible. Unlike his radio character, Jim was an enthusiastic and handy doer and fixer.

For her part, Marian acknowledged that being relieved of her usual household duties was a work of love. It would hasten the time when she could resume her role as wife and mother.

During the summer, when not finding things to do around the house, Jim spent as much time as possible with Marian, helping her to relax. He used some of that time to discuss an idea that he'd been toying with while she was confined. They both had been impressed with the places they had been able to visit while in Hollywood, and with the beauty of the West Coast area in general. Jim was certain that the climate and fresh air there would be conducive to Marian's recovery and her long-term health. He had only to make the suggestion and Marian agreed that she would very much like to relocate there.

When the program resumed in September, Jim began floating the idea among their regular cast members. Almost all agreed that they'd be happy to tag along. Jim next approached the NBC people and informed them of his plan. They assured him that the program could continue without interruption by moving the broadcast to their Hollywood studios.

Despite her previous one-time appearance on the program, Marian was not yet sufficiently recovered to rejoin the cast. So Don Quinn had Fibber put down his cigar, get up out of his easy chair, and venture outside more regularly.

Since he normally spent most of his time at home with Molly, the source of Fibber's income was a mystery that never was revealed in the long course of the program. However, in a series of adventures that followed, the boastful but usually bumbling McGee tried his hand at a variety of working-man endeavors.

Thanks to Don Quinn's vivid imagination, he became, albeit for very brief periods, a life guard, a football coach, a justice of the peace, a police reporter, an assistant fireman, even the quiz master of a radio program called *So You Think You're Smart, Eh?* Amazingly, he reached the management level at a travel bureau, a riding academy, a hamburger stand, a hotel, *and* the Bijou Theatre! Needless to say, all of these occasional occupations were short-lived. One broadcast, to be exact.

The October 11 broadcast was a milestone. In one of his outings, Fibber bumped into the Old Timer. In their brief chat, Fibber told a rather corny joke that prompted a perhaps merely polite chuckle from the old gent. He then replied in his wheezed voice, "That's pretty good, Johnny. But that ain't the way I heared it. The way I heared it, one feller says t'other feller, say-ay-ay, he sez…." He then proceeded to tell his own joke, which was as corny as McGee's, but funnier. After the laugh, he said, "Well, so long, Johnny" and moved on.

The exchange drew such a good laugh from the audience that Quinn thereafter incorporated a similar exchange in almost every Old Timer visit to the McGee residence. The phrases "That's pretty good, Johnny," and "That ain't the way I heared it," together and separately, were soon to become a frequent part of the general population's conversation.

The holidays were approaching. Marian yearned to rejoin Jim on the program, but they agreed that she still was not quite ready. Jim began coordinating with the cast and the NBC people in anticipation of the planned move out West. On January 24, 1939, *Fibber McGee and Company* made its last broadcast from WMAQ in Chicago.

Bill Thompson, Isabel Randolph and Harold Peary joined the Jordans in their move to a sunnier environment. Announcer Harlow Wilcox and Billy Mills and his orchestra also made the trip.

On the first Tuesday in February, the show aired from NBC's Hollywood studios. Hugh Studebaker had elected to stay in Chicago, so McGee was without his houseboy, Silly Watson. Apart from that, if they had not read about the move somewhere, the listening audience would have noticed no change.

Nevertheless, the network arranged to get some publicity out of the move. The January 28 issue of *Radio Guide* magazine included a comic photograph of Jim. In his "hick" attire, with his thumb out, he stands beside a roadside sign that says "Hollywood -- 2,500 Miles." His beat-up suitcase has the name "Fibber McGee" printed on it in large letters. In anticipation of some fun in the sun, he carries tennis rackets, golf clubs, fishing pole and a large jug labeled "Sun Tan Lotion."

Hal Peary, Isabel Randolph and the multiple voices of Bill Thompson enabled Don Quinn to supply McGee with more than enough characters with whom to spar or trade gags. Local actors occasionally stepped in for random appearances. Being in Hollywood also resulted in guest appearances from numerous film and radio stars. Though they were not credited on the air, most listeners probably recognized the voices of Frank Nelson, Verna Felton, Jim Backus, Mel Blanc, Walter Tetley and others.

Even with Molly's prolonged absence, the program continued to enjoy high ratings. When *Radio Guide* magazine announced its most recent poll, it ranked in fourth place. In April, an arrangement between NBC and the Canadian Broadcasting System enabled twenty-seven Canadian stations to tune in. The show's humor may have been lost on some French Canadian listeners, but the response from others was gratifying.

Meanwhile, continued rest, and perhaps the California climate, were having a beneficial effect on Marian's health. Her new California doctor agreed that she was much improved. Summoning the confidence to make her announcement, she told Jim that she was ready to return to the program. It took a bit of reassuring, but Jim agreed. He trusted her judgment, and sensed that if she felt up to it, being back on the show would add a mental boost to her physical recovery.

Jim informed Don Quinn. Don had the next show's script almost written, but he enthusiastically rehashed it to include Marian. Meanwhile, Jim spread the word to the rest of the cast and crew.

On April 18, the program was again introduced as *Fibber McGee and Molly.*

Before the broadcast, Marian was greeted with a "Welcome Back" that overwhelmed her. The walls of the NBC studio were all but covered by a high bank of flowers. A nearby table was covered with telegrams from friends who had been told of her return. They all welcomed her back, wished her well, and promised to be listening.

Marian was moved to tears. She composed herself as air time approached. In the pre-program time, when the cast gathered on stage, she was again greeted by a hearty burst of applause as the audience realized that "Molly" was back.

The program went well. By mutual consent, Marian and Jim did not linger to celebrate afterward. Rather, they went home straightaway lest she become weary. Although she acknowledged being tired, Marian felt it was from the anticipation beforehand and the excitement of again being a part of the program.

Thereafter, Marian resumed appearing on a regular basis. At Jim's insistence, she continued to sit at rehearsals and broadcasts. She gradually became less easily tired and assured him that being there was good for her recovery.

Once again Molly sat across from Fibber in the living room at 79 Wistful Vista. Ever the patient, loving wife, she chastised him when his temper flared and allowed his overblown narratives to go just so far before shooting him down.

Listeners around the country wrote to NBC to express their pleasure at having her back. Many also noted that they enjoyed the return of Teeny and the visits in which she left Fibber's nerves frazzled.

When they made the move to California, the Jordan's were fortunate to find and rent a house that was a modest size but adequate.

Having decided that this was to be a permanent relocation, they kept their eyes out for something that would be right for them to own.

In May, Jim and Marian took a Sunday drive through the San Fernando Valley area of Los Angeles. In the little community of Encino, they spied a house on Rancho Street. It was a Monterey style, painted white, with a large, beautiful garden. Posted out front was a "For Sale" sign.

Jim slowed the car and looked over at Marian. She was beaming. "Look, Jim!" she exclaimed. "It's our dream house!"

The lovely house was the centerpiece of a lot that covered almost three acres. Scattered throughout were fruit and nut trees, berries and grapes. In the rear, a little bridge spanned a narrow creek. Beyond it was a smaller building that housed a corner fireplace, a miniature kitchen, a game room and a fully equipped workshop.

In the main house, all the first floor rooms opened onto a terrace that stretched across the entire rear. Upstairs, all the bedrooms opened onto a long balcony in front. It was a setting that would offer fresh countryside breezes and the opportunity to soak up much of the good California sunshine.

One survey of the property was all it took to convince the Jordans that their next stop was the real estate office. A week later, it was theirs.

Unlike his fumble-fingered radio persona, Jim was skilled with tools and an enthusiastic handyman. He referred to the workshop as his "temple of sawdust." He soon had a large barbeque pit built under a tall oak tree in the rear. Many of the program's cast and crew settled in Encino or not far from the Jordans' new residence. Before long, Jim and Marian were having them over for barbeque picnics.

Marian's health continued to improve. When the show resumed in the Fall, she was again a regular participant and feeling much more like her old self. It was good that Molly was back on the scene, because the McGees soon had another frequent visitor with whom Fibber was continually at odds. Molly served as the intermediary, calming things down when their verbal contests grew heated.

On October 17, 1939, Harold Peary appeared for the first time as the McGee's next door neighbor Thockmorton P. Gildersleeve. "Gildy," as Fibber soon nicknamed him, had a bit of a superiority complex, which made him a natural foe of the boastful McGee. He often spoke with pride of his Great Dane, Hamlet. Fibber observed that "a Great Dane is a dog who has the house broken before he is."

Peary, who had a fine singing voice, also had a marvelous laugh that could run up and down the scale. He used it to project multiple emotions: irritation, surprise, worry, genuine amusement and, in his verbal bouts with Fibber, contempt. Their conflicting personalities led Gildersleeve and McGee to disagree on just about everything, regardless of how unimportant the topic.

Molly avoided getting into their debates, simply uttering an occasional "Dear, dear," or "Oh, my," from the sidelines. When an argument reached fever pitch, she would intervene with a chastising, "Boys, boys!" That would cause them both to take a deep breath and apologize to Molly, not to each other.

Fibber usually aimed one last wisecrack at Gildersleeve to make clear that his opinion, whatever the disagreement, was unchanged. Gildy would then respond, "Oh, you're a ha-aa-rr-rd man, McGee." It became one of many phrases that were repeated often on the program and usually prompted some audience laughter.

The soft-spoken Molly had two expressions that were uniquely her own. In the heat of Fibber's arguments, or while listening to one of their visitors recount some outrageous tale, she was wont to exclaim, "Heavenly days!" On other occasions, when subjected to a pitiful effort by Fibber to get a laugh from her, she would inform him, "'T'ain't funny, McGee."

Fibber: Now, Molly, I need a cigar a darn sight worse than I need a glass of Guernsey Gruel. (Laughs) Don't ya get it, Molly? Instead of using the word "milk," I called it "Guernsey Gruel."

Molly: 'T'ain't funny, McGee.

Fibber: 'T'ain't?

Molly: 'T'ain't.

Fibber: Ah, pshaw

The program continued to enjoy good ratings as the 1939-1940 season progressed. On February 6, a group of newcomers added another highlight to the broadcast. The King's Men was a male quartet headed up by arranger/composer and bass singer Ken Darby. In the show's opening number, backed up by Billy Mills' orchestra, they burst onto the scene singing "Holy Smoke, Can't You Take a Joke?"

Later in the show, they sang a novelty version of "Old MacDonald Had a Farm" arranged by Darby. It was typical of fun-filled special lyrics and arrangements he would bring to the program over the years. Among the modified lines:

"With a salesman here, and a salesman there, HARLOW WILCOX everywhere!"

Billy Mills had heard the group perform elsewhere. He liked their style and brought them on the show for what was meant to be a one-time guest shot. Their two numbers drew such an enthusiastic response from the studio audience that he had second thoughts. He conferred with the Jordans, who agreed that they were perfect for the show. They were invited to return, and they did, becoming the only vocalists on the program for most of the next thirteen years.

Actor Gale Gordon began making frequent appearances on the program early in 1940. Gordon was a handsome and versatile actor whose voice was familiar to listeners from dozens of radio programs on which he appeared. Until now, most of his roles had been serious and well suited to his deep authoritative-sounding voice. His only starring role had been as the first Flash Gordon when that serialized program began in 1935. The opportunity to do comedy was a welcome change of pace for him.

In his early appearances, Gordon was seldom heard twice as the same character. Just between February and May, the imaginative Don Quinn had him portray a pompous headwaiter, an optometrist (Dr. Cyclops), a cheeky mailman, the latter half of a legal firm called Habeas and Corpus, even the owner of a circus.

Gordon would later play two important and recurring roles on *Fibber McGee and Molly*. In addition, he would become the overbearing principal of Madison High School, whose primary function, it seemed, was to make life difficult for Connie Brooks (Eve Arden) on *Our Miss Brooks*. Still later, he was the nemesis of Lucille Ball on her television series *The Lucy Show*, followed by *Here's Lucy* and the short-lived *Life with Lucy*. He also played the grumpy Mr. Wilson, who lamented the frequent visits of that neighbor kid, *Dennis the Menace*.

On March 5, 1940, the program introduced one of radio's most famous running gags—perhaps *the* most famous.

Running gags were a staple of radio comedy. Some were gag lines that got repeated frequently. Mr. Dithers summoning Dagwood

Bumstead into his office always meant that Dag was in trouble: "Bumstead! Come into my office!" Lou Costello always got a laugh calling for his partner, Bud Abbott: "Heeeyyy, Abb-bott!"

As The Mad Russian, Bert Gordon's entry line always was: "How dooo you do?" Red Skelton's Junior, "the mean widdle kid," would plot some trick to play on his grandma and say, "If I dood it, I'll get a lickin'." Then, as the audience knew he would, he'd say, "Aw, I'll dood it anyway."

Other running gags involved sound effects. Don Ameche produced his own long, loud snoring as John Bickerson. More elaborate was the squeeking, clanking sound of Jack Benny's ancient Maxwell. Another Benny gag that audiences loved was his underground vault. When Jack needed a little cash, he descended steps down to a cavern area where his footsteps echoed. He had to cross a moat and identify himself to the guard, Ed, who seemingly had been there for decades. Then he could be heard working the combination lock, after which there was a long wailing alarm that sounded as the door opened.

As far back as Jim and Marian's days together on *The Smith Family*, the "boing!" sound of a broken sofa spring had been inserted into the script from time to time for the amusement of listeners. Don Quinn and Jim had experimented with a couple of things such as a window shade snapping up and flapping, but nothing they'd tried had been funny enough to bear frequent repeating.

On that March program, Fibber for the first time opened the hall closet that was perpetually jammed to the ceiling with things for which the McGees had no other storage space. While hunting for a dictionary, he thoughtlessly threw open the hall closet door.

That was the sound man's cue. Stationed high on a tall wheeled staircase, he began pouring items from a huge box perched on the top. The noise being captured by a nearby microphone came from a barrelful of broken crockery, ten empty oil cans, two boxes of old kitchenware, an egg beater, three cowbells, half a dozen pie pans, and a handful of other items meant to produce as much clankety-clank noise as possible. When the last item seemingly had fallen and the noise subsided, after a pause, came a small tinkling bell.

The audience erupted in uproarious laughter. Jim waited them out. When it tapered off he uttered the line that was to become a classic: "Gotta straighten out that closet one of these days."

That program when the overstuffed closet was opened for the first time was doubly memorable for listeners because of an unannounced visit by Gracie Allen. She was in the midst of her "Gracie for President" campaign, and stopped in to ask the McGees for their votes.

Perhaps to gauge the response to the closet gag, Don Quinn found a way to insert it twice into that program. Near the end of the show, Fibber has succeeded in getting everything stuffed back into the closet. Then he realizes that he has put away the dictionary that he was seeking originally. Impulsively, he opens the closet door again, with the same result.

Molly:	Heavenly days!
Fibber:	I'm buried here, Molly, but I'm okay. Hey, Molly!
Molly:	Yes?
Fibber:	Hand me that dictionary....How do you spell annihilated?

The hall closet became a much-anticipated and hoped-for part of the program. Knowing it was a sure-fire laugh-getter, Don Quinn wrote it into the script from time to time, but spaced far enough apart so that audiences never knew when to expect it.

Occasionally, one of the McGees would forgetfully open the door. If Fibber was the victim, he was apt to discover his old mandolin among the debris. He then would pick it up and strum a few bars of an old tune called "Pretty Red Wing."

Most often, however, a visitor would say his or her goodbye and start to leave. Molly would frantically call out, "No, not that door! That's the hall closet!" But too late. The sound effects man would then get the show's biggest laugh. Fibber's muttered comment about straightening out that closet usually would be the cue for a musical interlude.

When the show took its summer break, the Jordans embarked on a bit of an adventure. Since settling in Encino, they had heard several friends and neighbors enthuse about vacations involving house trailers. It sounded like fun. They visited a trailer sales lot and inspected a few. They drove off the lot pulling a trailer that was a modest size but adequate.

After making arrangements for their home to be watched over, they set off on what would be a 6,000-mile journey through the Northwest. The sightseeing of that area's scenic landscapes was a joy, but trailer life took some getting used to.

There were few trailer camps in 1940. As Jim later recalled for friends, "We often had to drive to the edge of a town to find a place to park at night." The kitchen was adequate but cramped, with little storage space for food. Frequent stops were required to replenish the larder in small quantities.

In Oregon, they camped on the Wall River to do some fishing. While they took lunch at a local restaurant, a fisherman came in displaying a large trout that he was certain was going to qualify as a record, fourteen pounds, six ounces. He asked several diners to sign a certificate attesting to its size. Jim playfully signed "Fibber McGee." The man became quite angry, thinking this would cause people to not believe the certificate. He calmed down and even chuckled when Marian reassured him in her Teeny voice that this was the *real* Fibber McGee.

On their way home, the Jordans wanted to see San Francisco. Jim was leery of hauling the trailer up and down that city's many tall hills. Luckily they found a trailer court just outside of town. They parked the trailer and did the tourist routine.

After dinner in a fancy restaurant, they decided they'd like to spend a night at one of the city's better hotels. They had no luggage, so Marian purchased a couple of cheap suitcases at a discount store. Jim later recalled that when a bellhop hurried to their car and was handed those empty suitcases, he gave the Jordans a very suspicious look.

Upon their arrival at home, they agreed that it had been a wonderful vacation but they had had enough of trailer living for awhile. The trailer got parked in back of the house, where it stayed for several years.

The first half of the 1940-1941 season went smoothly, or as smoothly as things ever go at 79 Wistful Vista. Fans of the McGees had to wait until October for their return, but they remained loyal. They were rewarded with the rousing new theme song, "Wing to Wing," composed by Billy Mills. Except for a few programs where other tunes were used for a change of pace or to suit an episode's story line, it became the familiar long-running theme throughout the show's remaining half-hour tenure.

On that opening show, fans also were treated to the awesome sight of the uppity Mrs. Uppington dancing a lively rumba to music provided by the Mills orchestra. Of course, listeners had to envision the dance in their imaginations, and given Uppy's high-toned personality it must have taken a vivid imagination. During the Fall, the Jordans were able to work around the program schedule to make their second film. Paramount Pictures had been pleased with the audience response to their appearance in *This Way Please* and had offered a contract for them to do several more films. Marian's illness had made it impossible for them to go forward with the idea and the offer was dropped. Now came an unexpected invitation from RKO Radio Pictures to do a film in which they would be the stars. Living now so close to Hollywood, how could they say "No"?

The film was titled *Look Who's Laughing*. The Jordans' friend, ventriloquist Edgar Bergen, would star with them and bring along his wooden pal, Charlie McCarthy. A young newcomer named Lucille Ball played Bergen's romantic interest. Hal Peary, Bill Thompson, Isabel Randolph and Gale Gordon all appeared in various roles they played on *Fibber McGee and Molly*. Even Harlow Wilcox popped in as (you guessed it) a salesman.

The plot of the film is both complicated and silly. It simply serves as a vehicle for the stars to bring their radio personas to the screen. Bergen, a licensed pilot in real life, plans to partner with a friend and build an airplane factory in the Midwest. On his way, he gets lost in a storm and lands at the Wistful Vista airport.

Naturally, he meets Fibber and Molly, who invite him to dinner and a sleepover at their house. When they learn of his plan, the McGees convince Bergen that an abandoned factory near the airport can easily be converted and would be perfect for the plant he envisions.

Before that happens, however, there is a sub-plot in which Gildersleeve tries to steer Bergen to another property. It happens to belong to a friend of Gildy, who will reward him handsomely. Later there is an improbable episode, reminiscent of Abbott and Costello, in which Fibber accidentally takes off in a plane that he has no idea how to land. Bergen and a friend pursue him in another plane and Edgar wing-walks to get to Fibber and bring him down safely.

It's pure nonsense, but exciting and funny.

The new year got off to a gratifying start for Jim. He and Marian had gotten to know many folks in the Encino neighborhood and felt accepted as just plain folks. They loved the area, and with a sense of civic pride, Jim joined the Encino Chamber of Commerce. When asked to take on the role of President, he agreed.

On January 28, 1941, he was installed at the town's Grace Haye's Lodge. A news photo shows Marian standing beside him as he doffs a western hat. They are surrounded by other Chamber members and guests, including a grinning Bob Hope off to one side.

With Marian's improved health, the Jordans were pleased to take part in more activities and events, including some guest appearances on radio programs other than their own. On February 24, they were starred in a comedy called "The Whole Town's Talking" on the popular *Lux Radio Theatre*. In March, they joined a dozen other stars for a variety show presented by the *Screen Guild Players*.

On April 15, 1941, Don Quinn and Bill Thompson conspired to introduce another memorable and lovable neighbor of the McGees, the woebegone Wallace Wimple. When he made his entry, it was always with a greeting of "Hello, folks."

Shy and soft-spoken, Wimple was a mousy little fellow whose domineering and abusive wife was twice his size. She had been, he once reported, a jujitsu instructor for the police force.

A lover of birds and an avid bird-watcher, he often referred to his bird book, which he pronounced with an emphasis on the B's and a bit of a lisp. He also was fond of poetry. Something in the discourse with the McGees often prompted him to announce that he had written a poem on the subject. The McGees, of course, would ask to hear it, and Wimple would recite it for them. It would be a bit of whimsy that somehow combined a little wisdom with some nonsense.

What most endeared Wimple to listeners, almost from day one, was the way that he endured the harsh treatment of the woman he called "Sweetie Face." When about to relate some recent incident to the McGees, he would begin by saying, "Sweetie Face—that's my big old wife...." As if the McGees didn't know.

Fibber: Well, what's new at your house, Wimp?
Wimple: Well, Mr. McGee, last night, Sweetie Face—that's my big old wife—threw a little party out in our back yard.
Molly: Oh, that must have been fun.
Wimple: Not for me, Mrs. McGee. I'm the little party that she threw out there.

Wimple's visits almost always entailed some account of being manhandled by his big old spouse. Occasionally he would attempt some devilish (in his mind) form of revenge. These never worked out as planned.

Wimple: Sweetie Face—that's my big old wife—had me washing windows all day today.
Fibber: It oughtn't to take that long, Wimp.
Wimple: It does when I do it her way—with a piece of wet cotton on a toothpick.
Molly: Heavenly days! What on earth is the idea of that?
Wimple: Punishment, Mrs. McGee. (Chuckles.) I was naughty this morning.
Fibber: Were you really, Wimp? What'd you do? Sneak out and inhale a dubeb?
Wimple: No, Mr. McGee. At breakfast this morning, Sweetie Face told me to eat all the crust of my toast or I wouldn't have curly hair, and when she turned her back I made a face at her.

Molly:	That was safe, wasn't it?
Wimple:	(Chuckles) That's what I thought, Mrs. McGee. But she saw my face in the coffee pot.
Fibber:	And then what?
Wimple:	And then I saw the coffee pot in my face!

Given Fibber's teasing nature, it didn't take him long to nickname Wimple and begin addressing him as "Wimp." That may well have been the origin of the term *wimpy*, as in "Don't be a wimp."

Despite his henpecked and woebegone nature, Wimple at times was tickled by some comment made by Molly or Fibber. He would then chuckle and say, "Oh, that's just peachy." The comment and/or the way he said it always got a laugh.

Sweetie Face was one of a number of invisible characters who were never, or seldom, actually heard. Fibber frequently had recollections of his two old pals in Peoria, Fred Nitny and Egghead Vanderween.

Molly's Uncle Dennis was a bit of a tippler, who also may not have been playing with a full deck. His recent exploits often were a topic of the McGees' conversation in between visitors. For a time, Uncle Dennis was a guest in Fibber and Molly's spare upstairs bedroom.

His "appearances" would be created by the sound effects man. First would be heard the sound of the back door closing. The McGees would hush as his stumbling steps got him through the rear hall and started up the stairs. Three or four steps up, then he would fall back a couple of steps. This was repeated several times until he finally made it to the upstairs and stumbled into his bedroom. As his shoes were dropped on the floor, Molly would observe: "Uncle Dennis is home early tonight."

Uncle Dennis was good for one or two gags during any time a program had a minute or so to fill. He almost never was actually heard. On a couple of rare occasions, Bill Thompson became Uncle Dennis, but his lines were spoken in such a mumbled fashion that only Fibber and Molly knew what he said. Everyone agreed that he was funnier when left to the listeners' imagination.

The McGees sometimes spoke of the Toops family, all of whom were interesting characters. The most interesting, though, was young Willie, who was spoken of by Teeny on most of her visits, while he waited outside on the sidewalk.

Undoubtedly the most favorite of the unseen characters was Myrt, the telephone operator. However many operators Wistful Vista may have had on its local switchboard, it somehow was always Myrt who responded when Fibber had to make a call.

Before rotary dial phones became common, McGee would pick up the phone and start to place his call with the operator….

    Fibber: Hello, operator? I need to call Wistful Vista 2, 9—oh, z'at you, Myrt? How's ever little thing, Myrt? (Pause.) You don't say. Uncle Horace took a spill, did he?

    Molly: Oh, dear. The poor man.

    Fibber: Smashed his face and busted one his hands, did he?

    Molly: Heavenly days!

    Fibber: And that's the second watch he's broken this year.

Sometimes the routine had Molly hearing one side of the conversation and asking McGee for clarification, so that he had to repeat what he'd just heard.

    McGee: How's ever little thing, Myrt? Your kid brother, hey? Broken back?

    Molly: Oh, heavenly days! What happened?

    McGee: He was hitchhiking to Chicago. Got as far as Peoria and ran out of money. Now he's broke 'n' back.

**Molly listens as Fibber chats with Myrt the telephone operator.
CREDIT: Photofest**

Keeping up with the times, the McGees later got one of those rotary phones. That didn't end Myrt's tenure, however. Fibber would occasionally want to make a call and not know the number, so he'd have to dial the operator. Guess who.

Wistful Vista's small town status apparently accounts for the McGees knowing most of its residents. The heart of the town was 14th and Oak. The town's park and most of its businesses apparently were somehow crammed into the area around that intersection. When leaving their house, whether they were headed for the Bon Ton, Doc Gamble's office, the county courthouse, the library, the Post Office, the railroad station, the Elks Club or Kremer's Drugstore, Fibber or Molly would mention that they were headed for 14th and Oak.

Listeners in Peoria took special pleasure in hearing Kremer's mentioned. There was an actual Kremer's Drugstore in Peoria. Jim and Marian often had stopped there for sodas while dating.

In May, 1941, the Jordans took part in an NBC program celebrating Jack Benny's tenth year on the air. Among the many other celebrants were Bob Hope, Edgar Bergen, Rudy Vallee, George Jessel, George Burns and Gracie Allen.

They dedicated their own June 17 program to Billy Mills. Mills had been active in radio for sixteen years and the broadcast marked a milestone, his ten thousandth.

During the program's summer break, the Jordans again embarked on an adventure into the great outdoors. They chartered a small yacht and enjoyed a relaxing and scenic trip to Juneau, Alaska. They were joined by Jim Jr. When they reached their destination, all three engaged in a few days of competitive fishing. Their best catches were served up as delicious dinners for themselves and the yacht's crew.

Kay Jordan did not join the yachting trip. Earlier in the year she had decided to try her luck as a radio performer. With no prior experience, and without mentioning her relationship to the network's popular couple, she built up her nerve to take an audition at NBC. To her surprise and great pleasure, she was given a supporting role in a continuing series called *Vance and Lila*. Sometime later she was given a small role on the *I Love a Mystery* series.

While the show was off for the summer, Gildersleeve left town without any prior announcement. Hal Peary's character had become one of the most popular on the program. With the Jordans' blessing, he left to star on his own show in what was the first "spin-off" of a radio character.

The Great Gildersleeve premiered on August 31, 1941, on NBC. Producer Cecil Underwood and Director Frank Pittman, both of whom had worked on the *McGee* program, joined Peary in their respective roles.

The story line involved Gildersleeve moving to the nearby town of Summerfield to become the guardian of his orphaned niece Marjorie and nephew Leroy. They begin living together and reordering their lives, with much help from their cook/housekeeper, Birdie.

Gildersleeve becomes the town's water commissioner and accumulates a group of male friends who comprise the Jolly Boys Club. The club's main purpose seems to be solving each other's problems and harmonizing in song. As on the McGee program, Throckmorton is quickly nicknamed "Gildy."

Though he at times had mentioned an unseen wife to the McGees, he is a confirmed bachelor on the new show. Numerous episodes involve him almost being trapped into marriage by women he dates. He is also frequently challenged by having to help his wards make important decisions and resolve their problems.

Marjorie, the older, is more level headed and less trouble prone. The part of Leroy was played by Walter Tetley, who was possessed of a perpetually boyish voice. He hovered around ten or eleven years of age through most of the series.

Frequent episodes had Leroy trying his uncle's patience in one way or another. When Gildersleeve tried to set him straight, Leroy was prone to make feeble attempts at defending his actions, saying, "Yeah, but Unc…" or "But gee whiz, Unc…" Gildy would endure a couple of such objections before his patience ran out. Then, in his deep, stern voice, he would say: "Leeeee-rooooooy!" End of discussion.

The program was sponsored by Kraft Foods. Most of the commercials were devoted to promoting Parkay margarine. The show proved so popular that Harold Peary starred in four feature films as Gildy. Many of the radio characters, although included in the films, were played by other actors. Walter Tetley, who was an adult, could not appear as Leroy.

Throckmorton P. Gildersleeve was a creation of Don Quinn, but neither he nor the Jordans objected to Hal Peary appropriating him to start up another program. In fact, the McGees later would pay him a visit in Summerfield.

To promote the coming release of *Look Who's Laughing*, an episode titled "Amusement Park" had the McGees spending a day at said park. They are followed around by an RKO Radio Pictures agent, played by Gale Gordon. He believes they would be perfect to play an ideal American couple in a movie that will star Edgar Bergen and Charlie McCarthy.

Again, on the day before the film's actual release, the program has it opening in Wistful Vista. Who should make guest appearances but Edgar and Charlie.

On September 8, *Look Who's Laughing* had its premiere. Initial response was good. To keep up public interest as the film circulated, Edgar and Charlie again made a guest visit to the McGees on the November 11 show.

On September 30, Gildersleeve returned to Wistful Vista to tie up some loose ends. Naturally, he stopped in to say goodbye to the

McGees. For once "the boys" were able to exchange some gentle joshing without Molly having to interpose. The visit was, of course, an opportunity to plug Peary's new show.

Don Quinn made certain that Throckmorton's departure was a fitting one and would be remembered. As he was about to leave, Gildy mistakenly opened the door to the notorious hall closet.

On the October 21 broadcast, Fibber did actually get around to straightening out that closet. Alas! It was not to stay uncluttered for long. Nevertheless, Don Quinn took a devilish pleasure in sometimes doing a twist on the various running gags.

On the two occasions when McGee actually got the closet straightened out, a visitor started to exit. Molly frantically cried, "No, no, not that door! That's the hall closet!" Then the sound of a door opening, followed by a breathless pause as the audience waits for the outpouring of debris. Finally, Fibber breaks the silence to say, "Oh, I forgot to tell you, Mollie. I straightened that closet out today." It got as much laughter and applause as the anticipated avalanche.

On another program, Fibber got a rare treat from his spouse. After years of telling jokes and hearing her say, "'T'ain't funny, McGee," he told another, and Molly actually laughed. It all but left him speechless.

Another deviation from the norm occurred on a program in which Fibber told one of his gags to the Old Timer. O.T. gave his pleased chuckle and said, "That's pretty good, Johnny. And that's *exactly* the way I heared it!"

On November 15, the Jordans joined a host of other stars on a special program called "Free For All." It was a celebration of the NBC network's fifteenth anniversary.

Then came December 7. A date that will live in infamy. The Japanese invasion of Pearl Harbor.

Radio broadcasting in America underwent an overnight change. There were frequent special news reports as the nation went on a wartime alert. Like many other programs, *Fibber McGee and Molly* began on December 9 with an announcement that the program might be interrupted for any important bulletin.

In place of one of the commercials, Harlow Wilcox read a telegram from the president of S. C. Johnson & Sons in which he said, "…(we) believe it is in the public interest to continue a program as entertaining as *Fibber McGee and Molly*. They have a place in the national morale." The program ended with Jim stepping out of character to lead the cast and the studio audience in singing "My Country 'Tis of Thee."

On the following week's program, Harlow Wilcox told the McGees that he was planning to buy a world globe as a Christmas gift for his nephew.

Molly: Do you want one with Japan on it?
Wilcox: Well, yes, I guess so….
Molly: Then you'd better find one FAST!

The audience responded with cheers, whistles and thunderous applause that lasted for three minutes. With the show running over, Jim preempted the usual closing and led the audience in singing "America the Beautiful" as they went off the air.

On subsequent programs, Don Quinn's scripts frequently managed to work in comments by the McGees or visitors encouraging support of the Red Cross, buying Defense Bonds, and refraining from hoarding or wastefulness. The term "Jap" was not politically incorrect and was freely used. Fibber once tells Mayor LaTrivia that he has a swell slogan for the war bond drive: "Every time you buy a bond, you slap a Jap across the pond."

In a closing of one program, Jim again stepped out of character to speak to listeners as a fellow American. "This is not an invitation to a tea party or a bingo game," he said. "This is WAR. It is going to cost a lot more than mere money to win it, but it would cost a lot more than mere money to lose it. This isn't the other fellow's fight. It's yours and mine. So, here it comes again: Buy Defense Bonds and Defense Stamps!"

A welcome diversion in 1942 was an invitation from RKO Radio Pictures to do another film. Once again the McGees would be the stars, joined by a number of other familiar characters. Isabel Randolph and Hal Peary were back as Mrs. Uppington and Throckmorton P. Gildesleeve. Bill Thompson appeared as Wallace Wimple and Gale Gordon as Molly's long-ago beau, Otis Cadwallader. For good measure, Edgar Bergen returned with his pesky companion, Charlie McCarthy.

The plot of *Here We Go Again* is a hodge-podge that would require a back-page addendum to explain. It hinges on Fibber and Molly celebrating a twentieth anniversary at a resort hotel they can not afford. Key nonsense includes a race between a buggy and a covered wagon. Bergen and Charlie trespass onto an Indian reservation, and are in danger of being roasted until Bergen causes a totem pole to speak to the tribe and instruct them to free the palefaces.

Don Quinn provided much of the McGees' material. The implausible plot not withstanding, making the film was a pleasant opportunity for the various cast members to regroup and enjoy some time together between takes.

During the summer of 1942, the Jordans embarked upon a bold new venture in a field far removed from the world of show business. They became cattle ranchers.

In the Green Horn Mountains area near Bakersfield, California, they purchased 1,000 acres and a small herd of Black Angus cattle. They spent most of the summer making repairs and developing the property.

Since his youthful days as a farm boy, Jim had a liking for animals. He began to studiously bone up on the ranching business. Hired hands and neighbor ranchers gave him guidance that eventually led to his raising some prize-winning animals. He told friends that his success as a rancher made him prouder than the compliments he often heard about the radio program.

Over the next few years, the Jordans purchased neighboring properties as they became available. The size of their herd grew and their spread eventually encompassed 4,000 acres.

The ranch became their "weekend" get-away place. In their case, the weekend was from Wednesday morning through early Saturday, when they would drive back to Encino for the first sit-down with Don Quinn to prepare for the next broadcast.

When the *McGee* program resumed in September, it was heard by servicemen overseas via shortwave radio. A hit of the first broadcast was the Kings Men singing "Praise the Lord and Pass the Ammunition."

Here We Go Again was released on October 9, 1942. The Jordans were pleased to see that the New York City premiere was at the famed Palace Theatre. Reviews were mostly favorable, although one critic noted that "the radio stars are not as funny on the screen as they are on the air." Nevertheless, for a "B" picture, it did well at the box office.

With their neighbor Gildersleeve gone, that pleasantly preposterous verbal sparring between he and Fibber was missed by both audience and cast. To fill the void, Don Quinn gave Gale Gordon a role that became one of the most popular visitors to the McGee residence: Mayor Charles LaTrivia.

For Gordon, who had played only dramatic roles prior to coming onboard, it proved to be one of his most memorable characters. His good diction and authoritative voice were perfect for the somewhat self-important public servant. He had a habit of making off-handed comments that enabled him to pat himself on the back for his most recent mayoral accomplishment.

The McGees took him with a grain or two of salt. Molly did politely address him as "your honor" or "Mister Mayor." Fibber, however, as was his wont, quickly took to abridging his name and addressing him as "LaTriv."

Without actually embracing the fact that Fibber never had a visible means of income, the mayor would sometimes extend him a job offer. These always turned out to be less prestigious than they sounded. A job "looking in on the higher-ups at City Hall" turned out to involve washing windows. When offered an "undercover" job that required wearing a disguise, Fibber ended up playing Santa Claus for the kiddies at a town hall party.

There was an unspoken conspiracy between Fibber and Molly to confound the mayor by misunderstanding when he expounded upon something using some cliché phrase or figure of speech, as he often did. In recounting his effort to lose some excess weight, LaTrivia explained that he had gone on a serious diet for several weeks and succeeded in losing ten pounds.

LaTrivia:	I no longer had difficulty getting my belt around my middle, and I was so pleased that I rewarded myself with a dish of ice cream for dessert. I must say that I ate it with relish.
Molly:	Sounds like a strange combination to me.
LaTrivia:	I beg your pardon.
Fibber:	She means putting relish on your ice cream, LaTriv. Most folks would prefer some crushed nuts or a little whipped cream.

LaTrivia: No, no. What I meant was ---
Molly: (interrupts) Well, everyone to their own taste, I always say. My Aunt Clara used to cover her scrambled eggs with ketchup.
LaTrivia: Yes, but you see —
Fibber: (interrupts) You're right, kiddo. I remember my cousin Otto slapping slices of banana between crackers and smearing them with peanut butter.

Gale Gordon delighted in his new comic role, and he was perfect as Mayor LaTrivia. He was a master of the slow burn. As the McGees continued to ignore his efforts to explain, his voice began to rise. He had trouble getting words out, and when he did they became garbled. Soon the McGees were hushed as he began to shout, but nothing that he said came out right.

His furious rant was apt to come out as something like: "Every time I stake a simple matement…make a staple mintment…stinkel satement…minkle statement…." When he was about to burst, he would stop and take a long, deep breath to calm himself. Then, in a deep, calm, measured, voice:

LaTrivia: McGeeeeee.
Fibber: (innocently) Yes, LaTriv?
LaTrivia: Oooooooo! Good day!
Sound: Door slams.

During one of his visits, His Honor used the phrase "playing possum." The McGees pounced. The result was another raving rant.

LaTrivia: I don't want to balk a stossum. Squawk a blossom. Look. When I said I was playing posse possum, I merely meant I was lowing lye! Er, lying low. I never said I was …

you're the one that always misconwords my strues ... strue remarks my words! You're the one ... I ... You ...."

Finally at the boiling point, he stopped to calm himself before continuing.

LaTrivia: McGeeeee?
Fibber: Yes, LaTriv?
LaTrivia: Would you be willing to serve as a volunteer at the police firing range?
Fibber: Sure, LaTriv. Wanna use me as an instructor?
LaTrivia: No. A target. Good day!

After the mayor's departure, there usually was a brief exchange between Fibber and Molly about him seeming a bit edgy. It was clear that they had teamed up to burst the poor fellow's balloon.

Why His Honor subjected himself to such regular abuse is anyone's guess, but Gale Gordon was so perfect as Mayor LaTrivia, and the character was so popular, that he became one of the McGees' most frequent visitors, although with two extended absences.

Just as we were getting to know him, Gordon left the show in December to join the U. S. Coast Guard. He served until the war's end as a gunnery instructor. His commanding voice no doubt got the attention of new recruits.

Fibber and Molly's popularity was due in large part to the fact that they came across as regular folk. Despite Fibber's boastful and argumentative nature, listeners felt that the comical couple were not much different than many of their relatives or friends. During 1942, the show's producers sought to get their own feel for listenership apart from various polls. They invited listeners to write in telling them where they thought 79 Wistful Vista was located. The overwhelming majority responded with some variation of the comment: "Just down the street."

The program ended the year at the top of the Crosley ratings. It's weekly audience was estimated at 30 million listeners.

The McGees began 1943 by making a visit to the town of Summerfield, where they looked in on Gildersleeve and his niece and nephew. There were some gags exchanged, but it was a more amiable visit than when they were neighbors.

In February, Bill Thompson enlisted in the U. S. Navy. Given his background, he was assigned to special duty entertaining troops at various bases, as well as sick and wounded in hospitals.

That same month, Don Quinn hired Phil Leslie as a co-writer. A talented writer with a gift for comedy, Leslie had been scripting NBC's "Major Hoople" program. He was a fan and loyal listener of the McGees. He and Don Quinn clicked, and Leslie quickly adapted to the style of the *McGee* programs and its characters. By the second week in March, he had written a complete script on his own with only a few suggestions from his mentor/boss.

In the absence of Harold Peary, Gale Gordon and Bill Thompson, the program was minus a number of regular visitors to 79 Wistful Vista. Don Quinn sensed that listeners especially missed Fibber's verbal duals with Gildersleeve, as did he. To fill the gap, he brought in Arthur Q. Bryan to be Doctor George Gamble.

Although Bryan had filled a number of radio roles previously, his voice probably was most familiar to the junior theater audiences who heard a lisping version of it in Looney Tunes cartoons. He provided the voice of Elmer Fudd, who was forever being teased and tricked by "that wascally wabbit," Bugs Bunny. Not long after Gildersleeve resettled in Summerfield, Bryan became Floyd Munson, the barber, one of Gildy's buddies in the Jolly Boys Club.

Phil Leslie recommended Bryan to Quinn to fill the Doc Gamble role. Bryan had been starring as Major Amos Hoople in the radio series based on the popular comic strip "Our Boarding House" and scripted by Leslie.

Hoople was an old windbag who claimed to have been a leader in numerous military organizations, in addition to being a descendant of various English nobility. Bryan came across sounding very much as one would imagine the cartoon character to sound. His boastfulness was on a level with that of McGee.

Doc Gamble, however, was a much different and more likeable fellow. Mild mannered and soft spoken, he never raised his voice or lost his cool in confronting McGee's fanciful boasting. He always was polite to Molly, usually addressing her as "my dear," but he could hold his own when Fibber attempted to engage him in verbal combat. Which was often.

Upon his arrival at the McGee dwelling, Fibber was apt to combine a greeting with some cheery insults: "Hiyah, Arrowsmith. Kick your case of corn cures in the corner and compose your corpulent corpus on a convenient camp chair." He spoke of or to the doctor with insulting alliterative descriptions: "tummy thumper," or "serum salesman." Seldom did he fail to poke fun at the good doctor's ample middle.

While always maintaining his cool, the doctor often took note that Fibber also carried some extra baggage. His entry line was apt to be something like: "Hello, Molly... and good day to you, Pantry Paunch." He would nonetheless begin their meeting by addressing Fibber as "old chum."

Fibber, however, could not restrain himself from calling Gamble "bone bender" or "the mortician's friend." He once asked, "Is it true, butcher boy, that you misplaced your satchel last week, and three patients got well before you found it?" On another occasion, he told Molly, "The ol' epidemic chaser here studied sewing under Omar the tentmaker."

When taunted thus, Doctor Gamble would counter by addressing McGee as "Neanderthal," or "Gutter-nose" or "Marblehead." When Fibber took it into his head that he had a great poet hidden inside himself, the doctor scoffed: "Poetry my peritoneum! You couldn't rhyme moon and June if you understudied with Ira Gershwin. You haven't got a sonnet in your bonnet that would bring ten cents at a literary rummage sale!"

Nevertheless, they actually had a fairly amiable relationship, even fishing together on occasion. The insults and arguments were more amiable than those McGee once had with Gildersleeve. Molly, who always politely addressed the pudgy physician as "Doctor Gamble" or just "Doctor," never had to interpose with her "Boys, boys!"

August 31 was the Jordans' twenty-fifth wedding anniversary. NBC and the Johnson's Wax family treated them to a gala celebration at Hollywood's Ambassador Hotel. They found themselves surrounded by cast members, staff and dozens of close friends.

Ransom Sherman joined the cast in the Fall. Sherman's radio experience dated back to 1923. In 1937, he created the *Club Matinee* program, in which he co-starred with Garry Moore. He also wrote and starred in *Hap Hazard*, the McGees' 1941 summer replacement. He now became Sigmund Wellington, the snooty manager of Wistful Vista's Bijou Theatre. When he visited the McGees, his snobbish demeanor made him an apt target for put-down gags by Fibber.

On the side, Wellington did movie reviews for the local radio station. On one program, the McGees listened in as he reported: "You should have seen the picture we played at the Bijou last week. *Here We Go Again*, with Edgar Bergen and three dummies. It was a cinematic canine that shouldn't happen to anybody."

Throughout the year, indeed, through the duration of the war, the

McGees did what they could to support the war effort, on their own program and elsewhere. They had a visit from film actress Claudette Colbert, whose guest appearance was used to promote the sale of War Bonds.

Don Quinn and Phil Leslie concocted a number of scripts in which Fibber attempts to deal with his frustrations with meat rationing, gas rationing, various shortages and other wartime inconveniences. He invariably is obliged to admit by show's end that he was behaving selfishly. The Jordans then closed the program in a more serious mode, urging Americans to pull together for victory. Molly sometimes reminded housewives to collect the grease and fats from their cooking and take them to the local butcher. These were used in producing ammunition for the troops.

There was a housing shortage during the war. Uncle Dennis had apparently departed the McGees' spare bedroom. They rented it to a sweet young aircraft plant worker named Alice Darling, played by Shirley Mitchell. A veteran radio actress, Mitchell had been heard on the *First Nighter* program, *The Life of Riley* and various supporting roles on a number of daytime soap operas. In her most memorable role, she later became Southern belle Lelia Randsom on *The Great Gildersleeve*. In her flirtatious cooing manner, she sought to win the heart and the hand of the elusive Gildy.

When radio fell victim to television, Mitchell made the switch. Although she never starred in any series, she appeared as a regular or recurring character on such shows as *I Love Lucy, Perry Mason* and *Petticoat Junction*.

As Alice Darling, Mitchell got to ham it up a bit. Alice was man-crazy, and thus thrilled by the abundance of handsome young fellas in uniform. A bit ditzy, but delightfully so, she was prone to uttering such excited explanations as "Creepers!" and "Crim-in-iny!" The sometimes grumpy McGee couldn't resist teasing her about her excess of sweetness and innocence.

By the beginning of 1944, the program was being heard on 133 NBC stations and affiliates. Despite the fact that Fibber never seemed to have a steady job, the McGees were able to take on a maid.

Though it was never stated, Beulah obviously was a black lady. The part was played by a white male actor named Marlin Hurt, who had the voice and the dialect down to perfection. Beulah usually would be introduced by Fibber or Molly wanting to make some request of her and calling her in from the kitchen.

Listeners at home may have wondered why her entry prompted such a burst of laughter from the studio audience. Marlin Hurt would be standing with the other actors, following the script. A little before his line, he would turn and appear to be gazing absently at the clock or control room. At his cue, he would quickly turn back, lean into the mic and almost shout his line: "Somebody bawl for Beulah?" The studio audience, taken completely by surprise, would let out a scream and then laugh uproariously.

Beulah was a treat for Fibber, too. Visitors seldom laughed at his feeble jokes, and Molly never hesitated to inform him, "'T'ain't funny, McGee." Beulah, on the other hand, always chuckled at his wisecracks. When he aimed one in her direction, she would laugh and then enthuse: "LOVE that man!"

Beulah had her own distinctive sense of humor. Not long after her arrival, she told the McGees, "I been bendin' over a stove for fifteen years now. The job is new, but the position ain't."

The character proved so popular that CBS lured Hurt away the following year to star in his own weekly comedy series. That gave the *McGee* program the distinction of being the first to generate two "spin-off" series. Unfortunately, Hurt's success was cut short by a heart attack. He died barely a year later.

On March 28, 1944, Jim Jordan was confined to hospital with pneumonia. For the first time in his career, he missed a broadcast. Don and Phil hastily concocted a script in which Gildersleeve and his nephew, Leroy, return for a visit and meet several of the Wistful Vista regulars.

With some juggling of their schedules, Jim and Marian found time to film their third and last picture for RKO, *Heavenly Days*. The screenplay was coauthored by director Howard Estabrook and Don Quinn. Other than the Kings Men, who appear as singing soldiers, none of the Wistful Vista gang appear.

Fibber and Molly are on their way to visit a cousin in Washington, D.C. On the way, they meet and get acquainted with the noted pollster, Dr. George Gallup, who is conducting a project to find "the average American man." One thing leads to another, Gallup decides he has found his man, and Fibber ends up making a rousing speech to Congress along the lines of *Mister Smith Goes to Washington*. Jim gets to play both Fibber and the ghost of the fife player from the famous Revolutionary War painting.

On June 6, NBC devoted much of its broadcast day to reports of the D-Day invasion at Normandy and salutes to the Allied forces and our American troops. The Jordans turned their program over to Billy Mills and the Kings Men for a half hour of patriotic music.

During the program's summer break, Jim and Marian spent almost all of their fifteen weeks at the cattle ranch. When Jim donned his ranch foreman's hat, Marian worked on a bountiful garden she was creating. She was blessed with the proverbial green thumb and was especially proud of her prize African violets. It was a combination work and relaxation vacation. They enjoyed hosting weekly barbeque cookouts with cast members and other friends.

The program resumed on October 10 at the peak of its popularity. In the *Radio Daily* annual poll of favorite programs, *Fibber McGee and Molly* took first place as the top "Comedy Team."

Heavenly Days was released in August. It did well at the box office, but not as well as its two predecessors. Some fans may have skipped it when they learned that it was missing all the usual suspects from Wistful Vista.

On November 7, the show did a special broadcast from the Navy Pier in Chicago. It was performed before an audience made up mostly of enlisted men stationed there. Navy man Bill Thompson was able to make a one-time return to the cast. It was a delight for the McGees and their listening audience to have both the Old Timer and Wallace Wimple pay them another visit.

As 1945 began, the McGees trailed Bob Hope by a slim margin for top-rated program in the polls.

Isabel Randolph had left the show in June, 1943, to focus her efforts on a film career. Opening the hall closet door by mistake, she truly made a grand exit. Mrs. Uppington had been one of the McGees' few female visitors, and she was missed. Bea Benaderet proved to be an apt replacement when she joined the cast on March 6 as Mrs. Millicent Carstairs.

Benaderet's radio resume included dozens of programs, on which she provided hundreds of voices. She was Lucille Ball's gal pal Iris Attebury on *My Favorite Husband*. On *The Great Gildersleeve*, she played school principal Eve Goodwin, one of Gildy's lady friends. Perhaps her best remembered radio role was that of Gertrude Gearshift, the telephone operator with a Brooklyn accent who frequently got on Jack Benny's nerves.

She began a series of television roles even as radio was breathing its last. She was hotel owner Kate Bradley on *Green Acres*. On the Burns and Allen series she was Gracie's next-door neighbor and sometime co-conspirator, Blanche Morton. She was considered for the role of Granny on *The Beverly Hillbillies*, but was deemed too young and attractive. She settled for the role of Cousin Pearl Bodine. That, however, led to what may be her best remembered role, as the star of the popular series *Petticoat Junction*.

McGee's jibes at Mrs. Uppington's highfalutin airs had mostly gone over her head. Although also a snobbish upper crust type, Mrs. Carstairs was much quicker on the draw. She responded to Fibber's jabs with witty and sharp ripostes. This made her even more fun for Fibber to engage and prompted more audience laughs.

Americans were stunned when President Franklin D. Roosevelt died suddenly on April 12 at his retreat in Warm Springs, Georgia. On April 15, NBC presented a special two-hour tribute to the beloved FDR. Amos and Andy, Bob Hope, Dinah Shore, Bing Crosby and Jack Benny participated in the salute, along with many others. Marian and Jim did a poignant skit in which Fibber must explain the president's death to Teeny.

May 8 was declared V-E Day. Victory in Europe was formalized by the German army's surrender just days after Adolph Hitler took his own life. In the U.S.A., the announcement was tinged with a somber sense of regret that FDR had not lived to celebrate the victory with his fellow Americans.

Meanwhile, there was another cause for joy in the Jordan family. Daughter Kay was now Mrs. Adrian Goodman. In the Spring, she presented Jim and Marian with their first grandchild, a daughter named Diane. The Goodmans were living nearby in Encino, so Marian and Jim had ample opportunity to visit and fuss over the new arrival. During that summer's break, they spent a little less time at the ranch so as to get in practice being grandparents.

On September 2, aboard the USS Missouri in Tokyo Bay, General Douglas MacArthur accepted the formal surrender of Japanese officials. President Truman officially declared V-J Day. Spontaneous wild celebrations took place in the streets across America. In San Francisco, two women jumped naked into a pond at the Civic Center, to the cheers of nearby soldiers. In New York's Time Square, a sailor kissed a nurse in the midst of a rejoicing crowd, and the resulting *Life* magazine photo became an iconic image.

The world breathed a sigh of relief. World War II was ended.

When the program resumed on October 2, Gale Gordon was once again free to rejoin the cast. Mayor LaTravia's return was greeted by the same dual attack on his sanity that the McGees had inflicted upon him in the past.

On October 30, *Fibber McGee and Molly* made its first ever "foreign" broadcast. In conjunction with the Ninth Canadian Victory Loan Drive, the program aired from Toronto, Canada. The cast then made a side trip to New York City for a two-week visit and broadcast two shows from the NBC studios there before returning to California. While there, Jim and Marian also took part in a *Command Performance* program.

At the beginning of 1946, America was in recovery mode. It would be awhile before all the troops came home, but life was beginning to get back to normal. At the McGee mansion, Alice Darling was no longer renting the extra bedroom. She may have managed to lasso one of those good looking young men in uniform.

One of those, Bill Thompson, was newly discharged and wearing "civvies" again. He returned to the show in January, bringing with him the Old Timer and Wallace Wimple. For a change of pace, he occasionally became an Irish policeman, complete with a heavy brogue and a voluminous bag of blarney:

"Ah, Macushla, sure and your beautiful Irish eyelashes are just like the shadows of lovely birds flying over the magnificent blue lakes of Killarney."

On the April 30 program, Don Quinn found an opportunity to work in a song by Jim. He raised his rich tenor voice in a solo rendition of "Dear Old Girl."

Not long after Thompson's return, Jim Jr. received his military discharge. Upon returning home, he decided to give radio acting a try. Although he was able to obtain parts on a few shows, he soon shifted to working as a producer. This proved to be a more gratifying field for him, and it later led to television production roles.

During the show's summer break, Marian and Jim took some time off from spoiling their granddaughter and working on the ranch. They returned to their "regular folks" roots and climbed aboard with some other tourists for a relaxing and scenic boat trip down the Current River in the Ozarks.

In November, they visited the Johnson Wax Company headquarters in Racine, Wisconsin. The company was celebrating its sixtieth anniversary, and they were greeted by the president himself. That week's program aired from the company's Memorial Hall. The audience included over 1,800 employees and their guests.

Fibber McGee and Molly began 1947 still at its peak. After conducting a nationwide poll, *Radio Daily* named it "Most Popular Comedy Radio Program of the Year." Their listening audience surpassed even those of Bob Hope and Jack Benny. The January 28 show was a milestone: their 500th broadcast.

On February 10, Jim and Marian once again starred on the CBS *Screen Guild Theatre*, this time in a radio adaptation of *Heavenly Days*.

During the Spring, as if running a cattle ranch was not enough to keep them busy, the Jordans branched out. They purchased a commercial tree nursery on the outskirts of Encino.

On the other hand, there was a post-war housing shortage. Kay and Jim Jr. were both now off on their own. Marian and Jim decided that they did not need the sprawling property and large house where they were currently living. They found and purchased a modest bungalow in another part of town, with a breathtaking view of the San Fernando Valley. It needed some up-dating inside and Marian wanted a bedroom added, just in case. While the work was being done, the house trailer that had long been parked at their Rancho Street house proved to be a perfect temporary dwelling.

The continued success and popularity of their program did not blind Jim and Marian to the fact that things can change, sometimes quickly. Moreover, Jim was at the half-century mark and Marian was getting close. Their at-home conversations began to include thoughts about the future.

Unlike his on-air persona, Jim actually was blessed with a natural business sense. As far back as 1938, he had partnered with his brother Byron to purchase a bottling plant for the popular Nesbitt's Orange Drink. It serviced several counties in the Peoria area. Byron, who had been with the Hires Company for nine years, took charge of the operation. Jim became a more-or-less silent partner, visiting when able and going over the business with his brother.

Over the years, Jim's business ventures included a partial interest in a sand-blasting equipment factory in Peoria and a construction firm in Nevada. He also had a keen eye for real estate, purchasing prime properties that he later resold at a profit when the areas were developed.

In recent months, CBS had been seeking to gain ground on NBC, offering enticing contracts that lured top stars away from their chief rival. The Jordans had been approached, but they chose to continue their long-standing and agreeable relationship with NBC.

Now, although they had no near-term plan to retire, they began to look to the future. From the beginning, the Jordans had maintained all rights to their program and their characters' names. Jim now began a series of negotiations with the network's top brass. The outcome was a contract that gave NBC all rights to the names *Fibber McGee and Molly* and to the program's concept and literary rights.

In return, the Jordans received a one-time payment of $2 million. In today's dollars, it would be a modest fortune. In 1947 dollars, it was a nest egg that they felt confident would suffice through their old age.

If anything, the sale of their property rights added to the Jordans' job security. NBC now had a vested interest in continuing to broadcast the program, and no one but Jim and Marian could ever pass as Fibber and Molly.

For the next few years, *Fibber McGee and Molly* went on with little change, part of an NBC Tuesday night line-up that boasted several of the most popular comedy shows. During station breaks, announcers would often remind listeners: "Tuesday night is laugh night on NBC!" Newspapers back then listed schedules for radio programs just as they do today for television. In 1947, the Tuesday listing for Chicago's NBC station WMAQ was:

7:00 p.m. Milton Berle Show
7:30 p.m. A Date with Judy
8:00 p.m. Amos and Andy
8:30 p.m. Fibber McGee and Molly

9:00 p.m. Bob Hope

9:30 p.m. Red Skelton

Gale Gordon changed hats for awhile. New York City's Mayor LaGuardia died in September, 1947. Although Mayor LaTrivia's character was not modeled on LaGuardia, his name was inspired by that of the beloved "Little Flower." Out of respect, LaTrivia was temporarily omitted from scripts.

Gordon became F. Ogden Williams, the weatherman. The ever-uncertain Williams was ever-apologetic for the weather, be it hot or cold, sunny or raining. Asked his opinion, he was apt to answer: "If you must know, and I don't know why you should, UN-officially, and off the record, weather conditions will PROBABLY be about GENERAL, if not better. Or worse. One never knows for sure. Sometimes it's this, sometimes it's that. Or both. Usually. One or the other. But not DEFINITELY."

McGee quickly dubbed the poor fellow "Foggy." His usual exit line was: "I must go home and feed my groundhog. Well, good day. Probably."

On October 30, appearing as Fibber and Molly, Jim and Marian were guest stars on a *Family Theatre* program. In a story titled "Advice to the Lovelorn," written by Phil Leslie, they helped a young couple resolve a romantic dispute.

In March, 1948, Chicago's station WMAQ was celebrating its twenty-fifth anniversary. The Jordans participated by sending a transcription on which they recalled their days at the station and repeated a skit from the *Smackout* program.

On April 14, they were Bing Crosby's guests on *Philco Radio Time*. Don Quinn supplied some witty back-and-forth. Along with Bing, they harmonized on "I Had a Dream, Dear." It had been some years since they had sung together on the air, and they never again did so.

The next day, Marian turned fifty. An unusual "party" took place at St. Joseph's College in Collegeville, Indiana. With hundreds of spectators filling the college theater, the Jordans were presented with honorary doctorates for their many years of wholesome, mirth-filled entertainment.

In September, as part of its "March of Time" series, 20th Century-Fox released a film called *Is Everybody Listening?* It was a combination of entertainment and a not too subtle promotion of various radio programs. Jim and Marian appeared in a brief clip from their show, along with such stars as Bob Hope, Jack Benny, Fred Allen and their old friends Edgar Bergen and Charlie McCarthy.

To the delight of the McGees and their audience, Mayor LaTrivia returned on October 5. Despite the torment to which he was subjected at 79 Wistful Vista, he continued as a regular visitor until mid-1953.

As part of the holiday festivities, Fibber and Molly made a guest appearance on December 16 on the *Sealtest Variety Theatre*, hosted by Dorothy Lamour.

They got 1949 off to a creepy start with a rare dramatic performance on *Suspense*. In a story called "Back Seat Driver," they play a couple driving home after seeing a movie. They pick up a hitchhiker who then begins acting strangely. Then they hear on the car radio that an escaped murderer is on the loose.

In February, Richard LeGrand became another frequent McGee visitor in the person of Ole Swenson. Originally the janitor at City Hall, Ole later took up the same job at the Wistful Vista Elk's Club, where Fibber frequently hung out with some of the other male regulars.

Either Ole was not paid well or he put in a lot of extra hours without being compensated. In his exaggerated Swedish accent, his classic line when discussing his labors at the club was: "I'm yust donatin' my time." His children all had typically Swedish monikers: Lars, Nels,

Sven and Kristina. Discussing Doctor Gamble with the McGees, Ole described him as "a great kidder. He delivered all my kids."

Richard LeGrand was a fine dramatic actor. In various roles, he was heard on many programs, including the continuing series *One Man's Family* and *I Love a Mystery*. His voice probably is most recognized as that of Mr. Peavy, the mild-mannered druggist on *The Great Gildersleeve*. When Gildy was expounding on some subject and expressed an opinion, Peavy was wont to respond, "Well, now. I wouldn't say that." Which frequently prompted the exasperated Gildy to snap back: "Well, then what *would* you say?"

Throughout 1949, *Fibber McGee and Molly* enjoyed an estimated audience of 40 million every week. That may have inspired the Jordans to treat themselves to a summer vacation in Ireland. Their show was not heard there, so they were able to blend in with other tourists as just two more American Irishers visiting "the old sod."

Meanwhile, Jim Junior's work as a producer had taken him into the film field, where he met a lovely young actress named Peggy Knudsen. Born Margaret Ann Knudsen, she began her career on Broadway, appearing in *My Sister Eileen*. Soon after, she migrated to Hollywood, where she got off to a good start appearing with Bette Davis in the 1946 film *A Stolen Life*.

Although she never achieved the star status that enjoyed top billing, she appeared in numerous films opposite such stars as Joan Crawford and Errol Flynn. She later found ample opportunities for supporting roles on many television series.

Soon after they met, Peggy and Jim Jr. began dating. It did not take long for a full-fledged romance to blossom. Jim Senior and Marian soon welcomed Peggy into the family as their new daughter-in-law. At the wedding reception, Jim lent his tenor voice to a heartfelt rendering of "I Love You Truly."

On a Friday evening, September 16, NBC presented a special one-hour program celebrating fifteen years of *Fibber McGee and Molly*. In addition to most of the regulars, there were return visits by Harold Peary as Gildersleeve and the now-famous singer, Perry Como. Other guests included Dinah Shore, Phil Harris, Alice Faye, Dennis Day, William Bendix and Bob Hope. The Kings Men sang a medley of songs that Jim and Marian had sung in their vaudeville and early radio days.

In November, Bill Thompson introduced a new character, a streetcar conductor who called out the up-coming street names in such an incomprehensible mumble that no one could make out what he said. Cliff Arquette returned, playing the Old Timer's girl friend Bessie. A Southern gal with a heavy accent, Bessie was so talkative that O.T. seldom got a word in. Her usual parting line was: "'Bye, ya-all."

Perhaps because the Old Timer was more comical, Bessie accompanied him for just a few visits. Arquette, however, hung around and played several dozen characters with outrageous Quinn-inspired names, each of whom showed up only once or twice.

As for Don Quinn, he dropped a bit of a bombshell on the Jordans during the summer. He would soon be resigning as head writer.

Quinn had been at work creating a new program that was worlds apart from the *McGee* comedy. Titled *The Halls of Ivy*, it had been accepted by NBC and would begin airing in January with stars Ronald Coleman and his wife, actress Benita Hume.

It would be a continuing series in which President William Todhunter Hall deals with a range of events and problems at Ivy College, with behind-the-scenes advice from his wife, the former British stage actress, Victoria Cromwell.

The program was an engrossing mixture of drama and soft humor.

It proved popular enough to last several years, after which it became a television series that ran through September, 1955.

Don Quinn stayed on board through the end of the year. The Jordans were sorry to see him go. He was not just a writer and co-worker. He was a dear friend. It was a sad parting but an amiable one, and the three would remain close.

By the time Phil Leslie took up the reins as chief writer at the beginning of 1950, he was so tuned in to the comedy style of the McGee program that no one could have detected any change.

In the Spring, Jim and Marian returned to their old home town, Peoria. Among other nostalgic stops were their old schools and St. John's church, where that fateful choir practice had brought them together. They even partook of ice cream sodas at their favorite after-date source, Kremer's Drug Store. *Look* photographers trailed them around town, and a story later appeared in the magazine. It was a most pleasant visit, during which they reconnected, however briefly, with many friends from their days as locals.

Not long after, an even more pleasant event occurred. Jim Jr. and Peggy presented them with another grandchild, their daughter Janice.

Meanwhile, another small cloud was forming. Television sets were finding their way into more and more American homes. Thus far the new medium had had no impact on the McGees' popularity, but the flickering screens were drawing many people away from their radios. The S. C. Johnson & Sons executives perceived a trend and were anxious to take advantage of the advertising possibilities. They asked the Jordans to consider adapting their program for television.

Jim and Marian had anticipated that the suggestion would be made, although not just yet. In its early years, the quality of television programs and their reception was such that Fred Allen quipped, "They call it a medium because nothing on it is done well."

The Jordans agreed that transforming *Fibber McGee and Molly* to a televised presentation would be a daunting task. For starters, television would require a much larger crew and more demanding rehearsals. Radio audiences painted their own imaginary picture of the program's colorful characters. Costumes, make-up and probably more cast members would be needed to present those characters looking somewhat like what the radio audience imagined. And how could you ever produce on live television the imagined disaster that was the mistakenly-opened hall closet?

Moreover, they were comfortable with the radio domain and confident that, for now at least, they still enjoyed a loyal audience. Some years later, telling an interviewer about their reluctance, Jim said, "Our friends advised us, 'Don't do it until you need to. You have this value in radio. Milk it dry.'" After considering all the pros and cons, the Jordans advised the Johnson people that they felt their particular show was meant for radio, not television.

The Johnson folk accepted their decision, but opted to move ahead with sponsorship of two television programs, *Saturday Night Review* and a dramatic series, *Robert Montgomery Presents*. On May 23, Jim and Marian performed their last program with Johnson's Wax as sponsor. As with Don Quinn, it was a sad parting, but amiable. They had enjoyed a wonderful working relationship with the Johnson company for fifteen years.

With a still loyal listening audience, the program had no problem attracting a new sponsor. When it resumed in September, that role was assumed by Pet Milk Company. Fibber's "Pet" name for Harlow Wilcox became "Milky."

Nevertheless, television was luring more and more sponsors away from radio. By 1952, it was estimated that more than 24 million families had television sets in their home. As more big name entertainers entered the field, people who once were regular radio listeners were spending more time watching the flickering tube.

Pet Milk carried the program through June, 1952. When it returned to the air in October, the Reynolds Aluminum Company assumed sponsorship. Reynolds was already promoting its products on television. For whatever reason, the company chose to sponsor the program for a season, but departed in June, 1953.

Because Marian was again experiencing some health problems and fatigue in 1954, the program underwent a significant change. In August, it became a 15-minute program, airing five nights a week, Sunday through Thursday. In its Friday night time slot, NBC was broadcasting boxing matches sponsored by Gillette. The following Spring, the show switched to Monday through Friday broadcasts.

The revised format was easier on Marian. The shows were recorded in a studio with no audience. The Jordans could do all five shows in one day, allowing much more time for Marian to rest the remainder of the week.

Phil Leslie took on a couple of part-time assistant writers. Scripting was adapted for some short episodes that were complete in one show, but most were continuing stories that carried out over several shows. One lasted for fourteen episodes.

In the new format, the only regular supporting cast members were Arthur Q. Bryan and Bill Thompson. Thus, the McGees' most frequent visitors were Doctor Gamble, the Old Timer, Wallace Wimple and, of course, Teeny. For the first program, Wallace wrote the McGees a poem:

"Welcome to Mr. and Mrs. McGee,

Back again on NBC.
As I look ahead,
It makes me shriek.
What'll you do
FIVE TIMES a week?!"

Many of the old cast members returned periodically for one program, or several that comprised a continued story line. In addition, Phil Leslie created novel personalities for dozens of stars who made guest appearances, including William Conrad, Pat O'Brien, Parley Baer, Herb Vigran, Mary Jane Croft, Marvin Miller and the Jordans' daughter-in-law, Peggy Knudsen.

The prevalence of single-sponsor programs was coming to an end. During the show's tenure as a quarter-hour program, it had multi sponsors that included Paper-Mate Pens, RCA Appliances, Richard Hudnut Home Permanents, Dial Soap, Prudential Insurance, Armour and Company, Brown and Williamson (the tobacco company), and Miles Laboratories (Alka Seltzer). In its last year, the latter two took over most of the program's commercial segments. NBC and the various sponsors benefited from rebroadcasts of the recorded shows during the Jordans' contractual vacation time.

The new format entailed more time on the air than in the past. Yet, for the Jordans, it required just a bit more work and allowed them much more free time. The shows were transcribed, with multiple shows being recorded at one session. Jim and Marian made but a few guest appearances on various programs during this period. They thus reaped the benefit of many more leisure hours for family visits and relaxing at home or on their ranch.

NBC elected to discontinue the program after the March 23, 1956, broadcast. In the quarter-hour format, there had been 577 programs.

Overall, the program had had an enviable record of endurance, wholesome entertainment and listener loyalty.

Retirement appeared to be the next episode in Jim and Marian's lives. They could well afford it. For a time, they enjoyed doing whatever they chose whenever they chose. Then *Monitor* came calling.

In a last-ditch effort to hold onto their listeners, NBC Radio launched *Weekend Monitor* in June, 1955. With a smorgasbord offering of news, sports, interviews, comedy, music and miscellaneous from around the world, it aired for forty hours, from 8:00 a.m. Saturday until midnight Sunday. It was promoted as "a true magazine of the air."

Eventually, nothing could save radio from the fascination that the flickering images on the television screen held for the viewing audience. Yet a large and loyal audience listened to *Monitor*, either sporadically or without touching the dial. It enabled listeners to tune in at random for a wide range of entertainment and information throughout the weekend. It maintained a respectable presence on radio until January, 1975, by which time television was the main source of income for both NBC and its rival networks.

In the Spring of 1957, NBC invited Jim and Marian to bring Fibber and Molly back. They might have declined, but another format change made it like getting paid for just having a little fun. Jim was willing, largely because he was proud of their contribution to radio comedy and appreciated the opportunity to present it again to a loyal audience that he knew was still out there. For her part, Marian simply viewed the easy assignment as a bit of a lark.

NBC's concept was a series of five-minute skits scattered throughout the weekend. Five would be aired on Saturday and another five on Sunday. There would be no other characters appearing, although many of them would be invoked as fodder for the conversations in which Fibber and Molly exchanged back-and-forth about comic adventures.

An NBC staff writer named Tom Koch was assigned to preparing scripts. He was a native of Charleston, Illinois, just down the road from the Jordans' home town of Peoria. Koch was a long-time fan who remembered listening to the McGees as a boy. He thus was familiar with their comedy formula and took pleasure in emulating it in the abbreviated scripting.

Again the format proved to be more fun than work for Jim and Marian. They could produce a week's worth of tapes in one day. The skits were taped in a recording studio set up on the Jordans' ranch, then sent to New York, where the program originated. As Jim recalled years later: "We sold 'em like you sell eggs, I guess, by the crate."

Their first appearance on Monitor was on June 1, 1957, and they continued producing crates of the short skits until September 6, 1959. Somewhat ironically, the last program had a series of connected skits titled "McGees as TV Stars," in which Fibber imagines Molly and himself as stars of a television Western series.

Fans may have yearned for more of Fibber and Molly. They continued to be a popular segment of *Monitor's* varied offerings. Yet for some reason NBC did not offer to renew their contract. The network did, however, continue to air reruns of the skits throughout 1960.

Jim and Marian continued to partake of the benefits of retirement, including a vacation trip to New York City in February, 1960. While there, they visited old friends at the NBC studios. To their surprise, NBC management then took them aside and offered to give them a new three-year contract to continue the short skits. Marian had again been feeling poorly for awhile, however, and the Jordans declined.

To her credit, Marian had refrained from all forms of alcohol after her long treatment at the sanitarium. So this new decline in her health was of great concern to both of the Jordans. When they returned home, Marian visited her physician and had a thorough check-up. It was found that she had a malignant ovarian tumor.

The Jordans spent the next year quietly at home. When her strength permitted, Marian found some distraction puttering in her garden. Jim hovered nearby and watched over her closely. Their children stayed in close contact.

On a Friday morning, Marian told Jim she was experiencing pain more severe than usual. Soon the family was gathered around her bedside. Later that day, April 6, 1961, she quietly breathed her last.

No more would a weary world hear the gentle Molly McGee say sweetly, "Good night, all."

Marian Jordan was laid to rest in Holy Cross Cemetery following a quiet funeral service at Our Lady of Grace Church in Encino.

With the love of his life gone, Jim accepted the fact that he was retired. Even if radio were to experience an unlikely revival, the Wistful Vista twosome would not be part of it. No one but Marian could ever be Molly.

He made what he thought might be his last personal appearance as a guest of Jack Paar on television's *Tonight Show* in July, 1961. He was joined by his old friend and sometime cast member Cliff Arquette.

He then determined to embrace retirement. Caring for Marian in her final months had been both physically and emotionally exhausting. To give himself some time to recover, he left for a solo vacation in Hawaii.

While relaxing there, he met a lady named Gretchen Stewart, who also was vacationing alone. Gretchen was no stranger to show business. Although she had never performed herself, she was the widow of

Harry Stewart, a popular dialectician and comedian. Stewart created and portrayed the heavily accented character Yogi Yorgesson. His recordings of "Yingle Bells" and "I Yust Go Nuts at Christmas" became classics that are heard frequently every year during the holidays.

Jim and Gretchen spent much time together while in Hawaii, finding that they shared many interests. Back home, Gretchen lived in Los Angeles, and their retiree status made it easy for them to get together frequently. The initial attraction that began in Hawaii became a close and romantic relationship. In January, 1962, they returned to Honolulu and were married there. They then took a leisurely extended honeymoon in the Orient.

For most of the 1960s, Jim and Gretchen kept a low profile, enjoying the benefits of being a well off and happy retired couple. Jim's woodworking skills would have provided steady employment had he not been in show business. In his "temple of sawdust," he created chairs, book shelves and small tables with a craftsman look to them. He even succeeded once in producing a four-wheeled wooden wagon.

In 1967, Jim and Gretchen decided their home was much bigger than the two of them needed. They sold it and moved to a smaller, more manageable home in a quiet, remote area of Beverly Hills.

Their tranquility was disturbed in 1970 when Jim began experiencing health problems. The culprit was his heart. He underwent open heart surgery and had a mechanical aortic valve implanted. The surgery went well. His doctors were pleased with how quickly he recovered, and impressed with his cheery efforts to entertain the staff while he was there.

In 1972, he agreed to film some television commercials for his old friends at the Johnson's Wax Company and for General Motors. He also was coaxed into appearing in a PBS television special called

The Great Radio Comedians. At a New York City news conference to promote the latter, he and Harold Peary (as Gildersleeve) presented a short McGee-style skit. A representative of New York City presented Fibber with a key to the city. In return, Fibber presented him with a key to the infamous hall closet.

In 1974, with the help of a fellow named Chuck Schaden, Jim made a comeback of sorts.

Chuck Schaden, a younger fellow who loved old time radio, had accumulated a collection of over five hundred recordings. Believing that other former listeners missed radio as much as he did, he talked his way into a small station near Chicago, where he began to produce and host a program called *Those Were The Days.* Every Saturday, he aired four hours of classic old time radio programs. In between the tapes, he provided listeners with background information on the shows themselves and the performers.

The program was an immediate hit and soon moved to a larger Chicago station with many more listeners. Private collectors and people who had worked in radio soon began finding more recordings for Schaden. His library of tapes grew. When he retired from his program after almost forty years on the air, he donated the master tapes for 50,000 individual programs of every genre to Chicago's Museum of Broadcast Communications.

During his hosting of the program, Schaden began tracking down people who had worked on radio, either before the mic or behind the scenes. He recorded interviews with them and aired these for his listeners to augment shows when he scheduled programs on which they had worked.

In July, 1973, Chuck connected with Jim Jordan for what was one of his most treasured interviews. In his amiable, guy-next-door fashion, Jim took him on a verbal tour of his and Marian's careers, from that fateful choir meeting, to their vaudeville days, the early radio days and their wonderful run as Fibber and Molly. Chuck later aired it on a show that was four hours of the *McGee* program and others on which Jim and Marian appeared as guests.

Jim and Chuck struck up a friendship that resulted in them staying in contact by phone and letter. Early in 1974, with the help of former writer Phil Leslie, they put together a program called *Fibber McGee and the Good Old Days of Radio*.

The series of seven hour-long shows had Schaden visiting McGee at his Wistful Vista residence. Fibber would be fiddling with his old super heterodyne radio. As he explained, those old radio programs were still floating around somewhere out there in the ether, if he could just tune them in. Then, voila! One of them would begin to come forth through the old mesh speaker.

Drawing upon Schaden's vast collection of tapes, they "tuned in" to segments of numerous programs and chatted about the shows and their stars. The series aired on seven Sundays, each week zeroing in on programs that had been on a specific day or night of the week. Sponsored by Chrysler Home Air Conditioning, the series was aired during the summer, with commercials touting Chrysler's Air Temp line.

Each week, about halfway through the program, announcer Larry Thor interrupted the proceedings when he popped in for a visit. As in days of old, something in the conversation would prompt him to begin extolling the benefits of having a Chrysler Air Temp home air conditioner. Larry wasn't quite as natural and loose as Harlow Wilcox, but he did get into the spirit of the sneakily inserted plug.

Later that year, Jim and Harold Peary appeared with Tom Snyder on his *Tomorrow* television show. Along with dramatic actor Les Tremayne and famed radio writer Arch Obler, they presented a sixty-minute program called "A Salute to Old Time Radio."

To some extent earlier, and especially in the 1970s, there was a ground swell of interest in what became known as "The Golden Age of Radio." Former listeners, now middle-aged or seniors, had a nostalgic connection. They were joined by many younger folk who grew up with television, but "discovered" radio thanks to programs like Schaden's that replayed the old programs on various stations around the country. Over the next decade, Jim Jordan repeatedly stepped briefly out of retirement to participate in various radio remembrances.

In March, 1976, he was one of dozens of old radio hands gathered at tables in the audience for a ninety-minute television special called *The Good Old Days of Radio with Steve Allen*. Steve had each of the veteran radio folk stand as he introduced them. When Jim was called, he stood and said. "Did you ever see so many old people?"

Wait for the laugh. Then: Does anybody here remember *Stoopnagle and Budd*?"

When several dozen hands went up: "Then you're older than I am!"

That Fall, Jim made his first and only cameo appearance in a television series. On *Chico and the Man*, he played an aging mechanic forced into retirement. A reviewer noted: "At 80, Jordan is remarkably trim and compact, with a neat bush of gray hair. The voice is exactly the same muted oboe of McGee, double-edged, with bravado and guilt."

Early in 1977, Hollywood called again. This time it was the Walt Disney studio, no less. Jim provided the voice for a somewhat pathetic albatross named Orville in the film *The Rescuers*.

Later that year he signed on with a California savings and loan association to lend his familiar voice to a series of commercials to be aired locally. He also was selected as a perfect candidate to do a commercial for the American Association of Retired People (AARP). He did so in his guise as Fibber, and the commercial incorporated the familiar hall closet gag.

In December, he appeared with a number of old radio friends in a three-hour program called "The Golden Days of Radio." It was presented at the Los Angeles convention of the AFL-CIO, held at the luxurious Bonaventure Hotel.

In August, 1978, Jim and many *McGee* fans were delighted when Johnson's Wax began a year-long series of repeat broadcasts over station WRJN in Racine. The company had its commercials edited out. In their place were inserted public service announcements for various community organizations in the area.

On November 17, one day after he turned eighty-two, Jim was the guest of honor at a special luncheon of the Pacific Pioneer Broadcasters Association. He was the belated recipient of their Diamond Circle Award, honoring members who have reached the age of seventy-five. Noting its tardiness, Jim quipped that he was glad he was able to stick around until the plaque was ready.

Acknowledging the interest in old time radio, CBS was at that time running a series of new one-hour dramas called *Sears Radio Theatre*. In February, Jim starred in a comedy story called "The Trouble Maker." He was his old playful self as a retiree who stirs up a hornet's nest when corporate finagling threatens to cost him his pension. Produced by Elliott Lewis and hosted by Andy Griffith, the show reunited Jim with such old friends as Mary Jane Croft, Shirley Mitchell, Frank Nelson and Herb Vigran.

On May 16, 1980, Jim joined other former radio performers to present a "Salute to the Golden Days of Radio" for members of the Pacific

Pioneer Broadcasters. In a McGee-style skit, he was joined by Frank Nelson as a mailman and Shirley Mitchell in her old Alice Darling role.

In December, 1983, Jim had the pleasure of attending the unveiling of a star on the Hollywood Walk of Fame honoring Marian and himself. Former cast members Shirley Mitchell and Gale Gordon were in attendance, along with writer Phil Leslie. Because Jim and Marian were best known to radio and film audiences as their Wistful Vista counterparts, the names on the star were Fibber McGee & Molly.

In March, 1987, he took part in a program by the Pacific Pioneer Broadcasters to honor the work of the Armed Forces Radio Service (AFRS). The organization also used the occasion to recognize Frank Bresee, who for twenty years had aired a program on AFRS called *Golden Days of Radio*.

Jim had been a guest on Bresee's program several times. He was recruited to make the presentation. In concluding his comments, he said, "I'm tickled to death to give this award to Frank. He told me if I gave it to him, he would give me a ride home."

Jim's heart and other ailments were slowing him down in the 1980s. As a result, his personal appearances were few. He was, however, a regular attendee of Pacific Pioneer Broadcasters meetings. Jim was a long-time member and for several years served as chairman of the group's board of directors. Fellow members recall that when business meetings sometimes became disorganized, Jim's usually cheerful countenance changed to one of stern disapproval.

Although somewhat frail and slow, Jim remained bright and quick of wit. He and Gretchen led a quiet at-home life, sometimes dining out, sometimes having a few friends over to visit.

In March, 1988, Jim suffered a bad fall at their home. He was taken unconscious to Beverly Hills Medical Center, where he was diagnosed with a blood clot to in his brain. He was hospitalized and in a coma for more than a week.

Gretchen and other family members were continually at his side. They felt that he was aware of their presence, although he was unable to acknowledge it. On Friday, April 1, he died without ever having regained consciousness. He was ninety-one years old.

Jim was buried next to Marian at Holy Cross Cemetery in Culver City. The feisty Fibber had gone to join his gentle Molly.

* * * * * * * * *

Gretchen Stewart/Jordan continued to reside at the Beverly Hills home she and Jim had shared until her death on July, 12, 1998, at age eighty-nine. She was buried with her first husband, Harry Stewart, in Grand View Memorial Park, Glendale, California.

* * * * * * * * *

The marriage of Jim Jordan Jr. and Peggy Knudsen ended in 1960. Prior to their divorce, they had three children. In 1962, he married Beverly Tyler, with whom he had four more children.

In part because he had a heart problem, Jim had abandoned show business in 1972. He took up the real estate business and became a successful land developer in the Reno, Nevada, area. He was sometimes assisted by his father, who had some experience and expertise in the real estate world.

Jim Jr. was still married to Beverly when he died of a heart attack on December 24, 1998.

* * * * * * * * *

Kathryn (Kay) Jordan's first marriage ended in divorce. Her second marriage, to Doctor Victor Newcomer, lasted over fifty years, until his death in 2002. Kathryn inherited her mother's green thumb and spent much of her later years nurturing the magnificent rose and herb gardens at her Malibu home. She died on February 9, 2007.

* * * * * * * * *

Peggy Knudsen's career was cut short when she developed a crippling arthritis. In her last years, she was cared for by actress Jennifer Jones, with whom she had developed a close friendship.

She later also suffered from cancer, which was the cause of her death on July 11, 1980. She was buried in San Fernando Mission in Mission Hills, California.

She is honored with a star on the Hollywood Walk of Fame for her contribution to the television industry.

* * * * * * * * *

The *Fibber McGee and Molly* show has a star on the Hollywood Walk of Fame at 1500 North Vine Street, just outside the building where the program was once broadcast from the NBC studio.

The program itself was inducted into the Radio Hall of Fame the year after Jim Jordan died.

* * * * * * * * *

Jim Jordan was once asked how he would like to be remembered. He replied that it was not the memories of his radio audience that he thought about in that regard. "I only think about my peers," he said. "I only want to be remembered by the people I spent my life working with. I want to be remembered as somebody who was 'on the square.' I just want to be respected by the people I worked with."

Jim actually outlived most of those people. Yet during their lifetimes, they surely regarded him and Marian that way and more so. The Jordans were as straightforward and homespun as any couple that one might know from next door or just down the block in Anytown, U.S.A. Without the easygoing, outgoing natures that they shared, it's unlikely that they would have developed into the radio personalities that became their alter egos.

During eighteen years in its half-hour format, *Fibber McGee and Molly* drew a faithful audience of listeners in small towns, big cities and in between. For seven of those years, they were rated the top comedy show, surpassing even Bob Hope and Jack Benny. At its peak, the program was estimated to have a listening audience of 48 million. Its 15-year sponsorship by Johnson Wax Company ranks as one of the longest on radio.

Their program produced the first "spin-off" on radio: *The Great Gildersleeve*. It later repeated that feat when the McGees' maid Beulah became the star of her (actually actor Marlin Hurt's) own show.

In an era when radio was referred to as "the theater of the mind," Jim and Marian Jordan, a.k.a. Fibber McGee and Molly, provided millions of listeners with a weekly half-hour of entertainment that was wholesome, lively and good for many a laugh. Those truly were heavenly days.

Acknowledgements

This book would not have happened were it not for the thoughtfulness of Teresa McGuire, wife of my cousin Mark. Aware of my interest in old time radio and my penchant for nostalgic rambling, she passed along her copy of *George Burns and the Hundred-Year Dash*. As I read it, I found myself remembering George and Gracie and the other four couples who were wed both on and off the stage.

A seed was planted. It prompted much additional reading and researching. My initial intent was an article for *Nostalgia Digest*, but I soon had accumulated far too much material for one magazine article. Eventually, the seed bore fruit in these chronicles of those five couples' collective contributions to that wonderful yesteryear medium, radio.

The possibility of putting a lot of time and effort into a project that might never see print was intimidating. Publisher Ben Ohmart's thumbs up response to my proposal gave me the encouragement and the impetus to plod ahead. (At my age, I no longer charge ahead.)

Although he has retired after thirty-nine years of broadcasting, old time radio historian Chuck Schaden continues to offer OTR memories and programs on his website, *www.SpeakingofRadio.com*. Schaden was the perfect proofreader and fact-checker for my first draft. With his encyclopedic knowledge of the programs and performers, he spotted passages that needed correcting, provided background on some areas where I was hazy, and offered a few anecdotes that I was pleased to splice in at appropriate spots.

George Ulrich is a devoted fan of Alice Faye and co-creator of a neat website modestly named *The Official Alice Faye Fan Club*. He kindly agreed to critique the Phil Harris/Alice Faye section of the book. His thorough review saved me from some inaccurate reporting about Alice and shed light on some areas where I had only sketchy information.

Film historian Bob Kolososki perused the portions of the book that dealt with the various couples' films. In addition to spotting some inaccuracies, he offered some interesting tidbits about the films and the stars. When told not to take too much time from the business that puts food on his table, he replied, "I love this stuff!"

Steve Darnall is host and producer of *Those Were the Days*, broadcasting four hours of old time radio programs every Saturday afternoon over Public Radio Station WDCB (90.9 FM) in Glen Ellyn, Illinois. In his spare time (?), he also is editor and publisher of the quarterly *Nostalgia Digest*. In addition to writing the Foreword that graces the front pages of this book, Steve dug into his voluminous photo file and provided almost all of the photos that appear herein.

As always, the folks at the Bensenville Community Public Library were very patient and helpful in tracking down numerous books, some long out of print, that I requested as I gathered information. They found every one of them.

The husband/wife team of Daniel and Darlene Swanson proved to be a dynamic duo in getting the finished book ready for the printer. Darlene supplied me with a neatly formatted first proof and then worked dilgently and patiently with me to correct a bountiful batch of punctuation and spelling errors and make numerous minor changes.

Acknowledgements

Daniel took a wisp of an idea I suggested and produced a front cover that is a work of art. Then he metamorphosed my feeble attempt at a back cover to give it a polished professional look.

My thanks and appreciation to all those who gave encouragement to my efforts in this endeavor and lent their knowledge, skills and advice to enabling its completion. If the finished product is not best-seller quality, it ain't their fault.

Finally, a special thanks to the love of my life, who from time to time reminds me that housewives do not get to retire. During the many hours when I absented myself in the back room that has become my computer den, she steadfastly maintained our household routine, making sure that I had clean underwear and sox and ate three well-balanced meals per day. You couldn't buy better elder care.

Dan McGuire

References

Alice Faye: A Life Beyond the Silver Screen; by Jane Lenz Elder; University Press of Mississippi; 2002

And There I Stood with my Piccolo; by Meredith Willson; Doubleday & Company, Inc.; 1948

The Better of Goodman Ace; by Goodman Ace; Doubleday & Company, Inc.; 1970

CBS: *Reflections in a Bloodshot Eye*; by Robert Metz; Playboy Press, distributed by Simon & Schuster; 1975

Frank and Anne Hummert's Radio Factory; by Jim Cox; McFarland & Company; 2003

Funny Ladies; by Stephen M. Silverman; Harry N. Abrams, Inc., Publishers; 1999

George Burns and the Hundred-Year Dash; by Martin Gottfried; Simon & Schuster; 1996

Gracie: A Love Story; by George Burns; Putnam's; 1988

The Great American Broadcast: A Celebration of Radio's Golden Age; by Leonard Maltin; published as a Dutton book by Penguin Books Ltd.; 1997

The Great Radio Sitcoms; by Jim Cox; McFarland & Company; 2007

Heavenly Days! by Charles Stumpf and Tom Price; World of Yesterday Publications; 1987

Ladies and Gentlemen: Easy Aces; by Goodman Ace; Doubleday & Company, Inc.; 1970

Nostalgia Digest magazine; various issues and articles

On the Air: The Encyclopedia of Old-Time Radio; by John Dunning; Oxford University Press; 1998

Out of the Blue; by John Crosby; Simon and Schuster; 1952

Ozzie; by Ozzie Nelson; Prentice-Hall; 1973

Radio Comedy; by Arthur Frank Wertheim; Oxford University Press; 1979

Raised on Radio; by Gerald Nachman; Pantheon Books; 1998

Speaking of Radio; interviews by Chuck Schaden; Nostalgia Digest Press; 2003

Who's Who in Comedy; by Ronald L. Smith; Facts on File/Roundhouse Publishing Ltd., Oxford, United Kingdom; 1992

About the Author

Dan McGuire is a long-time contributor to *Nostalgia Digest* magazine. He was a featured columnist for ten years. When he noticed that he was beginning to repeat himself, he backed off to make room for other nostalgia buffs. He nonetheless continues to appear frequently in the magazine.

After retiring from his day job, McGuire collected some of his favorite pieces from the *Digest*, expanded upon them here and there, and published them as a book called *Now, When I Was A Kid…*. His "nostalgic ramblings" recall a time when Mom shopped at nearby mom-and-pop stores, kids rode balloon-tire bikes and clamped metal roller skates onto their shoes, folks gathered on someone's front porch to chat and share neighborhood news on summer evenings, and the family's "entertainment center" was a table radio or a Philco console in the living room—all of this as seen through the eyes of a kid growing up in that bygone era.

McGuire hawks the book at his online store, *www.backwhenbooks.com*. For good measure, he offers 300 other selections with a "yesteryear" theme, including some BearManor favorites.

As this book goes to press, Dan and his wife, Joy, are approaching sixty years of togetherness. They still reside in the house where they reared their elder daughter Laurie and twins David and Jennifer.

www.ingramcontent.com/pod-product-compliance
Lightning Source LLC
Chambersburg PA
CBHW071950220426
43662CB00009B/1077